Obesity and the Economics of Prevention

Fit not Fat

Franco Sassi

Senior Health Economist
Organisation for Economic Co-operation and Development
(OECD)
Paris, France

In association with the OECD

Edward Elgar
Cheltenham, UK • Northampton, MA, USA

Published by
Edward Elgar Publishing Limited
The Lypiatts
15 Lansdown Road
Cheltenham
Glos GL50 2JA
UK

Edward Elgar Publishing, Inc.
William Pratt House
9 Dewey Court
Northampton
Massachusetts 01060
USA

A catalogue record for this book
is available from the British Library

Library of Congress Control Number: 2010939215

ISBN 978 1 84980 860 6 (cased)
      978 0 85793 171 9 (paperback)

Printed and bound by MPG Books Group, UK

Foreword

"There was a fat boy in our street. People called him fatso", observes the main character in Kieron Smith, Boy, a novel by James Kellman narrated from the point of view of a child from the time he is 4 to almost 13. Through his eyes, we see a picture of life in Glasgow in the 1960s – and get an idea of the changes taking place. At the time, obesity was unusual enough to draw attention. Yet now more than a third of Scottish 12-year-olds are overweight, a fifth are obese and over one in ten severely obese. The statistics for adults are even worse, with almost two-thirds of men and more than half of women overweight. The situation is better in the other OECD countries, apart from the United States, but obesity is a concern almost everywhere, in the OECD area and beyond.

If economics is "the study of human behaviour as a relationship between ends and scarce means which have alternative uses"[1] it must have something to say on lifestyles, health and, above all, on the epidemic of obesity that has developed over the past 30 years, one of the largest epidemics in the history of mankind. Indeed, obesity has become a favourite subject for economists in various parts of the world, but the role of economics in addressing the determinants and consequences of individual health-related behaviours has been interpreted rather narrowly by many, including some economists. This book is a humble attempt to explore the broader scope of the potential contribution of economics to the design of effective, efficient and equitable approaches to chronic disease prevention, with a focus on diseases linked to unhealthy diets, sedentary lifestyles and obesity.

The public health paradigm, which still inspires and guides the field of chronic disease prevention, is well reflected in Geoffrey Rose's famous statement "It is better to be healthy than ill or dead. That is the beginning and the end of the only real argument for preventive medicine. It is sufficient."[2] To an economist, Rose's argument is of critical importance, but it is not sufficient. And no sensible economist would claim that what is missing is the "economic argument" that prevention will be a "money-saver", dismissed as "misleading, or even false", by Rose himself. This book provides ample evidence that Rose's stance on this type of economic argument is well founded. The role of economics is to ensure that prevention improves social welfare and its distribution across social groups. This is what an economist would regard as a "sufficient" argument for prevention. Health is one dimension of social welfare, but not the only one, and not always the most important. Human behaviours are driven by many "ends", to use Lionel Robbins' word, which are all in competition with each other because resources to pursue them are scarce. If so many people in the OECD area and beyond have been *gaining weight to the point that their health and longevity are affected, it may mean that ends other than the pursuit of good health have taken a higher priority at a certain point in time, or it may mean that people's priorities have been increasingly constrained by environmental influences, which they have not been able to handle. The role of economics is to determine what mechanisms have been at play in the development of the obesity epidemic and whether implementing actions that have the potential to reverse current trends in obesity would generate an improvement in social welfare.*

This book is the result of work undertaken at the OECD since 2007, following a mandate received from the OECD Health Ministers at a meeting in Paris in 2004. The book presents a wealth of data and analyses carried out by the OECD with the aim of supporting the development of policies for tackling obesity and preventing chronic diseases by its member countries. Some of these analyses were designed and undertaken in close partnership with the World Health Organisation.

Notes

1. Lionel Robbins (1932), "An Essay on the Nature and Significance of Economic Science", Macmillan Facsimile, London.

2. Geoffrey Rose (1992), *The Strategy of Preventive Medicine*, Oxford University Press.

Acknowledgements

M any deserve credit for the contents of this book, but two deserve it above all: Michele Cecchini and Marion Devaux, whose tireless efforts have given substance to the work presented herein. Michele's work is behind the analyses of the impact of prevention strategies discussed in Chapter 6, while Marion's is behind all of the statistical analyses presented in Chapters 2 and 3. Without them, this book would not have been written. The author is also especially grateful to Jeremy Lauer and Dan Chisholm, who have made an invaluable contribution to the assessment of the impact of prevention strategies and have helped to establish, along with David Evans and Tessa Tan-Torres, a most productive collaboration between the OECD and the WHO on the economics of chronic disease prevention. Other OECD colleagues who provided valuable contributions to the work at various stages of the Economics of Prevention project include Jeremy Hurst, Linda Fulponi, Mark Pearson, Peter Scherer, Elizabeth Docteur, John Martin, Martine Durand, Elena Rusticelli, Christine Le Thi and Francesca Borgonovi, as well as Anna Ceccarelli, Jody Church, Amrita Palriwala, Ji Hee Youn, Fareen Hassan, Romain Lafarguette, Angelica Carletto and Lucia Scopelliti who worked on the Economics of Prevention project during internships in the OECD Health Division. Members of the Expert Group on the economics of prevention nominated by OECD countries, too many to list individually, as well as members invited by the OECD Secretariat, including Donald Kenkel, Marc Suhrcke, Evi Hatziandreu, Edward Glaeser, Francesco Branca, Thomas Philipson, Tim Lobstein, Klim McPherson, Julia Critchley, Taavi Lai, Godfrey Xuereb, and Mike Murphy have greatly improved the quality of the work presented in this book. Several of them have contributed directly to the book, in the "special focus" sections which follow some of the chapters. The author is also grateful to representatives of the food and beverage industry and of the sports and exercise industry who provided comments on project plans and outputs through the Business and Industry Advisory Committee to the OECD (BIAC). Country analyses of the impact of prevention strategies were made possible by inputs received from Sylvie Desjardins, Jacques Duciaume and Peter Walsh (Canada), Peter Dick and Francis Dickinson (England), Giovanni Nicoletti and Stefania Vasselli (Italy), Nobuyuki Takakura, Kaori Nakayama, Shunsaku Mitzushima, Tetsuya Fijikawa and Hitoshi Fujii

(Japan), Fernando Alvarez Del Rio, Cristina Gutierrez Delgado, Gustavo Rivera Pena and Veronica Guajardo Barron (Mexico), who also helped to interpret the findings of the analyses. Finally, the author acknowledges the continued support, encouragement and helpful comments received from the OECD Health Committee, chaired by Jane Halton, throughout the duration of the Economics of Prevention project.

Special thanks go to Tracey Strange and Marlène Mohier for their most valuable editorial contributions, to Patrick Love for contributions at an earlier stage in the development of the book, and to Kate Lancaster and Catherine Candea for their help in transforming an editorial project into a real publication. Further editorial assistance was provided during the course of the project by Gabrielle Luthy, Christine Charlemagne, Elma Lopes, Aidan Curran, Judy Zinnemann and Isabelle Vallard.

The Economics of Prevention project was partly funded through regular contributions from OECD member countries. Additional voluntary contributions to the project were made by the following member countries: Australia, Canada, Denmark, Italy, Japan, Mexico, Netherlands, Sweden, Switzerland and United Kingdom. The project was also partly supported by a grant from the Directorate General for Public Health and Consumer Affairs of the European Commission. The contents of this book do not necessarily reflect the views of the Commission.

Table of Contents

Abbreviations

ADLs	Activities of daily living
APC	Age-period-cohort
ANGELO	Analysis grid for environments linked to obesity
BMI	Body mass index
CDP	Chronic Disease Prevention
CEA	Cost-effectiveness analysis
CHD	Coronary heart disease
CHOICE	Choosing interventions that are cost effective (WHO project)
COI	Cost of illness
CONAPO	Consejo Nacional de Población (Mexico)
DALY	Disability-adjusted life year
DGIS	Dirección General de Información en Salud (Mexico)
EPODE	Ensemble, Prévenons l'Obésité des Enfants (European Project)
FSA	Food Standards Agency (United Kingdom)
GBP	Great Britain Pound
GCEA	Generalised cost-effectiveness analysis
GDP	Gross domestic product
GEMS	Girls Health Enrichment Multi-site Studies (Stanford)
HBSC	Health behaviour in school-aged children
HFSS	High in fat, salt and sugar
HSE	Health Survey for England
IARC	International Agency for Research on Cancer
IFBA	International Food and Beverage Alliance
IOM	Institute of Medicine (United States)
IMSS	Instituto Mexicano del Seguro Social (Mexico)
ISTAT	Istituto Nazionale di Statistica (Italy)
LY	Life year
MCBS	Medicare Current Beneficiary Survey (United States)
MoH	Ministry of Health
NBGH	National Business Group on Health (United States)
NGO	Non-governmental organisation
NHANES	National Health and Nutrition Examination Survey (United States)
NHIS	National Health Interview Survey (United States)
NIPH	National Institute of Public Health (Japan)

NLEA	Nutrition Labelling and Education Act (United States)
OPIC	Obesity Prevention In Communities
PHAC	Public Health Agency of Canada
PPPs	Purchasing power parities
QALY	Quality-adjusted life year
RR	Relative risk
RRa	Relative rate
SES	Socio-economic status
USD	American dollar
USDA	US Department of Agriculture
WFA	World Federation of Advertisers
WHO	World Health Organisation

Executive Summary

Obesity is a major health concern for OECD countries. Using a wide range of individual-level and population data from OECD countries, this book presents analyses of trends in obesity, explores the complex causal factors affecting the epidemic and develops an assessment of the impacts interventions to combat the problem. The book provides new information on what prevention strategies are most effective and cost-effective, discussing the respective roles of individuals, social groups, industry and government, and the implications of these findings for the development of policies to address one of the largest public health emergencies of our time.

The book presents an economic approach to the prevention of chronic diseases, which recognises the importance of human goals that are potentially in competition with the pursuit of good health and the social and material constraints which influence individual choice and behaviours. An economic approach aims at identifying possible factors, technically market failures, which limit opportunities for people to make healthy lifestyle choices, and devising suitable strategies to overcome such failures.

What are the health and economic costs associated with obesity?

Chapter 1 places obesity in the context
of the growing burden of chronic disease
and discusses the extent of the problem

Much of the burden of chronic diseases is linked to lifestyles, with tobacco smoking, obesity, diet and lack of physical activity being responsible for the largest shares of such burden. Research has shown that people who lead a physically active life, do not smoke, drink alcohol in moderate quantities, and eat plenty of fruits and vegetables have a risk of death that is less than one fourth of the risk of those who have invariably unhealthy habits. Mortality increases steeply once individuals cross the overweight threshold. The lifespan of an obese person is up to 8-10 years shorter (for a BMI of 40-45) than that of a normal-weight person, mirroring the loss of life expectancy suffered by smokers. An overweight person of average height will increase their risk of death by approximately 30% for every 15 additional kilograms of weight. In ten European countries, the odds of disability, defined as a limitation in activities of daily living (ADL), are nearly twice as large among the obese as in normal weight persons.

An obese person generates higher health care expenditures than a normal-weight person and costs increase disproportionately at increasing levels of BMI. However, over a lifetime, existing estimates suggest that an obese person generates lower expenditures than a person of normal weight (but higher than a smoker, on average).

What are the trends in obesity – past and future?

Chapter 2 looks at the development
of obesity over time and its relationship
to changes in diet and lifestyle

Height and weight have been increasing since the 18th century in many of the current OECD countries, as income, education and living conditions gradually improved over time. Surveys began to record a sharp acceleration in the rate of increase in body mass index (BMI) in the 1980s, which in many countries grew two to three times more rapidly than in the previous century. While gains in BMI had been largely beneficial to the health and longevity of our ancestors, an alarming number of people have now crossed the line beyond which further gains become more and more detrimental. Before 1980, obesity rates were generally well below 10%. Since then, rates have doubled or tripled in many countries, and in almost half of OECD countries 50% or more of the population is overweight.

Rates of overweight and obesity vary considerably across OECD countries, but have been increasing consistently over the past three decades everywhere. If recent trends in OECD countries continue over the next ten years, projections suggest that pre-obesity rates (a BMI above the normal limit of 25 but below the obesity level of 30) for the 15-74 age group will stabilise progressively, and may even shrink slightly in many countries, while obesity rates continue to rise.

On the one hand, obesogenic environments, including physical, social and economic environments, have contributed to higher obesity rates over the past 30 years by exerting powerful influences on people's overall calorie intake, on the composition of their diets and on the frequency and intensity of physical activity at work, at home and during leisure time. On the other hand, changing individual attitudes, reflecting the long-term influences of improved education and socio-economic conditions, have countered environmental influences to some extent.

Which groups are the most affected by obesity?
What are the social impacts of obesity?

Chapter 3 looks at how age, gender
education and socio-economic status affect
obesity rates and, conversely, at how obesity
affects labour market opportunities
and outcomes

There does not appear to be a uniform gender pattern in obesity across countries. Worldwide, obesity rates tend to be higher in women than in men, other things being equal, and the same is true, on average, in the OECD area. Male obesity rates have also been growing faster than female rates in most OECD countries. The gender dimension is especially important because of its significant interactions with other individual characteristics, such as socio-economic condition or ethnicity.

A complex relationship exists between socio-economic condition and obesity. For example, this relationship changes as economies become more developed, with poorer people more likely to be affected in rich countries. Analyses of data from more than one third of OECD countries show important social disparities in overweight and obesity in women and lesser or no disparities in men. Social disparities within countries are larger in obesity than in overweight, but when comparisons across countries are made, the size of disparities is not related to countries' overall obesity rates. With few exceptions, social disparities in obesity remained remarkably stable over the past 15 years.

Social disparities are also present in children in three out of four countries examined, but no major differences between genders are observed in degrees of disparity. The gap in obesity between children who belong to ethnic minorities and white children in England and in the United States is larger than that observed in adults.

Disparities in labour market outcomes between the obese and people of normal weight, which are particularly strong in women, are likely to contribute to the social gradient in overweight and obesity. The obese are less likely to be part of the labour force and to be in employment. Discrimination in hiring decisions, partly due to expectations of lower productivity, contributes to the employment gap. White women are especially disadvantaged in this respect. The obese are likely to earn less than people of normal weight. Wage penalties of up to 18% have been associated with obesity in existing research. The obese tend to have more days of absence from work, a lower productivity on the job and a greater access to disability benefits than people of normal weight. The need for government intervention to protect the obese in labour markets and ensure they enjoy the same opportunities as anyone else in terms of employment, type of job, sector of occupation and pay naturally follows the evidence presented in Chapter 3.

How did obesity become a problem?

Chapter 4 explores some of the key dynamics that have contributed to the obesity epidemic, including the role of factors which have made it difficult for individuals to handle increasing environmental pressures

The obesity epidemic is the result of multiple, complex and interacting dynamics, which have progressively converged to produce lasting changes in people's lifestyles. The supply and availability of food have changed remarkably in the second half of the 20th century, in line with major changes in food production technologies and an increasing and increasingly sophisticated use of promotion and persuasion. The price of calories fell dramatically and convenience foods became available virtually everywhere at any time, while the time available for traditional meal preparation from raw ingredients shrunk progressively as a result of changing working and living conditions. Decreased physical activity at work, increased participation of women in the labour force, increasing levels of stress and job insecurity, longer working hours for some jobs, are all factors that, directly or indirectly, contributed to the lifestyle changes which caused the obesity epidemic.

Government policies have also played a part in the obesity epidemic. Examples include subsidies (*e.g.* in agriculture) and taxation affecting the prices of lifestyle commodities; transport policies, some of which have led to an increased use of private means of transportation; urban planning policies leaving scarce opportunities for physical activity, or leading to the creation of deprived and segregated urban areas that provide fertile grounds for the spread of unhealthy lifestyles and ill health.

The question must be asked of whether the changes that fuelled obesity and chronic diseases in the past decades are simply the outcome of efficient market dynamics, or the effect of market and rationality failures preventing individuals from achieving more desirable outcomes. In the design and implementation of prevention policies special attention must be placed on the role of information, externalities and self-control issues, including the role of "social multiplier" effects (the clustering and spread of overweight and obesity within households and social networks) in the obesity epidemic. Evidence of similar failures is reviewed and the scope for prevention to address some of the consequences of those failures is discussed in the book.

What can governments and markets do to improve health-related behaviours?

*Chapter 5 looks at the broad range of actions
taken in recent years to improve nutrition
and physical activity in OECD countries*

Governments can increase choice by making new healthy options available or by making existing ones more accessible and affordable. Alternatively, they can use persuasion, education and information to make healthy options more attractive. These are often advocated as minimally intrusive interventions, but governments may not always deliver persuasion effectively and in the best interest of individuals, and it is difficult to monitor whether they do so. Regulation and fiscal measures are more transparent and contestable interventions, although they hit all consumers indiscriminately, may be difficult to organise and enforce and may have regressive effects. Interventions that are less intrusive on individual choices tend to be more expensive, while interventions that are more intrusive have higher political and welfare costs.

A survey of national policies in 2007-08 covering all OECD and EU countries shows that governments acknowledge that individuals are often exposed to large amounts of potentially confusing information on health and lifestyles from a variety of sources, and assert that it is primarily their responsibility to act as a balanced and authoritative source of information, thus providing clear guidance to individuals who struggle to cope with increasingly powerful environmental influences.

Many governments are intensifying their efforts to promote a culture of healthy eating and active living. A large majority of them have adopted initiatives aimed at school-age children, including changes in the school environment, notably regarding food and drink, as well as improvements in facilities for physical activity. The second most common group of interventions involves the public health function of health systems. These interventions are primarily based on the development and dissemination of nutrition guidelines and health promotion messages to a wide variety of population groups through numerous channels, as well as promotion of active transport and active leisure. Governments have been more reluctant to use regulation and fiscal levers because of the complexity of the regulatory process, the enforcement costs involved, and the likelihood of sparking a confrontation with key industries.

The private sector, including employers, the food and beverage industry, the pharmaceutical industry, the sports industry and others, has made a potentially important contribution to tackling unhealthy diets and sedentary lifestyles, often in co-operation with governments and international organisations. Evidence of the effectiveness of private sector interventions is still insufficient, but an active collaboration between the public and the private sector will enhance the impact of any prevention strategies and spread the costs involved more widely. Key areas in which governments expect a contribution from the food and beverage industry are: food product reformulation; limitation of marketing activities, particularly to vulnerable groups; transparency and information about food contents.

What interventions work best and at what cost?

Chapter 6 presents a comprehensive analysis of the impacts of nine different health interventions on obesity and related chronic diseases in five OECD countries: Canada, England, Italy, Japan and Mexico

Interventions aimed at tackling obesity by improving diets and increasing physical activity in at least three areas, including health education and promotion, regulation and fiscal measures, and counselling in primary care, are all effective in improving health and longevity and have favourable cost-effectiveness ratios relative to a scenario in which chronic diseases are treated only as they emerge. When interventions are combined in a multiple-intervention strategy, targeting different age groups and determinants of obesity simultaneously, overall health gains are significantly enhanced without any loss in cost-effectiveness. The cost of delivering a package of interventions would vary between USD PPPs 12 per capita in Japan to USD PPPs 24 in Canada, a tiny fraction of health expenditure in those countries, and also a small proportion of what is currently spent on prevention in the same countries.

Most of the interventions examined have the potential to generate gains of 40 000 to 140 000 years of life free of disability in the five countries together, with one intervention, intensive counselling of individuals at risk in primary care, leading to a gain of up to half million life years free of disability. However, counselling in primary care is also the most expensive of the interventions considered in the analysis. Interventions with the most favourable cost-effectiveness profiles are outside the health care sector, particularly in the regulatory and fiscal domain. Interventions, especially those aimed at children, may take a long time to make an impact on people's health and reach favourable cost-effectiveness ratios.

Interventions add years of healthy life to people's health expectancy, reducing health care costs. However, the health benefits of prevention are such that people also live longer with chronic diseases, and years of life are added in the oldest age groups, increasing the need for health care. The interventions assessed may, at best, generate reductions in the order of 1% of total expenditure for major chronic diseases. At the same time, many such interventions involve costs which outweigh any reductions in health expenditure. These costs may arise in different jurisdictions. Some are typically paid through public expenditure, but do not necessarily fall within health care budgets (*e.g.* the costs associated with regulatory measures, or interventions on the education or transport systems). Others fall outside public budgets altogether (*e.g.* most of the costs associated with worksite interventions).

The distributional impacts of interventions are mostly determined by differences in morbidity and mortality among socio-economic groups. Fiscal measures are the only intervention producing consistently larger health gains in the less well-off. The distributional impacts of other interventions vary in different countries.

Those reported in Chapter 6 are likely to be conservative estimates of the impacts to be expected in real world settings. Key drivers of success for preventive interventions include high participation (on both supply and demand sides), long-term sustainability of effects, ability to generate social multiplier effects, and combination of multiple interventions producing their effects over different time horizons.

How can an unhealthy societal trend be turned around?

Chapter 7 outlines the role of information, incentives and choice in designing policies to combat obesity and discusses the relevance of a multi-stakeholder approach to chronic disease prevention

The main question addressed in this book is how to trigger meaningful changes in obesity trends. The short answer is by wide-ranging prevention strategies addressing multiple determinants of health. The reality is that every step of the process is conditioned not just by public health concerns, but by history, culture, the economic situation, political factors, social inertia and enthusiasm, and the particularities of the groups targeted.

Individual interventions have a relatively limited impact; therefore, comprehensive strategies involving multiple interventions to address a range of determinants are required to reach a "critical mass" – one that can have a meaningful impact on the obesity epidemic by generating fundamental changes in social norms. The development of comprehensive prevention strategies against obesity needs to focus on how social norms are defined and how they change; on the influence of education and information on obesity but also on the potential for government regulation to affect behaviours; and on the role of individual choice and values. A sensible prevention strategy against obesity would combine population and individual (high-risk) approaches, as the two have different and complementary strengths in the pursuit of effectiveness, efficiency and favourable distributional outcomes.

The adoption of a "multi-stakeholder" approach is increasingly invoked as the most sensible way forward in the prevention of chronic diseases. But while few if any of those involved would argue with this in theory, the interests of different groups are sometimes in conflict with each other and it is not always possible to find a solution where nobody loses out. Yet at the same time, no party is in a position to meaningfully reduce the obesity problem and associated chronic diseases without full co-operation with other stakeholders.

Chapter 1

Introduction: Obesity
and the Economics of Prevention

Unprecedented improvements in population health have been recorded in OECD countries during the past century, thanks to economic growth and to public policies in education, sanitation, health, and welfare. Yet industrialisation and prosperity have been accompanied by increases in the incidence of a number of chronic diseases, for which obesity is a major risk factor. This chapter looks at the impact of obesity on health and longevity and the economic costs that obesity generates, now and for the future. It examines the role of prevention in mitigating these effects and presents a case for how an economic perspective on the prevention of chronic diseases linked to lifestyles and obesity can provide insight into better ways of addressing the obesity epidemic.

Obesity: The extent of the problem

Unprecedented improvements in population health have been recorded in OECD countries during the past century. Life expectancy has increased on average by as much as 25-30 years. Major infectious diseases have been eradicated. Infant mortality rates have been dramatically reduced. People have gained in height and weight over time, with a substantial number moving out of under-nutrition. Economic growth has played an important role in these achievements, and so have public policies in education, sanitation, public health, and the development of welfare systems. However, industrialisation and prosperity have been accompanied by increases in the incidence of a number of chronic diseases. Advances in medical care have, in some cases, prevented increasing incidence from translating into higher mortality, but industrialised societies bear growing burdens of disability, which are contributing to rising health care expenditures.

Lifestyles have played an important part in the health changes described here. In high-income countries, smoking alone is estimated to be responsible for 22% of cardiovascular diseases, and for the vast majority of some cancers and chronic respiratory diseases. Alcohol abuse is deemed to be the source of 8-18% of the total burden of disease in men and 2-4% in women. Overweight and obesity account for an estimated 8-15% of the burden of disease in industrialised countries, while high cholesterol accounts for 5-12% (WHO, 2002).

Studies conducted in the 1970s and 1980s in the county of Alameda, California, showed that healthy habits concerning aspects of diet, physical activity, smoking, alcohol consumption and sleeping patterns could reduce mortality rates by 72% in men and 57% in women, relative to rates observed in those who had mostly unhealthy habits (Breslow and Enstrom, 1980). A recent study in England produced similar findings, suggesting that combining healthy habits has the strongest impact on mortality. People who lead a physically active life, do not smoke, drink alcohol in moderate quantities, and eat plenty of fruits and vegetables have a risk of death that is less than one fourth of the risk of those who have invariably unhealthy habits (Khaw *et al.*, 2008). In Ireland, almost half of the reduction in CHD mortality rates during 1985-2000 in the age group 25-84 was attributed to declining trends in the number of smokers and in the mean levels of cholesterol and blood pressure (Bennet *et al.*, 2006). Active lifestyle change may reap large benefits, as demonstrated, for instance, by a 25-year intervention on adult men in

Finland, named the North Karelia project, which is purported to have led to a 68% decline in cardiovascular disease mortality, 73% in coronary heart disease, 44% in cancer, 71% in lung cancer, and to a 49% decline in deaths from all causes (Puska *et al.*, 1998).

Among the many epidemics that hit the world in the 20th century, two have contributed to a substantial proportion of the burden of chronic diseases, especially in high-income countries: tobacco smoking and obesity.

Cigarette smoking was a phenomenon of negligible importance in the early 1900s, but smoking rates increased steadily during the course of the century, in line with the mass production of cigarettes. The increase was particularly large between the 1930s and the 1960s. During the 1960s and 1970s, smoking rates reached peaks of 50% or more in many OECD countries, before starting to decline.

Solid evidence of the harm caused by tobacco to the health of smokers has been available at least since the 1950s. In 1964, the US Surgeon General issued a landmark report outlining the sheer scope of the health risks associated with smoking. However, it took many more years for the addictive nature of tobacco and the dangers of passive smoking to be fully and widely recognised, amidst deceptive actions by the tobacco industry and a heavy involvement of the judiciary.

The obesity epidemic has developed more recently. Height and weight have been increasing since the 18th century in many of the current OECD countries, as income, education and living conditions gradually improved over time. Surveys began to record a sharp acceleration in the rate of increase in body mass index (BMI) in the 1980s, which in many countries grew two to three times more rapidly than in the previous century. While gains in BMI had been largely beneficial to the health and longevity of our ancestors, an alarmingly large number of people have now crossed the line beyond which further gains become more and more detrimental. Before 1980, obesity rates were generally well below 10%. Since then, rates have doubled or tripled in many countries, and in almost half of OECD countries 50% or more of the population is overweight.

Evidence of a link between body weight and mortality dates back to the early 1950s (Dublin, 1953), but the harmful effects of specific nutrients and those of increasingly sedentary jobs and lives has proved much more difficult to ascertain. It was only in recent years that a clear link between unsaturated (trans) fats, particularly hydrogenated oils, and coronary heart disease was established (Mozaffarian and Stampfer, 2010). But for most nutrients, including other types of fats, sugar and salt, the issue is rather to determine at what levels their consumption may become a health hazard. The factors that influence what people eat and the activities in which they engage are so many and so diverse that capturing the fundamental causes of the obesity epidemic and acting on the levers which may effectively and durably change the course of the epidemic is a considerable challenge.

Obesity, health and longevity

Obesity is a major public health concern because it is a key risk factor for a range of chronic diseases (Malnick and Knobler, 2006), with diabetes being the most closely linked. The severely obese have a risk of developing type 2 diabetes up to 60 times larger than those at the lower end of the normal weight spectrum. High blood pressure and high cholesterol are also more common as BMI increases. These links make the obese more likely to develop heart disease, particularly coronary artery disease, and stroke, and to die from these diseases. A large proportion of major cancers such as breast and colorectal cancer is linked to obesity and physical inactivity. Obesity also increases the chances of developing a number of respiratory and gastrointestinal diseases, as well as osteoarthritis, some mental conditions, and many other diseases and complaints, too numerous to list here. Some of the consequences of obesity may not even be known yet.

Chronic diseases are currently the main cause of both disability and death worldwide. They affect people of all ages and social classes, although they are more common in older ages and among the socially disadvantaged (WHO, 2002). Globally, of the 58 million deaths that occurred in 2005, approximately 35 million, or 60%, were due to chronic causes. Most deaths were due to cardiovascular disorders and diabetes (32%), cancers (13%), and chronic respiratory diseases (7%) (Abegunde et al., 2007). This burden is predicted to worsen in the coming years. A WHO study projected an increase of global deaths by a further 17% in the period 2005-15, meaning that of the 64 million estimated deaths in 2015, 41 million people will die of a chronic disease (WHO, 2005).

The burden of chronic diseases is proportionally even larger in OECD countries. In 2002, these caused 86% of deaths in the European region (WHO, 2004). However, the prevalence of many chronic diseases, including diseases of the circulatory system, digestive and respiratory diseases, was substantially lower at the end of the 20th century than it had been at the start of the century in countries such as the United States (Fogel, 1994). Mortality for cardiovascular diseases more than halved in the United States in the latter part of the last century, after the end of World War II. Deaths decreased by a further 13% between 1996 and 2006, as case fatality dropped by almost 30%. In many countries, mortality declined more rapidly among the better off. Social disparities in premature mortality from cardiovascular diseases and many cancers widened in countries such as Finland, Norway, Denmark, Belgium, Austria and England (Mackenbach, 2006).

Such a dramatic fall in mortality, which was not mirrored by comparable declines in disease incidence, and a general increase in longevity, led to a substantial growth of morbidity associated with chronic diseases in recent years. In Denmark, an estimated 40% of the population lives with long-term conditions (WHO Europe, 2006), while in the United States the majority of 70-year-olds is affected by at least one chronic condition, with cardiovascular diseases alone affecting 40% of males (Adams *et al.*, 1999). OECD research showed a generalised increase in the prevalence of diabetes among the elderly. Alarming trends were observed even in countries traditionally minimally affected by such disease. For instance, Japan saw a 5.3% average annual increase in the prevalence of diabetes in the period 1989-2004 (Lafortune and Balestat, 2007). Co-morbidities also increase with age, and populations are ageing rapidly in the OECD area. In western Europe, the number of people aged over 64 has more than doubled in the last 60 years, while the number of those aged over 80 has quadrupled. As a consequence, several chronic diseases can co-exist in many individuals. At least 35% of men over 60 years of age have been found to have two or more chronic conditions (WHO Europe, 2006), and of the 17 million people living with long-term chronic diseases in the United Kingdom, up to 70-80% would need support for self-care (Watkins, 2004).

Obesity, mortality and life expectancy

Unhealthy diets, sedentary lifestyles and obesity are responsible for a considerable proportion of the burden of ill health and mortality described here. The largest existing study of the link between obesity and mortality, covering close to one million adults in Europe and North America, came to the conclusion that mortality increases steeply with BMI once individuals cross the 25 kg/m^2 threshold (the lower limit of the overweight category) (Prospective Studies Collaboration, 2009). The lifespan of an obese person with a BMI between 30 and 35 is two to four years shorter than that of a person of normal weight. The gap increases to eight to ten years for those who are severely obese (BMI of 40-45), mirroring the loss of life expectancy suffered by smokers. An overweight person of average height will increase their risk of death by approximately 30% for every 15 additional kilograms of weight.

The link is not as strong beyond age 70 (Stevens *et al.*, 1998; Corrada *et al.*, 2006). Many cross-sectional studies of older individuals have even found a lower mortality among the overweight and those who are mildly obese than in normal weight individuals – the so-called "obesity paradox" – although detailed longitudinal studies have shown that this is mostly an effect of the weight loss associated with chronic diseases (Strandberg *et al.*, 2009).

The overall impact of the obesity epidemic on trends in life expectancy is still somewhat uncertain, despite the large amount of evidence gathered in recent years. A widely cited analysis published in a leading medical journal predicted that the rise in obesity will lead life expectancy to level off or even decline during the first half of this century in the United States (Olshansky *et al.*, 2005). Roughly at the same time, the UK Department of Health claimed that if the growth of obesity continued unchanged, projected increases in life expectancy to 2050 would have to be revised downwards by over five years (UK Department of Health, 2004). More recent estimates, however, are not so pessimistic. A detailed model-based analysis for England concluded that the loss of life expectancy due to increasing obesity will more likely be in the order of a fraction of a year by 2050 (Foresight, 2007). A US-based analysis estimated that the growth of obesity will offset the positive effects of falling smoking rates, but the net effect will be that increases in life expectancy projected by 2020 will be held back by less than one year (Stewart *et al.*, 2009). Overall, downward trends in mortality from a range of chronic diseases are likely to continue to prevail over the negative effects of the obesity epidemic, although it is unquestionable that progress in longevity would be much faster if fewer people were overweight.

However, a growing body of research shows that the impact of obesity on disability is far larger than its impact on mortality (Gregg and Guralnik, 2007). The obese not only live less than their normal weight counterparts, they also develop chronic diseases earlier in life and live longer with those diseases and with disability (Vita *et al.*, 1998). In ten European countries, the odds of disability, defined as a limitation in activities of daily living (ADL), are nearly twice as large among the obese as in normal weight persons. The odds are three to four times as large in men and women who are severely obese (Andreyeva *et al.*, 2007). In the United States, the obese did not benefit from general improvements in cardiovascular health as much as those with normal weight did. While disability decreased in the latter group, it increased among the obese between the late 1980s and the early 2000s (Alley and Chang, 2007). At age 70, an average obese person can expect to live over 40% of their residual life expectancy with diabetes, over 80% with high blood pressure and over 85% with osteoarthritis, while the corresponding shares for a normal weight person are 17%, 60% and 68% (Lakdawalla *et al.*, 2005).

The economic costs of obesity

The strong association between obesity and chronic diseases suggests that the obese are likely to make a disproportionate use of health care, leading to a substantially larger expenditure relative to normal weight individuals. A wealth of studies has shown this based on data from at least 14 OECD countries and some non-OECD countries, mostly focusing on medical care expenditures. However, the question of the economic impact of obesity is not so simple when addressed over the lifetime and at a population level.

Estimates based on widely different approaches and methods suggest that obesity is responsible for approximately 1% to 3% of total health expenditure in most countries, with the notable exception of the United States, where several studies estimate that obesity may account for 5% to 10% of health expenditures (Tsai *et al.*, 2010). At the individual level, an obese person incurs health care expenditures at least 25% higher than those of a normal weight person, according to a range of studies from a variety of countries (Withrow and Alter, 2010). When production losses are added to health care costs, obesity accounts for a fraction of a percentage point of GDP in most countries, and over 1% in the United States. The figure rises to over 4% in China, according to one study of the economic impact of overweight (rather than obesity), which estimated production losses in the region of 3.6% of GDP (Popkin *et al.*, 2006; Branca and Kolovou Delonas, forthcoming).

The lifetime perspective

Because of the time lag between the onset of obesity and related health problems, the rise in obesity over the past two decades will mean higher health care costs in the future. Taking the example of England, the costs linked to overweight and obesity could be as much as 70% higher in 2015 relative to 2007 and could be 2.4 times higher in 2025 (Foresight, 2007).

Only a few of the many studies exploring health care costs associated with obesity have taken a lifetime perspective. These are all model-based studies, and unfortunately their results are not fully consistent, leaving a great deal of uncertainty on the long-term impacts of obesity. Two studies published in 1999, both based on US data, suggest that obesity increases lifetime expenditures (Thompson *et al.*, 1999; Allison *et al.*, 1999). At least one of these studies (Allison *et al.*, 1999) accounts for the disease and health care implications of the longer life expectancy of people who are not obese, reaching the conclusion that after age 80 the expected health care expenditures of a non-obese person outgrow those of an obese person, as the gap in mortality between the two increases with age. However, the health care expenditures incurred by the obese at earlier ages are so much greater than those of the non-obese that, on balance, the obese still have higher lifetime costs.

This conclusion is in line with the findings of a later study (Lakdawalla *et al.*, 2005) that entailed a simulation analysis for a cohort of 70-year-olds based on data from the US Medicare Current Beneficiary Survey (MCBS). The study concluded, perhaps unsurprisingly, given its focus on individuals who were still alive at age 70, that an overweight (but not obese) person has health care expenditures about 7% higher than those of a normal weight person, during the course of their remaining life spans, while the expenditures of an obese person are over 20% higher than those of a normal weight person. However, a further study published in 2008, based on data from the

Netherlands, found that decreased longevity of the obese makes them likely to incur lower health care expenditures than the non-obese, over a lifetime (van Baal *et al.*, 2008). According to this study, an average obese person, during their entire life span, will incur 13% lower health expenditures than a normal weight person, but 12% higher than an average smoker. The sign of these differences did not change in the study under a wide range of assumptions.

Cost-of-illness (COI) studies like the ones described here do provide some useful information, but is this the information policy makers really need to devise sound prevention strategies? When a study claims that obesity is responsible for a given amount of health care expenditure, or that obesity is associated with X% higher health care expenditures, what these claims really mean is the following : "If there were a treatment that made all obese people non-obese and equivalent in health to people who had never been obese, and if this treatment cost nothing to apply, and it were given to all obese people, then in the immediately subsequent time period direct health care costs would be reduced by [X%]" (Allison *et al.*, 1999). This hypothetical situation, of course, is very different from the reality policy makers face. Any prevention programme, at best, will produce a marginal shift in people's levels of risk. If prevention is successful in moving a certain number of people from obesity to pre-obesity, or from the latter to normal weight, those who change their condition are likely to be the ones who used to be borderline above the threshold, and their change in weight will probably take them just slightly below the same threshold. The changes in health care expenditures following a real preventive intervention are unlikely to bear much of a relationship with the estimates provided by COIs.

In the work which led to this book, the OECD deliberately avoided producing new generic estimates of health care expenditures, or costs, associated with obesity. Rather, it focused on estimating how specific forms of prevention may potentially modify existing health care needs and expenditures, as part of a broader economic analysis in which the costs of prevention are contrasted with its effectiveness. The methods and findings of this work are illustrated in Chapter 6.

The implications for social welfare and the role of prevention

OECD health care systems offer a wide range of treatments for chronic diseases, aimed at minimising their consequences. Many treatments generate benefits that justify their costs, notably in terms of quality of life. Still, the need to develop ever better ways to improve quality of life must inevitably confront the question of resources: are there limits to what can be spent on improving the quality of life and extending the life expectancy of those who suffer from chronic diseases? How do investments in prevention fit into the equation?

Few countries, if any, have similarly organised systems for the prevention of chronic diseases, although many initiatives have been taken to counter specific risk factors. As the burden of chronic diseases increases, and as societal expectations in terms of quality of life and longevity also increase, prevention may offer a valuable alternative to treatment, especially since in principle, it has the potential for increasing well-being and longevity even more than treating existing disease.

However, the costs and benefits associated with prevention are not always as obvious as many would think. Unlike treatment, prevention does not target diseases, but aims at modifying the conditions that make disease possible or likely, such as living conditions, lifestyles and the education people receive. Changing these often involves some kind of individual sacrifice. Examples may include switching from motorised transport to walking or cycling; opting for home cooked meals rather than ready-made and fast food restaurant meals; walking an extra distance to buy fresh produce which may not be available in the neighbourhood; and many others.

Health is not everything

The obesity epidemic is at least in part the result of changes that may be positive in themselves. Food has become more plentiful and food prices have fallen dramatically. Food is produced and delivered in ways which have cut the time people have to spend preparing meals, at a time when employment among women, who have traditionally done and still do most of food preparation, has been steadily on the rise. "In 1965, a married woman who didn't work spent over two hours per day cooking and cleaning up from meals. In 1995, the same tasks take less than half the time" (Cutler *et al.*, 2003). For an increasing number of people, labour is no longer a synonym for work, as jobs have become less and less physically demanding. Motorised transport is commonplace, even to the local grocery store or school. Obesity, to a certain extent, is a side effect of these and other changes, which Philipson and Posner (2008) call the "positive aspects of the growth in obesity". If, hypothetically, those changes were to be reversed for the sake of a slimmer population, on the whole, people would be worse off.

A central tenet in an economic approach to prevention is the recognition that improving health is not the sole, and often not the most important, goal of human life. Individuals wish to engage in activities from which they expect to derive pleasure, satisfaction, or fulfilment, some of which may be conducive to good health, others less or not at all. Health is complementary with many forms of non-health-related consumption. It is necessary for individuals to flourish as consumers, parents, workers, and in other capacities. But activities from which individuals derive pleasure and fulfilment may also be in conflict with health. Some of these are fairly obvious, such as smoking, drinking to excess, or indulging in unhealthy eating. Prevention will inevitably affect the pursuit of activities that are in conflict with health. As a consequence, individuals will be inhibited to some degree from enjoying those activities.

The benefits of prevention over time and across social groups

Why should people change their ways of life? What does prevention have to offer in exchange for the sacrifices it imposes on individuals? The benefit people derive from prevention is not an immediately tangible improvement in their condition. Rather, it is the prospect of a reduced risk of developing certain diseases sometime in the future. Both the size of the risk reduction, often relatively small, and the time required for such risk reduction to materialise, make it difficult for people to fully appreciate the value of prevention. People's attitudes towards risk, and their preferences concerning outcomes that may occur at different points in time, have a great influence on the perceived value of prevention.

The impact of prevention on social welfare depends on the balance between the costs of prevention, including the sacrifices imposed on those whose environments and lifestyles are affected, and the value attached to future risk reductions. Good prevention practices are those which provide real opportunities for increasing social welfare, by ensuring the value of prevention is greater than its cost. This is the first and foremost goal of prevention. In addition, prevention may provide opportunities for improving the distribution of welfare, or some component of it, such as health, across individuals and population groups.

Health disparities are ubiquitous and persistent in OECD countries, and many governments have made commitments to reducing them on equity grounds. Prevention always has an impact on the distributional aspects of health and welfare. Different individuals have different probabilities of developing chronic diseases, and have different health expectancies once diseases occur. Different individuals also respond differently to preventive interventions, and some will gain more than others from prevention. These distributional effects need to be accounted for in assessing the value of prevention, and they should be an integral part of the motivation for delivering prevention programmes. Prevention can be an effective way of pursuing equity in health when interventions are carefully designed to achieve this goal.

What economic analyses can contribute

This book provides an economic perspective on the prevention of chronic diseases linked to lifestyles and obesity. That perspective is about more than counting the costs associated with diseases, whether medical care costs or productivity losses. And it involves more than assessing the cost-effectiveness of preventive interventions, although this is an important role for health economics. The potential for an economic approach to shape and inform the debate on prevention stretches beyond those aspects. It can also:

- Help in understanding the pathways through which chronic diseases are generated, which have at least as much to do with social phenomena as with human biology.

- Provide the tools for interpreting the individual and social choices that constitute a fundamental part of those pathways.

- Help in identifying opportunities for intervening on such choices with a view to improving social welfare.

- Help in understanding and addressing potential conflicts between the goals of increasing overall welfare and improving the distribution of health across individuals and population groups.

The economic approach proposed in this book provides a framework for analysing the consequences of prevention strategies and draws upon the contributions of other disciplines such as psychology, sociology, epidemiology, and public health. The proposed approach rests on the hypothesis that countering the obesity epidemic with appropriate prevention strategies may be preferable to treating the disease consequences of obesity. This hypothesis is subjected to rigorous testing based on the best existing knowledge and data, including new analyses undertaken by the OECD.

What do people want?

Identifying the potential for welfare gains from disease prevention means, above all, understanding what people value and why they value certain outcomes more than others. Lifestyles are the result of the balancing of multiple, sometimes conflicting objectives. The pursuit of each goal, including the maintenance of good health, finds a limit in the tradeoffs that emerge. Individuals who experience the consequences of unhealthy lifestyles, like obesity, or develop chronic diseases, may be willing to sacrifice the pursuit of other goals in order to improve their chances of preserving or restoring their own health. But when there is only a risk of disease, a more or less remote chance of developing disease in the future, individual priorities may be different and the relative importance attached to goals other than maintaining good health may increase substantially. An assessment of the role of prevention must not ignore those competing goals. To the extent that individuals are the best judges of their own welfare, the chances of success of any prevention programme will depend on how people value those goals.

On the other hand, the economic approach taken here recognises that individual lifestyles are subject to influences and constraints that may prevent people from making the choices that would maximise their welfare. The ability of individuals (obese and not obese) to make choices that would maximise their own welfare is limited. Even if all individuals were perfectly rational, the environment in which they live could still prevent them from making the best possible choices. O'Donoghue and Rabin (2003) emphasise that "economists will and should be ignored if [they] continue to insist that it is axiomatic that constantly trading stocks or accumulating consumer debt or becoming a heroin addict must be optimal for the people doing these things merely because they have chosen to do it". The same applies to obesity. It cannot be assumed that all those who become obese willingly accept this as a necessary consequence of behaviours from which they otherwise derive satisfaction and fulfilment.

Markets can fail

Economics interprets people's choices and interactions with their environment as market dynamics. There are strong indications, and some empirical evidence, as discussed in Chapter 4, that the market mechanisms through which individuals make their lifestyle choices (whether or not money is involved), may sometimes fail to operate efficiently. Obesity is partly the result of these failures, interpreted in this book as "market failures", potentially limiting the ability of individuals to maximise their own welfare.

Information failures provide a good example of what we mean by market failures. The assumption that the consumer has adequate information concerning the health effects of food and physical activity is not always tenable. But even if the information is complete and unambiguous, many consumers may not have the tools needed to use the information provided to their best advantage. For instance, many consumers would find it difficult to say whether "energy dense" and "high calorie" are the same thing. This is not just a question of lack of education. In a survey of 200 primary-care patients in the United States, two-thirds of whom had been to college, only 32% could correctly calculate the amount of carbohydrates consumed in a 20-ounce bottle of soda that had 2.5 servings in the bottle. Only 60% could calculate the number of carbohydrates consumed if they ate half a bagel when the serving size was a whole bagel. (Rothman et al., 2006).

The reasons most people gave for these misapprehensions were that they did not understand the serving size information, they were confused by extraneous material on the label, and they calculated incorrectly. Information failures may contribute to the adoption of unhealthy behaviours and lifestyles through inadequate knowledge or understanding of the long-term consequences of such behaviours.

The problem of self-control

Among the many reasons why people ignore sound advice on health and nutrition, even though they are aware of the economic and health costs involved, lack of what we commonly call self-control is an obvious one. People generally prefer an immediate benefit to a delayed one, even if the later one is larger. Likewise, they discount the longer-term negative consequences of an act that procures immediate gratification. Even if people understand the negative consequences of eating too much or not exercising, this counts less than the more immediate pleasure or other benefit they obtain from consumption (O'Donoghue and Rabin, 1999; Scharff, 2009).

A key characteristic of people who lack self-control is procrastination (Ariely, 2008, Chapter 6). Those who have poor self-control do not lack knowledge and information, they are often perfectly aware what they are doing or not doing is bad for their health in the long run, and they are willing and ready to change their behaviour, in the future. And they truly believe in their commitment to change. But when tomorrow comes, of course, they are no longer prepared to change. This inconsistency of preferences over time, which is the cause of procrastination, is what makes people with poor self-control especially vulnerable to the influences of an obesogenic environment.*

The importance of self-control and ability to delay gratification, is well exemplified by the famous "marshmallow experiment" (Mischel *et al.*, 1992). Pre-school children who were able to refrain from eating a marshmallow when they were offered one, in order to gain a second marshmallow reward later, grew up with fewer behavioural problems and a better school performance than children who were not able to delay gratification. Although obesity was not among the outcomes directly assessed in the study, the experiment is relevant to the issue of weight gain because it shows that self-control is an important feature of personality, linked to long-term behavioural and social outcomes, of which obesity is very likely to be one amidst ever increasing environmental pressures.

---

* O'Donoghue and Rabin (1999) observe that most behaviours suggesting the presence of self-control problems might also be explained in a framework of time-consistent preferences. For instance: "suppose a person becomes fat from eating large quantities of potato chips. She may do so because of a harmful self-control problem, or merely because the pleasure from eating potato chips outweighs the costs of being fat." Procrastination, however, is a clear sign of present-biased preferences and poor self-control. In practice, "the existence of present-biased preferences is overwhelmingly supported by psychological evidence, and strongly accords to common sense and conventional wisdom" and "even relatively mild self-control problems can lead to significant welfare losses".

External costs of obesity

The obese do not pay the full price attached to their condition. Society at large picks up the "externalities" bill. Externalities linked to obesity may result in the social or other costs and benefits not being fully reflected in their private costs and benefits to individual consumers. For example, a fat person needs more room on public transport than a thin one, but does not pay a higher price for the ticket (although some airlines are introducing extra charges for people who do not fit standard seats). This is a negative externality of being fat, as are the additional costs to health systems of obesity related diseases (or to hospitals of having to buy equipment to cope with larger patients).

Fiscal externalities are potentially the most important ones. When health care is funded through public expenditure, the cost of the additional health care needed by an obese person is borne by taxpayers. If an insurance plan or other third party payer is involved, the cost will be shared among all those covered by the plan, who pay a premium for their care. However, as discussed before, it is still unclear whether the additional health care expenditures generated by obesity may or may not be offset by decreased expenditures later in life, due to premature mortality.

Externalities are also associated with the social mechanisms which make unhealthy behaviours spread within families, social networks and peer groups as a true multiplier effect. These external costs are very difficult to quantify, but no less important than others which translate more easily into monetary figures.

Externalities generally provide a strong justification for considering interventions. Evidence of important externalities from smoking and alcohol abuse, among other things, has made possible the implementation of severe restrictions on tobacco and alcohol consumption. Virtually all market and rationality failures will translate either into an excessive or a too limited consumption of lifestyle commodities such as food and physical activity, relative to the levels that would be socially desirable. Actions aimed at correcting the effects of those failures may tackle directly the mechanisms through which failures manifest themselves, for instance, by providing information when this is lacking or by making individuals pay for the negative external effects of their own consumption, possibly through taxation.

However, it is not always possible, or effective, to act directly on those failures. Prevention may also tackle failures indirectly, by acting on any relevant determinants of health, to redress the initial overconsumption or underconsumption. For instance, when information is too complex to be communicated effectively, the effects of poor information on consumption may be compensated by using taxes or other financial incentives.

Identifying the determinants of obesity

An economic approach to obesity and prevention seeks to identify the determinants of obesity – those which have changed over time, contributing to the development of the obesity epidemic, as well as those which have not changed or have changed slowly, contributing mainly to disparities in obesity across individuals – and to find out whether failures like the examples above may have been at play.

The determinants of health and disease have become the objects of a field of study in its own right, to which many disciplines have contributed over the course of the past three decades. Studies have pointed to at least three important groups of determinants of the obesity epidemic:

1. *Supply-side factors*, including the changing roles of the industries that supply lifestyle commodities; their increased and increasingly sophisticated use of promotion and persuasion; and changes in production technologies, and productivity dynamics that have shaped trends in market prices.

2. *Government policies*, including subsidies (*e.g.* agriculture) and taxation affecting the prices of lifestyle commodities; transport policies, some of which have led to an increased use of private means of transportation; urban planning policies leaving scarce opportunities for physical activity, or leading to the creation of deprived and segregated urban areas that provide fertile grounds for the spread of unhealthy lifestyles and ill health.

3. *Changes in working conditions*, including decreased physical activity at work, increased participation of women in the labour force, increasing levels of stress and job insecurity, longer working hours for some jobs.

Education and socio-economic status are causally linked to powerful social disparities in obesity. However, the ways these determinants act is complex. They play an important role in women, but a much less important role in men. The way they affect obesity has changed over time. Obesity used to be a condition of the wealthy, and still is in many low- and middle-income countries. But in virtually all high-income countries obesity is now a condition of the poor and least educated. This is not because their individual characteristics are fundamentally different from those of people higher up the social ladder, but mainly because they are exposed to less favourable and more compelling environmental pressures.

Understanding the pathways through which diseases are generated is a necessary but not a sufficient condition for preventive action. If more women have taken up employment, and if they have been working such long hours that the time they used to dedicate to the preparation of meals for themselves and their families is now drastically reduced, it means that all those involved, women, their families, their employers, must have acted on the expectation that those changes would lead to a welfare gain, despite the possible negative consequences on health from poorer nutrition (Anderson *et al.*, 2002, showed that increased female labour force participation contributed to increases in child obesity, although Cutler *et al.*, 2003, disputed this claim). And a welfare gain has likely been attained, given that the trend has been consolidating over time. Acting on the labour market dynamics described above simply with the aim of preventing negative health effects, may result in a conflict with the aspirations of those who triggered those dynamics.

The prevention of chronic diseases inevitably interferes with lifestyles and social phenomena which are of value to many people. Some forms of prevention aim at widening choice by making new options available to consumers: healthier foods for a lower price; new opportunities for physical activity – for instance, more green spaces in urban areas, or new active means of transportation. In these cases, interference with individual lifestyles may be very mild. But prevention can be much more intrusive when the consequences of unhealthy lifestyles are particularly undesirable, or when specific circumstances make rational choices difficult or unlikely (for instance, when children are involved) or when information is lacking. In these cases prevention may impinge more heavily on individuals, up to the point of restricting their choices by banning options that present the highest risks for health.

The political costs of prevention, in the form of interference with individual choice, often follow an inverse pattern relative to the economic costs of prevention. Interventions that involve lower degrees of interference tend to have higher economic costs, and *vice versa*.

The book's main conclusions

Overweight and obesity rates have been increasing relentlessly over recent decades in all industrialised countries, as well as in many lower income countries. OECD analyses of trends over time, as well as projections of overweight and obesity rates over the next ten years, draw a grim picture about the present and possible future, contributing new evidence to a growing international literature. The circumstances in which people have been leading their lives over the past 20-30 years, including physical, social and economic environments, have exerted powerful influences on their overall calorie intake, on the composition of their diets and on the frequency and intensity of physical activity at work, at home and during leisure time. On the other hand, changing individual attitudes, reflecting the long-term influences of improved education and socio-economic conditions have countered increasing environmental pressures to some extent.

Social factors

OECD analyses confirm the existence of what has been described elsewhere as a "social multiplier" effect, corresponding to the clustering of overweight and obesity within households, social networks, and possibly other levels of aggregation (Cutler and Glaeser, 2007). This is likely to have contributed to the rapid spread of overweight and obesity, especially in high-income countries, making this expansion more and more similar to a classic epidemic. The social multiplier effect reflects externalities of lifestyles, particularly within households. The impact on other individuals' health may be less direct in this case than, for instance, in the case of passive smoking, but it is no less important. In a policy perspective, such externalities are likely to be more relevant than those associated with health expenditures, which remain somewhat controversial. The role played by education, health literacy and information as determinants of obesity suggests that lifestyle choices could be improved by changing individual endowments and the availability of information. There is also some evidence of rationality failures in choices concerning diet and physical activity, associated with lack of self-control and inconsistent preferences over time, which may have contributed to the obesity epidemic.

Many OECD countries have been concerned not only about the pace of the increase in overweight and obesity, but also about inequalities in their distribution across social groups, particularly by socio-economic status and by ethnic background. Large inequalities across social groups are observed in women, while substantially milder inequalities, or none at all, are observed in men. Acting on the mechanisms that make women in poor socio-economic circumstances so vulnerable to obesity, and women at the other end of the socio-economic spectrum much more able to handle obesogenic environments, is of great importance not just as a way of redressing existing inequalities, but also because of its potential effect on overall social welfare. The current distribution of obesity appears particularly undesirable, as it is likely to perpetuate the vicious circle linking obesity and disadvantage by intergenerational transmission.

Prevention needs consensus

The question addressed in this book, then, is how to trigger meaningful changes in obesity trends. The short answer is by wide-ranging prevention strategies addressing multiple determinants of health. The reality is that every step of the process is conditioned not just by public health concerns, but by history, culture, the economic situation, political factors, social inertia and enthusiasm, and the particularities of the groups targeted. For example, the fact that interventions and impacts may be asynchronous can create a political obstacle, especially during periods of cuts in public expenditures.

Politicians may be reluctant to approve spending when any benefit may not appear for several decades. Those designing and implementing a prevention strategy are faced with the difficult task of having to devise a mix of interventions that takes into account various tradeoffs, including those among available resources, distribution of costs and health effects across population groups, and interference with individual choice.

A wide consensus on what should be done, when and with what means would of course make things easier. However, although the contribution and co-operation of many agents is needed for the success of a prevention strategy, none of the agents potentially involved, at any point in time, possesses all the information, tools and power required for the planning of comprehensive chronic disease prevention strategies, and none of the agents is able to take a sufficiently long time perspective to make such planning possible.

Insufficient evidence

Governments in the OECD area have implemented a wide range of interventions at the national and local levels, particularly during the past five years. Governments have been taking action in response to calls by international organisations and pressure by the media and the public health community, but without a strong body of evidence of the effectiveness of interventions, and virtually no evidence of their efficiency and distributional impact. The opportunity cost of resources used by governments to promote healthy diets and physical activity may be high, and most governments have not yet engaged in open discussions of possible rationales for intervention. In the private sector, employers, the food and beverage industry, the pharmaceutical industry, the sports industry and others have made potentially important contributions to tackling unhealthy diets and sedentary lifestyles, often in co-operation with individual governments and international organisations, although there is still insufficient evidence of the effectiveness of such interventions.

The adoption of a "multi-stakeholder" approach is increasingly invoked as the most sensible way forward in the prevention of chronic diseases. But while few if any of those involved would argue with this in theory, the interests of different groups are sometimes in conflict with each other and it is not always possible to find a solution where nobody loses out. Yet at the same time, no party is in a position to meaningfully reduce the obesity problem and associated chronic diseases without full co-operation with other stakeholders.

Who pays?

The question of who pays for and who benefits from prevention strategies is a case in point. Economic analysis contrasts the costs involved in implementing preventive interventions with the expected health outcomes of those interventions, without distinction as to who might bear the costs. The conclusion that many such interventions are efficient is based on the assumption that the health outcomes generated by the interventions are of value to those who bear the relevant costs. This would be the case for governments that view the enhancement of individual and population health as one of the goals of their action.

However, at least some of the costs of preventive interventions might be shifted onto the private sector, as long as these interventions generate outcomes that may be of value to potential payers. Parents for example, increasingly expect schools to carry out a number of roles apart from teaching children academic subjects. They might be willing to pay for school-based initiatives from which their children could benefit, such as expanded sports facilities, better food in canteens, or personalised nutrition programmes. Here the funder – the parent – has a clear obligation to aid the beneficiary and can be expected to act altruistically. The argument is more complicated regarding business. Initiatives taken by the food industry, for instance in relation to self-regulation of advertising or nutrition labelling, have the effect of charging the industry with a significant portion of the cost of those actions. The cost may be transferred to consumers, but the impact of the action may be to damage profitability, either through the extra cost itself, or because consumers buy less of the product when they understand what it is made of. Of course, if, as mentioned earlier, the alternative is even harsher regulation imposed by public authorities, the industry may see the cost as worthwhile.

Most interventions are efficient, but none can solve the problem alone

Despite the many complications, the overall conclusion from our study is that most interventions are efficient, as illustrated by broad cost-effectiveness categories, relative to a scenario in which no systematic prevention is undertaken and chronic diseases are treated once they emerge. Some interventions can even lead to overall cost savings. However, if individual interventions were to be implemented in isolation, they would have a limited impact on the overall scale of the obesity problem, reducing the obese population, at best, by less than 10%, although they would all increase life expectancy and disability-adjusted life expectancy. Although the most efficient interventions are outside the health care sector, health systems can make the largest impact on obesity and chronic conditions by focusing on individuals at high risk. Interventions targeting younger age groups are unlikely to have any meaningful health effects at the population level for many years. The cost-effectiveness profiles of such interventions may be favourable in the long term, but remain unfavourable for several decades at the start of the interventions. In general, the scale of the impact of individual interventions is limited by the difficulties involved in reaching a large proportion of the national population, so the wider the range of actions included in prevention strategies, the greater their effectiveness.

In policy terms, the main lesson is that there is no magic bullet that will be effective against all the causes of obesity across all age and socio-economic groups. But effective interventions do exist in all the main areas of action, and this book will help policy makers to assess their options and combine them in a practical, cost-effective manner.

Overview of the remaining chapters

This book proposes an economic approach to the study of obesity and chronic disease prevention, based on work undertaken by the OECD, partly in collaboration with the World Health Organisation (WHO). The concepts and analyses presented here provide a basis for developing and evaluating policies to maintain and improve population health by reducing the occurrence and the impact of chronic diseases. The proposed economic framework is centred on the hypothesis that prevention may provide the means for increasing social welfare, enhancing health equity, or both, relative to a situation in which chronic diseases are simply treated once they emerge. The book develops the steps required for testing this hypothesis in relation to the prevention of chronic diseases linked to unhealthy diets, sedentary lifestyles and obesity.

The scale and characteristics of the obesity epidemic, which is the most immediate and visible reflection of changing patterns of diet and physical activity, are addressed in the next two chapters. The findings presented in these chapters reflect the ways in which obesity has spread among adults in recent decades and its distribution across population groups, mainly based on analyses of health survey data from 11 OECD countries. Historical trends and projections of overweight and obesity rates are presented in Chapter 2, along with a challenging analysis of the relative contributions of age, period and cohort effects in the development of the obesity epidemic. Social disparities in obesity along several dimensions are discussed in Chapter 3, followed by a comprehensive review of the impacts of obesity on employment, earnings and productivity.

A special contribution by Tim Lobstein follows Chapter 3 and completes the picture by expanding the child obesity dimension of the analysis of recent trends in obesity. Lobstein's discussion of the phenomenon adds to the findings of OECD analyses of child obesity in four countries, including projections of child overweight and obesity rates over the next ten years reported in Chapter 2 and analyses of social disparities in child obesity reported in Chapter 3.

Some of the key pathways through which obesity and chronic diseases are generated are discussed in Chapter 4. There the question is addressed of whether such pathways are simply the outcome of efficient market dynamics, or the effect of market and rationality failures preventing individuals from achieving more desirable outcomes. Special attention is placed on information, externalities and self-control issues, including a detailed discussion of the role of social multiplier effects in the obesity epidemic. Evidence of similar failures is reviewed and the scope for prevention to address some of the consequences of those failures is discussed.

Donald Kenkel provides a further in-depth analysis of the role of information in relation to obesity in a special contribution which follows Chapter 4.

Actions taken by OECD governments and by the private sector in response to the obesity epidemic are reviewed in Chapter 5, partly based on a survey undertaken by the OECD of recent government policies aimed at improving diet and physical activity. The main characteristics and potential impact of interventions are assessed in relation to the degree to which they are likely to interfere with individual choice.

In a further special contribution which follows Chapter 5, Francesco Branca and his co-authors provide an overview of the breadth and effectiveness of local-level initiatives to improve diets and physical activity and discuss how these relate to national programmes.

An economic analysis of a set of nine interventions aimed at tackling obesity by improving diets and physical activity is the subject of Chapter 6. The main focus of the chapter is on five OECD countries – Canada, England, Italy, Japan and Mexico. Interventions range from health education and promotion in various settings to fiscal measures and regulation, to counselling of individuals at risk in primary care. These were identified on the basis of their prominence in the current policy debate, and of the availability of sufficient evidence of their effectiveness. The analysis was based on a micro-simulation model designed in collaboration with the WHO to assess the impact of changes in risk factors on chronic diseases, quality of life, longevity and expenditure. The likely distributional consequences of such changes by age, gender and socio-economic status are also presented in Chapter 6.

The strengths and limitations of government regulation and self-regulation of food advertising to children, two of the preventive interventions assessed in Chapter 6, are presented in two special contributions which follow the chapter.

Finally, the relevance of the findings presented throughout the book for government policy aimed at tackling the growing obesity epidemic is discussed in Chapter 7. The conclusions of the book emphasise the distinct contribution of an economic approach to prevention, highlight the key messages which emerge from OECD work on obesity and the challenges countries will face in the future.

Key messages

- Major progress in health care and public health over the past century, associated with a sustained economic growth, has contributed to improvements in population health and longevity, but has not prevented an expansion of the burden of chronic diseases in OECD countries.

- Much of the burden of chronic diseases is linked to lifestyles, with tobacco smoking, obesity, diet and lack of physical activity being responsible for the largest shares of such burden.

- Existing evidence shows that mortality increases steeply with BMI once individuals cross the overweight threshold. The lifespan of an obese person is up to 8-10 years shorter (for a BMI of 40-45) than that of a normal-weight person, mirroring the loss of life expectancy suffered by smokers.

- An obese person generates higher health care expenditures than a normal-weight person and costs increase disproportionally at increasing levels of BMI. However, this does not provide a complete picture of the economic burden associated with obesity.

- Over a lifetime, existing estimates suggest that an obese person generates lower expenditures than a person of normal weight (but higher than a smoker, on average).

- Assessing opportunities to modify existing health care needs and expenditures at the margin (as done in Chapter 6) is more important than producing generic estimates of the costs associated with obesity.

- Prevention can be one of the most effective ways of improving population health, but the small size of the risk reduction, at the individual level, and the time required for this to materialise, make it difficult for people to fully appreciate the value of prevention.

- An economic approach to the prevention of chronic diseases recognises the importance of human goals that are potentially in competition with the pursuit of good health and the social and material constraints which influence individual choice and behaviours.

- An economic approach to prevention aims at identifying possible factors, technically market failures, which limit opportunities for people to make healthy lifestyle choices, and devising suitable strategies to overcome such failures.

Bibliography

Abegunde, D.O. *et al.* (2007), "The Burden and Costs of Chronic Diseases in Low-Income and Middle-Income Countries", *The Lancet*, Vol. 370, No. 9603, pp. 1929-1938.

Adams, P.F., G.E. Hendershot and M.A. Marano (1999), "Current Estimates from the National Health Interview Survey 1996", *Vital Health Statistics*, Vol. 200, pp. 1-203.

Alley, D.E. and V.W. Chang (2007), "The Changing Relationship of Obesity and Disability, 1988-2004", *JAMA*, Vol. 298, No. 17, pp. 2020-2027.

Allison, D.B., R. Zannolli and K.M. Narayan (1999), "The Direct Health Care Costs of Obesity in the United States", *Am. J. Public Health*, Vol. 89, pp. 1194-1199.

Anderson, P., K.F. Butcher and P.B. Levine (2002), "Maternal Employment and Overweight Children", NBER Working Paper No. 8770, Cambridge, MA.

Andreyeva, T., P.C. Michaud and A. van Soest (2007), "Obesity and Health in Europeans Aged 50 years and Older", *Public Health*, Vol. 121, No. 7, pp. 497-509, DOI: *http://dx.doi.org/10.1016/j.puhe.2006.11.016*.

Bennett, K., Z. Kabir, B. Unal, E. Shelley, J. Critchley, I. Perry, J. Feely and S. Capewell (2006), "Explaining the Recent Decrease in Coronary Heart Disease Mortality Rates in Ireland, 1985-2000", *J. Epidemiol. Community Health*, Vol. 60, pp. 322-327.

Branca, F. and V. Kolovou Delonas (forthcoming), "Review of Cost-of-illness Studies on Obesity in Countries of the WHO European Region and Comparison with Other Countries", WHO Organisation, Regional Office for Europe.

Breslow, L. and J.E. Enstrom (1980), "Persistence of Health Habits and Their Relationship to Mortality", *Prev. Med.*, Vol. 9, No. 4, pp. 469-483, July.

Corrada, M.M., C.H. Kawas, F. Mozaffar and A. Paganini-Hill (2006), "Association of Body Mass Index and Weight Change with All-cause Mortality in the Elderly", *Am. J. Epidemiol.*, No. 163(10), pp. 938-949, May.

Cutler, D.M. and E.L. Glaeser (2007), "Social Interactions and Smoking", NBER Working Paper No. 13477, Cambridge, MA.

Cutler, D.M., E.L. Glaeser and J.M. Shapiro (2003), "Why Have Americans Become More Obese?", *Journal of Economic Perspectives*, Vol. 17, No. 3, pp. 93-118.

Dublin, L.I. (1953), "Relation of Obesity to Longevity", *N. Engl. J. Med.*, Vol. 248, pp. 971-974.

Fogel, R.W. (1994), "Economic Growth, Population Theory, and Physiology: the Bearing of Long-Term Processes on the Making of Economic Policy", *American Economic Review*, Vol. 84, No. 3, pp. 369-395.

Foresight (2007), *Tackling Obesities: Future Choices, Project Report*, Foresight, London.

Gregg, E.W. and J.M. Guralnik (2007), "Is Disability Obesity's Price of Longevity?", *JAMA*, Vol. 298, No. 17, pp. 2066-2067.

Khaw, K.-T., N. Wareham, S. Bingham, A. Welch, R. Luben *et al.* (2008), "Combined Impact of Health Behaviours and Mortality in Men and Women: The EPIC-Norfolk Prospective Population Study", *PLoS Med.*, Vol. 5, No. 1, e12.

Lafortune, G. and G. Balestat (2007), "Trends in Severe Disability Among Elderly People: Assessing the Evidence in 12 OECD Countries and the Future Implications", OECD Health Working Paper No. 26, OECD Publishing, Paris.

Lakdawalla, D.N., D.P. Goldman and B. Shang (2005), "The Health and Cost Consequences of Obesity Among the Future Elderly", *Health Affairs*, Vol. 24, Suppl. 2, w5r30-41.

Mackenbach, J.P. (2006), *Health Inequalities: Europe in Profile*, European Commission, Brussels.

Malnick, S.D. and H. Knobler (2006), "The Medical Complications of Obesity", *QJM*, Vol. 99, No. 9, pp. 565-579, September, epub, Aug 17.

Mischel, W., Y. Shoda and M.L. Rodriguez (1992), "Delay of Gratification in Children", in G. Loewenstein and J. Elster (eds.), *Choice Over Time*, Russell Sage Foundation, New York, pp. 147-164.

Mozaffarian, D. and M.J. Stampfer (2010), "Removing Industrial Trans Fat from Foods", *British Medical Journal*, Vol. 15, No. 340, c1826, April, DOI: *10.1136/bmj.c1826*.

O'Donoghue, T. and M. Rabin (1999), "Doing It Now or Later", *American Economic Review*, Vol. 89, No. 1, pp. 103-124.

O'Donoghue, T. and M. Rabin (2003), "Studying Optimal Paternalism, Illustrated by a Model of Sin Taxes", *American Economic Review*, Vol. 93, No. 2, pp. 186-191.

Olshansky, S.J. *et al.* (2005), "A Potential Decline in Life Expectancy in the United States in the 21st Century", *New England Journal of Medicine*, Vol. 352, No. 11, pp. 1138-1145.

Philipson, T. and R. Posner (2008), "Is the Obesity Epidemic a Public Health Problem? A Decade of Research on the Economics of Obesity", NBER Working Paper No. 14010, Cambridge, MA.

Popkin, B.M., S. Kim, E.R. Rusev, S. Du and C. Zizza (2006), "Measuring the Full Economic Costs of Diet, Physical Activity and Obesity-related Chronic Diseases", *Obesity Reviews*, Vol. 7, pp. 271-293.

Prospective Studies Collaboration, (2009), "Body-Mass Index and Cause-specific Mortality in 900 000 Adults: Collaborative Analyses of 57 Prospective Studies", *The Lancet*, Vol. 373, No. 9669, pp. 1083-1096.

Puska, P. *et al.* (1998), "Changes in Premature Deaths in Finland: Successful Long-Term Prevention of Cardiovascular Diseases", *Bulletin of the World Health Organization*, Vol. 76, No. 4, pp. 419-425.

Rothman, R.L., R. Housam, H. Weiss, D. Davis, R. Gregory, T. Gebretsadik, A. Shintani and T.A. Elasy (2006), "Patient Understanding of Food Labels: The Role of Literacy and Numeracy", *American Journal of Preventive Medicine*, Vol. 31, No. 5, pp. 391-398.

Scharff, R. (2009), "Obesity and Hyperbolic Discounting: Evidence and Implications", *Journal of Consumer Policy*, Vol. 32, No. 1, pp. 3-21.

Stevens, J., J. Cai, E.R. Pamuk, D.F. Williamson, M.J. Thun and J.L. Wood (1998), "The Effect of Age on the Association Between Body Mass Index and Mortality", *N. Engl. J. Med.*, Vol. 338, pp. 1-7.

Stewart, S.T., D.M. Cutler and A.B. Rosen (2009), "Forecasting the Effects of Obesity and Smoking on US Life Expectancy", *N. Engl. J. Med.*, Vol. 361, No. 23, pp. 2252-2260, 3 December.

Strandberg, T.E., A.Y. Strandberg, V.V. Salomaa, K.H. Pitkälä, R.S. Tilvis, J. Sirola and T.A. Miettinen (2009), "Explaining the Obesity Paradox: Cardiovascular Risk, Weight Change, and Mortality During Long-term Follow-up in Men", *Eur. Heart J.*, Vol. 30, No. 14, pp. 1720-1727.

Thompson, D., J. Edelsberg, G.A. Colditz, A.P. Bird and G. Oster (1999), "Lifetime Health and Economic Consequences of Obesity", *Arch. Intern. Med.*, Vol. 159, pp. 2177-2183.

Tsai, A.G., D.F. Williamson and H.A. Glick (2010), "Direct Medical Cost of Overweight and Obesity in the USA: A Quantitative Systematic Review", *Obesity Reviews*, 6 Jan., epub ahead of print.

UK Department of Health, Economic and Operational Research (2004), "Life Expectancy Projections", Government Actuary's Department: estimated effect of obesity (based on straight line extrapolation of trends), Stationery Office, London.

van Baal, P.H.M., J.J. Polder, G.A. de Wit, R.T. Hoogenveen, T.L. Feenstra *et al.* (2008), "Lifetime Medical Costs of Obesity: Prevention No Cure for Increasing Health Expenditure", *PLoS Med.*, Vol. 5, No. 2, e29, DOI: *http://dx.doi.org/10.1371/journal.pmed.0050029.*

Vita, A.J., R.B. Terry, H.B. Hubert and J.F. Fries (1998), "Aging, Health Risks, and Cumulative Disability", *N. Engl. J. Med.*, Vol. 338, No. 15, pp. 1035-1041, 9 Apr.

Watkins, P. (2004), "Chronic Disease", *Clinical Medicine*, Vol. 4, No. 4, pp. 297-298.

WHO (2002), *The World Health Report 2002*, World Health Organisation, Geneva.

WHO (2004), *The World Health Report 2004: Changing History*, World Health Organisation, Geneva.

WHO (2005), *Preventing Chronic Diseases: A Vital Investment*, World Health Organisation, Geneva.

WHO Europe (2006), *Gaining Health. The European Strategy for the Prevention and Control of Non-communicable Diseases*, World Health Organisation, Regional Office for Europe, Copenhagen.

Withrow, D. and D.A. Alter (2010), "The Economic Burden of Obesity Worldwide: A Systematic Review of the Direct Costs of Obesity", *Obesity Reviews*, 27 Jan., epub ahead of print.

Special Focus I.
Promoting Health
and Fighting Chronic Diseases:
What Impact on the Economy?

by

Marc Suhrcke, University of East Anglia

Does better health lead to greater wealth, either for an individual or a society? The question can be tackled using at least three economic concepts (Suhrcke *et al.*, 2005; Suhrcke *et al.*, 2006):

- Social welfare costs and benefits, to capture the value people place on better health.

- Micro- and macroeconomic costs, a more limited but more tangible concept.

- Health care costs associated with chronic disease, the most limited but nevertheless widely applied cost concept.

Social welfare costs

From a welfare economic perspective, the most relevant cost concept is the value individuals attribute to health in general and chronic disease in particular, elicited for example by analysing how people act or how they answer certain questions related to real or hypothetical situations involving a trade-off between money and health. It turns out that the social welfare benefit of health is much higher than the other more conventional (but incomplete) measures, and far too high to be ignored in public policy decisions (Viscusi and Aldy, 2003; Usher, 1973; Nordhaus, 2003; Costa and Kahn, 2003; Crafts, 2008). This value also captures the intrinsic value of health, a feature not shared by the other concepts.

Evaluating the evolution in life expectancy in the European high-income countries (which grew appreciably between 1970 and 2003) in terms of the social welfare costs/benefits illustrates the monetary value of the gains. Since the majority of the improvement in life expectancy in rich countries can be attributed to the reduction in chronic diseases, those gains can almost entirely be interpreted as the welfare benefit from chronic disease reduction. When expressed as a percentage of per capita GDP, the values attributed to health gains far exceed each country's national health expenditures, and range from 29% to 38% of 2003 per capita GDP, or from USD 2 598 to USD 12 676 in terms of purchasing power parity.

Micro- and macroeconomic costs

The microeconomic perspective assesses costs at the individual or household level, asking, for example, whether being ill reduces an individual's labour productivity or the likelihood that they will be in work. Macroeconomic consequences are viewed from the national economy level, generally considering whether ill health damages a country's economic growth.

The vast majority of studies on the microeconomic consequences of adult health focus on labour market outcomes (Currie and Madrian, 1999). Ill health reduces labour productivity measured by earnings (Contoyannis and Rice, 2001; Jäckle, 2007) and is important in shaping labour supply (García Gómez, 2008; Gannon, 2005). Good health raises the probability of working in the first place, and health may even be the main, but not the sole, determinant of labour supply for older workers (Currie and Madrian, 1999; Sammartino, 1987; Deschryvere, 2004; Lindeboom, 2006; Hagan et al., 2006).

Although there is a significant literature on the impact of risk factors on labour market outcomes, surprisingly few studies have examined the labour market impact of smoking in itself, although several studies examine simultaneous effects of smoking and drinking (Auld, 2005; Lee, 1999; Lye and Hirschberg, 2004; van Ours, 2004). One study found that smokers earn 4-8% less than non-smokers (Levine, 1997), while a study in the Netherlands found that alcohol use was associated with 10% higher wages for males while smoking reduced them by about 10% (the study found no effects of either in females) (van Ours, 2004).

Several other studies confirm the somewhat counterintuitive, positive wage impact of alcohol consumption, although explanations vary. There may be a beneficial health effect of moderate alcohol consumption, but not in younger people who have little risk of cardiovascular disease. Another explanation is that alcohol is consumed during social networking with colleagues, which may influence chances or promotion or a wage increase by providing access to information or giving a positive image of commitment to the firm (MacDonald and Shields, 2001). The observed results could also be due to measurement problems. For instance, two studies showed that binge drinking reduced earnings among males and females in the United States (Keng and Huffman, 2007; Mullahy and Sindelar, 1995) and Finnish data demonstrate that alcohol dependence reduces the probability that a man (woman) would be in full- or part-time work by around 14 (11) percentage points (Johansson *et al.*, 2006; Johansson *et al.*, 2007).

In theory, being overweight should have effects similar to more general health variables on labour market outcomes, simply because of the adverse impact of obesity on health. The impact could be even greater if employers discriminate against obese job seekers or workers, but it is not possible to see this from most empirical studies, since they calculate the overall impact on labour market outcomes, without seeking to disentangle any discrimination effect from a productivity effect.

However, more research is needed to better explain why results vary among studies and countries, the interplay with labour market institutions, and the very complex nature of the relationship between obesity and socio-economic factors. Some of the differences may result from the imperfect measures used as a proxy for adiposity (Burkhauser and Cawley, 2008).

At the macroeconomic level, there is comparatively little work on health and growth in high-income countries. The WHO Commission on Macroeconomics and Health (WHO, 2001) sought to address this question several years ago. Noting that politicians have long accepted the case for investment in physical infrastructure and human resources as a means of promoting economic growth and reducing poverty, the Commission presented the case for making similar investments in health, focusing on the urgent public health crises in Africa, including infectious diseases (HIV/AIDS, malaria, tuberculosis) and maternal and child health issues. That focus was entirely justified, but it left unanswered how the relationship between health and economic outcomes plays out in the advanced countries and for the type of diseases more common in those countries, *i.e.* chronic diseases (including cardiovascular and lung disease, type 2 diabetes and cancer). Consistently with the findings of a large body of research, the Commissions work showed a robust impact of health on economic growth. However, some more recent work focusing on developing countries cautions against – and indeed reverses – the expectation of major growth dividends from improved health, arguing that most of the previous work on the subject has not properly addressed endogeneity in the relationship between health and economic growth (Acemoglu and Johnson, 2007; Ashraf *et al.*, 2008).

Three studies using health expenditures as a proxy for health in OECD countries found a positive association between health expenditure and economic growth or income levels (Beraldo *et al.*, 2005; Rivera and Currais, 1999a and 1999b). These results are intriguing, especially since expenditure on health emerges as substantially more important than that on education in explaining economic growth. On the other hand, two studies based on a sample of

22 developed countries between 1960 and 1985 found that health – measured by life expectancy – had no significant impact on economic growth (Knowles and Owen, 1997) or on per capita income levels (Knowles and Owen, 1995). Does this mean that, above a certain level of economic development, further health gains may either have no impact or even reduce subsequent economic growth? There is no ultimate answer to this question in sight.

Other research (Suhrcke and Urban, 2009), focusing on a health proxy that displays greater variation between rich countries than the life expectancy, finds a very robust causal impact on per capita growth rates in a sample of 26 high-income countries over the period 1960-2000. In one estimate, a 10% reduction in cardiovascular mortality was associated with a one percentage point increase in growth of per capita income, a seemingly small amount but one that has a large effect when summed over the long term. Further recent, more optimistic assessments of the impact of health on growth, if not specifically related to chronic diseases, include Aghion *et al.* (2010) and Cervellati and Sunde (2009).

Health-care costs

The expectation that preventing chronic disease will mitigate or even reverse the trend of increasing health expenditures cannot be supported by the research evidence. Even if better health may, in some circumstances, lead to lower health spending, other cost drivers, in particular technological progress, more than outweigh any such savings and will most likely contribute to sustained upward pressure on expenditures. Improvements in population health can, at best, be expected only to diminish the rate of increase in health spending. On the other hand, there is not much support for the hypothesis that better health by itself would be a major cost driver.

Conclusions

Although this discussion does not cover the costs or benefits of interventions, it does have important policy implications:

● Estimates of the costs of ill health can be thought of as the upper limit of the economic benefits that could be derived from interventions.

● By showing how chronic disease can reduce social welfare, act as a drag on the economic conditions of both individuals and entire countries, and can (possibly) exert upward pressure on health expenditures, it may be possible to capture the attention of policy makers outside the health system.

● While it is useful to show that better health produces tangible micro- and macroeconomic benefits, and may in some cases reduce future costs of health care, these economic benefits are small compared to the relevant economic gains expressed as the monetary value that people attribute to better health. It is the latter that should be factored into the economic evaluation of chronic disease prevention, as failure to do so risks understating the true economic benefits derived from health interventions.

Bibliography

Acemoglu, D. and S. Johnson (2007), "Disease and Development: The Effect of Life Expectancy on Economic Growth", *Journal of Political Economy*, Vol. 115, No. 6, pp. 925-985.

Aghion, P., P. Howitt and F. Murtin (2010), "The Relationship Between Health and Growth: When Lucas Meets Nelson-Phelps", NBER Working Paper No. 15813, Cambridge, MA.

Ashraf, Q.H., A. Lester and D.N. Weil (2008), "When Does Improving Health Raise GDP?", Economics Department, Brown University, Providence, RI.

Auld, M.C. (2005), "Smoking, Drinking and Income", *Journal of Human Resources*, Vol. 40, No. 2, pp. 505-518.

Beraldo, S., D. Montolio and G. Turati (2005), "Healthy, Educated and Wealthy: Is the Welfare State Really Harmful for Growth?", Working Paper in Economics No. 127, Espai de Recerca en Economia, University of Barcelona, Barcelona.

Burkhauser, R.V. and J. Cawley (2008), "Beyond BMI: The Value of More Accurate Measures of Fatness and Obesity in Social Science Research", *Journal of Health Economics*. Vol. 27, No. 2, pp. 519-529.

Cervellati, M. and U. Sunde (2009), "Life Expectancy and Economic Growth: The Role of the Demographic Transition", IZA Discussion Paper No. 4160, Bonn.

Contoyannis, P.and N. Rice (2001), "The Impact of Health on Wages: Evidence from the British Household Panel Survey", *Empirical Economics*, Vol. 26, pp. 599-622.

Costa, D.L., and M.E. Kahn (2003), *Changes in the Value of Life, 1940-1980*, Massachusetts Institute of Technology, Cambridge, MA.

Crafts, N. (2005), "The Contribution of Increased Life Expectancy to Growth of Living Standards in the United Kingdom, 1870-2001", London School of Economics, London, accessed 5 May 2008 at *http://wpeg.group.shef.ac.uk/documents/crafts.pdf*.

Currie, J. and B.C. Madrian (1999), "Health, Health Insurance and the Labour Market", in O. Ashenfelter and D. Card (eds.), *Handbook of Labour Economics*, Vol. 3, Elsevier Science, Amsterdam, pp. 3309-3415.

Deschryvere, M. (2004), "Health and Retirement Decisions: An Update of the Literature", ETLA Discussion Paper No. 932, Elinkeinoelämän Tutkimuslaitos (ETLA), Helsinki.

Gannon, B. (2005), "A Dynamic Analysis of Disability and Labour Force Participation in Ireland", *Health Economics*, Vol. 14, pp. 925-938.

García Gómez, P. (2008), "Institutions, Health Shocks and Labour Outcomes across Europe", FEDEA Working Paper No. 2008-01, Fundación de Estudios de Economia Aplicada, Madrid, accessed 6 May 2008 at *www.fedea.es/pub/Papers/2008/dt2008-01.pdf*.

Hagan, R., A.M. Jones and N. Rice (2006), "Health and Retirement in Europe", HEDG Working Paper No. 06/10, Health Economics Research Centre, University of York, York.

Jäckle, R. (2007), "Health and Wages: Panel Data Estimates Considering Selection and Endogeneity", Working Paper No. 43, Ifo Institute for Economic Research, University of Munich, Munich.

Johansson, E. et al. (2006), "Abstaining from Alcohol and Labour Market Underperformance – Have we Forgotten the 'Dry' Alcoholics?", Alcohol and Alcoholism, Vol. 41, No. 5, pp. 574-579.

Johansson, E. et al. (2007), "The Association of Alcohol Dependency with Employment Probability: Evidence from the Population Survey 'Health 2000 in Finland'", Health Economics, Vol. 16, No. 7, pp. 739-754.

Keng, S.-H. and W.E. Huffman (2007), "Binge Drinking and Labor Market Success: A Longitudinal Study on Young People", Journal of Population Economics, Vol. 20, No. 1, pp. 35-54.

Knowles, S. and P.D. Owen (1995), "Health Capital in Cross-Country Variation in Income per Capita in the Mankiw-Romer-Weil Model", Economic Letters, Vol. 48, pp. 99-106.

Knowles, S. and P.D. Owen (1997), "Education and Health in an Effective-labour Empirical Growth Model", Economic Record, Vol. 73, No. 223, pp. 314-328.

Lee, Y. (1999), "Wage Effects of Drinking and Smoking: An Analysis Using Australian Twins Data", Working Paper No. 99-22, University of Western Australia, Perth.

Levine, P.B., T.A. Gustafson and A.D. Valenchik (1997), "More Bad News for Smokers? The Effects of Cigarette Smoking on Wages", Industrial and Labor Relations Review, Vol. 50, pp. 493-509.

Lye, J.N. and J. Hirschberg (2004), "Alcohol Consumption, Smoking and Wages", Applied Economics, Vol. 36, pp. 1807-1817.

Lindeboom, M. (2006), "Health and Work of Older Workers", in A.M. Jones (ed.), The Elgar Companion to Health Economics, Edward Elgar Publishing, Cheltenham, pp. 26-35.

MacDonald, Z. and M.A. Shields (2001), "The Impact of Alcohol Consumption on Occupational Attainment in England", Economica, Vol. 68, No. 271, pp. 427-453.

Mullahy, J. and J.L. Sindelar (1995), "Health, Income, and Risk Aversion: Assessing Some Welfare Costs of Alcoholism and Poor Health", Journal of Human Resources, Vol. 30, No. 3, pp. 439-459.

Nordhaus, W. (2003), "The Health of Nations: The Contribution of Improved Health to Living Standards", in K.M. Murphy and R.H. Topel (eds.), Exceptional Returns: The Value of Medical Research, University of Chicago Press, Chicago, pp. 9-40.

Rivera, B. and L. Currais (1999a), "Economic Growth and Health: Direct Impact or Reverse Causation?", Applied Economics Letters, Vol. 6, pp. 761-764.

Rivera, B. and L. Currais (1999b), "Income Variation and Health Expenditure: Evidence for OECD Countries", Review of Development Economics, Vol. 3, No. 3, pp. 258-267.

Sammartino, F.J. (1987), "The Effect of Health on Retirement", Social Security Bulletin, Vol. 50, No. 2, pp. 31-47.

Suhrcke, M. and D. Urban (2009), "Are Cardiovascular Diseases Bad for Economic Growth?", *Health Economics,* epub ahead of print.

Suhrcke, M. *et al.* (2005), "The Contribution of Health to the Economy in the European Union", European Commission, Brussels.

Suhrcke, M. *et al.* (2006), *Chronic Disease: An Economic Perspective,* Oxford Health Alliance, London.

Usher, D. (1973), "An Imputation to the Measure of Economic Growth for Changes in Life Expectancy", in M. Moss (ed.), *The Measurement of Economic and Social Performance,* Columbia University Press for National Bureau of Economic Research, New York, pp. 193-226.

van Ours, J.C. (2004), "A Pint a Day Raises a Man's Pay; But Smoking Blows that Gain Away", *Journal of Health Economics,* Vol. 23, pp. 863-886.

Viscusi, W.K. and J.E. Aldy (2003), "The Value of a Statistical Life: A Critical Review of Market Estimates Throughout the World", NBER Working Paper No. 9487, Cambridge, MA.

WHO (2001), "Macroeconomics and Health: Investing in Health for Economic Development", WHO Commission on Macroeconomics and Health, World Health Organisation, Geneva.

Chapter 2

Obesity:
Past and Projected Future Trends

Obesity has risen to epidemic proportions in OECD countries during the last 30 years. In this chapter, the development of the epidemic is discussed in the light of evidence from a range of OECD countries. After a comparative overview of current obesity rates in OECD and selected non-OECD countries, the recent obesity epidemic is set in the context of historical developments in height, weight and body mass index (BMI). Using BMI as the reference measure to identify individuals who are overweight or obese, a detailed analysis is presented of how rates have grown in OECD countries in the past 30 years, accounting for differences in the likelihood of obesity across birth cohorts. The final section of this chapter presents OECD projections of further growth of overweight and obesity rates in the next ten years in adults and children.

Obesity in the OECD and beyond

It is no surprise that obesity has risen to the top of the public health policy agenda in virtually all OECD countries. The latest available data (up to 2007) collected by the OECD on overweight and obesity rates show that over half of the adult population is overweight in at least 13 countries, including Australia, the Czech Republic, Greece, Hungary, Iceland, Ireland, Luxembourg, Mexico, New Zealand, Portugal, Spain, the United Kingdom and the United States. In contrast, overweight and obesity rates are much lower in Japan and Korea and in some European countries, such as France and Switzerland. However, rates are also increasing in these countries.

In non-OECD countries such as Brazil, China, India, Indonesia, Russia and South Africa, rates are still somewhat lower than in OECD countries, but increasing at similarly fast rates. In China, where rapid changes in dietary habits are exacting a large toll (Baillie, 2008), overweight rates doubled from 13.5% to 26.7% between 1991 and 2006. The obese are a small proportion of these, but tripled over the same period of time (Lu and Goldman, 2010). New estimates suggest that the prevalence of diabetes, the chronic disease which is most closely linked with obesity, in China is as high as in the United States, with over 92 million cases (Yang et al., 2010). In Brazil, obesity rates grew threefold in men and almost doubled in women between 1975 and 2003 (Monteiro et al., 2007). Smaller increases in overweight were recorded in India (rates for women increased from 10.6 to 12.6 between 1998-99 and 2005-06), but increases were much steeper in west urban areas, where rates approached 40% in the early 2000s, almost doubling in less than ten years (Wang et al., 2009). Overweight and obesity have taken over as the predominant features of malnutrition in South Africa (Puoane et al., 2002), where one third of women and one tenth of men are obese (WHO Infobase), with highest rates among black women and white men. After the recent political and economic transition, obesity grew also in the Russian Federation, where one in four women and one in ten men are now obese, and rates are projected to grow fast in the coming years (WHO Infobase). The global dimension of the obesity epidemic is illustrated very well in Barry Popkin's book *The World is Fat* (Popkin, 2009).

The prevalence of obesity in adults varies more than tenfold among OECD countries, from a low of 1 in 33 in Japan and Korea, to one in three in the United States and Mexico. The number of people who are obese has more than doubled over the past 20 years in the United States, while it has almost tripled in Australia and more than tripled in the United Kingdom. Between one in four and one in five adults are obese in the United Kingdom, Australia, Iceland and Luxembourg, about the same proportion as in the United States in the early 1990s. Figure 2.1 shows a comparison of obesity rates available from OECD and selected non-OECD countries, for men and women.

Measuring obesity

According to the WHO, overweight and obesity are meant to reflect abnormal or excessive fat accumulation – also called adiposity – that may impair health. The measurement of adiposity is difficult, therefore proxies are normally used based on more easily measurable anthropometric characteristics. The body mass index (BMI),[1] a measure of body weight-for-height, is the most well known proxy for adiposity, dating back to the 19th century.

Modern use of BMI dates from 1972. Until then, obesity was defined by reference to an "ideal body weight" derived from life insurance actuarial tables. In 1972, obesity researcher Ancel Keys published the results of a study of almost 7 500 men in five countries. Keys compared a number of formulas to see which was the best predictor of body fat measured directly, and the equation proposed by Belgian scientist Adolphe Quetelet proved more accurate than alternatives such as weight divided by height. Keys renamed Quetelet's index "body mass index". Based on BMI data, the WHO concluded in 1997 that obesity had reached epidemic levels worldwide.

The US National Institutes of Health started defining obesity by BMI in the 1980s. In 1998, they defined a BMI of 25-29.9 as "overweight", and 30 and above as "obese". Based on these thresholds, a woman of approximately average height in the OECD (1.65 m, or 5 feet 5 inches) is overweight if she weighs 68 kg, and obese if she weighs 82 kg. A man of average height (1.75 m, or 5 feet 9 inches) is overweight if he weighs 77 kg, and obese if he weighs 92 kg. There are suggestions that lower thresholds should be used in Asian populations (WHO, 2004), as well as in certain ethnic minority groups, because increasing patterns of health risks have been observed in those populations starting from lower BMI levels.

BMI's main advantages are that it is simple and provides easily remembered cut-off points. But many researchers criticise it for not taking into account important factors such as age, sex and muscularity, so that using BMI alone can contribute to the so called "obesity paradox", where certain degrees of excess weight can even appear to offer protection against some conditions in certain population groups (Lewis *et al.*, 2009). Critics argue that waist measurement, for example, or the waist-to-hip ratio, are better indicators of abdominal fat and associated health risks. Keys himself stressed

Figure 2.1. **Obesity and overweight in OECD and non-OECD countries**

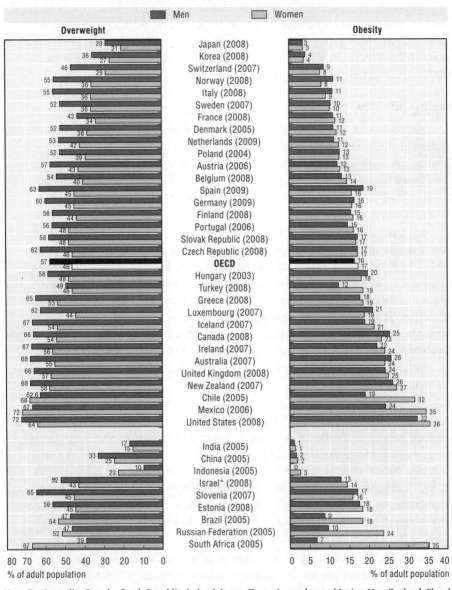

Note: For Australia, Canada, Czech Republic, Ireland, Japan, Korea, Luxembourg, Mexico, New Zealand, Slovak Republic, United Kingdom and United States, rates are based on measured, rather than self-reported, body mass index (BMI).

* The statistical data for Israel are supplied by and under the responsibility of the relevant Israeli authorities. The use of such data by the OECD is without prejudice to the status of the Golan Heights, East Jerusalem and Israeli settlements in the West Bank under the terms of international law.

Source: OECD Health Data 2010; and WHO Infobase for Brazil, Chile, China, India, Indonesia, Russian Federation and South Africa.

StatLink 〰〰 http://dx.doi.org/10.1787/888932315621

that BMI was useful for epidemiological research, but warned against using it for individual cases.

Despite continued controversy on the use of BMI as a marker of risk (Cawley and Burkhauser, 2006), a very large study of the link between obesity and mortality published in 2009 concluded that BMI is a strong predictor of mortality, and that different proxy measures of adiposity are more likely to be complements than substitutes, as each can provide additional information relative to others (Prospective Studies Collaboration, 2009).

Historical trends in height, weight and obesity

Height and weight have been increasing since the 18th century in many of the current OECD countries. Height increases have been closely related with economic growth (Steckel, 1995), although early industrialisation brought about periods of slight shrinkage of average height in countries such as Great Britain and the United States (Komlos, 1998). The British were the tallest population in Europe in the 18th century, on average they were about 5 cm taller and had a 18% larger calorie consumption than the French. Americans were even taller, by as much as 6-7 cm over the average height of a Briton, and continued to be the tallest until at least the second half of the 19th century, when their growth in stature slowed down, relative to northern European populations, and the latter took over as the tallest in the 20th century.

Over the same period of time, weight and body mass also increased gradually, until increases in BMI accelerated sharply in many OECD countries starting from the 1980s. Norwegian men aged 50-64 increased their body mass by approximately one point in the 18th century, by 3 points in the following century and by a further 3 points between 1870 and 1975 (Fogel, 1994). In the subsequent 25 years alone, average BMI in the same group grew by at least two additional points (Strand and Tverdal, 2006; Reas et al., 2007). American men of the same age increased their average BMI by 3.6 points between 1910 and 1985-88, and by almost the same amount in the following single quarter of a century. Average BMI increased by 1.5 points in England over 15 years, from the early 1990s to the mid-2000s, and by 1 point in France in the same period.

The changes described have clear implications on longevity. Nobel laureate and economic historian Robert Fogel makes use of Waaler curves, named after the Norwegian economist who developed them, to investigate the links between height, weight and mortality. In a three-dimensional view, Waaler curves draw a mountain-like shape (Mount Waaler, as Angus Deaton calls it – Deaton, 2006) where mortality is highest at the bottom and lowest at the top. Mankind has gradually climbed this mountain, progressively growing in height, weight and BMI, and enjoying an ever longer life span. But the trajectory of this journey does not aim straight to the top of the mountain. The ascent has been slowed down by an excessive gain in weight-for-height, and the current acceleration in BMI growth has further deflected the trajectory. The populations of most OECD countries are beginning to circle around the top of the mountain, rather than pointing straight to it.

Following the growth in BMI described above, overweight and obesity rates have been increasing consistently over the past three decades in all OECD countries. Obesity has been increasing at a faster pace in countries with historically higher rates, leading to a widening gap among countries over time. Conversely, pre-obesity[2] has been growing faster in countries with historically lower rates. In countries with high rates of overweight and obesity (*e.g.* United States, England) rates of pre-obesity stabilised or even began to shrink in recent years, while obesity rates continued to rise. The reason for the different trends in obesity and pre-obesity is explained below in the final section of this chapter. The size of the pre-obese category in a population depends both on the rate at which normal weight people become overweight (inflow) and on the rate at which pre-obese people become obese (outflow). The relative changes in the obese and pre-obese categories depend therefore on changes in the shape of the overall BMI distribution over time (see Figure 2.5 below).

The OECD carried out a detailed analysis of individual-level national health examination and health interview survey data, using surveys from the following 11 OECD countries: Australia, Austria, Canada, England, France, Hungary, Italy, Korea, Spain, Sweden and the United States. All of the available waves of these health surveys were used in the analyses, providing a temporal coverage that varies from 4 (Hungary) to 31 years (United States). The surveys used provide the most accurate and detailed information currently available on overweight and obesity, assessed with reference to the body mass index (BMI) , which is directly measured in three of the 11 countries (England, Korea and the United States) and based on self-reported height and weight in the remaining eight. Details about the surveys used and the years covered are available in Table A.1 in Annex A.

Figure 2.2 shows the pace of growth of obesity rates in the working-age populations of the above OECD countries, accounting for differences in the age structures of the relevant populations. Obesity rates have been increasing in all OECD countries in men (Panel A). Similar increases have been observed in women in Australia, Austria, Canada, England, France, Hungary, Sweden and the United States whereas the corresponding curves for Italy, Korea and Spain in Panel B are virtually flat or show minimal increases over time. Obesity rates in England and the United States are substantially higher than in the other countries, and over five times those observed in Korea. The same BMI thresholds were used in all countries to define overweight (BMI of 25 and over) and obesity (BMI of 30 and over). The two trend lines for the United States in the figures are based on two different surveys: the National Health and

Figure 2.2. **Age-standardised obesity rates, age 15-64, selected OECD countries**

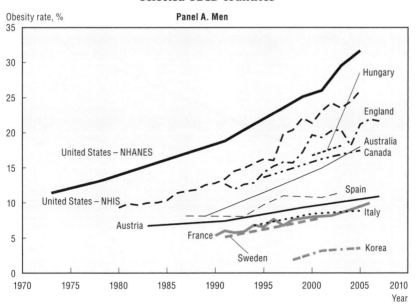

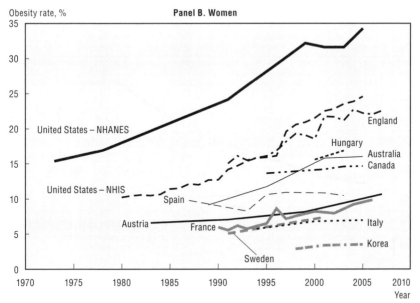

Note: For England, Korea and the United States (NHANES) rates are based on measured, rather than self-reported, body mass index (BMI). Rates are age-standardised using the OECD standard population.

Source: OECD analysis of national health survey data.

StatLink 🔗 *http://dx.doi.org/10.1787/888932315640*

Figure 2.3. **Age-standardised overweight rates, age 15-64, selected OECD countries**

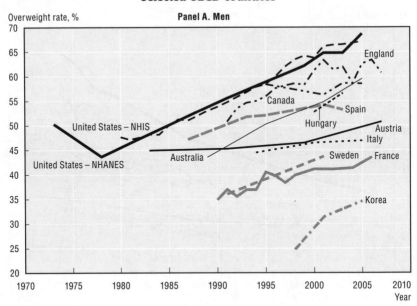

Panel A. Men

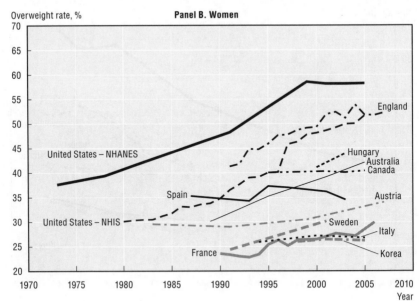

Panel B. Women

Note: For England, Korea and the United States (NHANES) rates are based on measured, rather than self-reported, body mass index (BMI). Rates are age-standardised using the OECD standard population.

Source: OECD analysis of national health survey data.

StatLink ⊞≣⊐ http://dx.doi.org/10.1787/888932315659

Nutrition Examination Survey (NHANES) using measured BMI, and the National Health Interview Survey (NHIS) using self-reported BMI. Self-reported rates from NHIS under-estimate obesity compared to actual rates reported in NHANES, but the time trends are the same.

Overweight rates, shown in Figure 2.3, have been increasing for men in all countries except in Canada. Overweight rates display less variation than obesity rates: US rates for overweight are twice as high as Korean rates, while the difference in obesity between the two countries is roughly eightfold. Overweight rates in women (Panel B) show an increase over the years except for Italy, Korea, and Spain, whose curves are virtually flat.

Cohort patterns in overweight and obesity

There is substantial evidence of the role of both individual characteristics and environmental influences in the development of overweight and obesity, but less is known about the way these factors have acted over time, and on the relative contribution they made to the current obesity epidemic. In an effort to fill this gap, we carried out a statistical analysis known as age-period-cohort (APC) analysis using individual-level health survey data for around 1.8 million individuals aged 15-65 from six OECD countries. The aim was to gain an improved understanding of how the obesity epidemic developed, disentangling the relative contributions to the epidemic of different types of factors (*e.g.* individual *vs.* environmental) which are likely to act differently over time. Failure to distinguish different temporal effects makes it difficult not only to interpret the observed relationship between BMI and age, but also to extrapolate observed time trends into the future.

The countries studied were Canada, England, France, Italy, Korea and the United States. The three time-related factors were:

- *Age*: biological and lifestyle changes typically characterise a given age group, for example physiological capacities, accumulation of social experience, or time spent on different activities such as exercise.

- *Period of observation*: period effects reflect events experienced at a given point in time, including cultural, economic, or environmental changes, which affect all individuals simultaneously. Environmental factors also affect every individual in a population at the periods when the surveys were undertaken.

- *Birth cohort*: individuals in a cohort are exposed to similar influences at key stages throughout their lives, for example nutrition received in the early years of life or the type of education, and share a number of characteristics that vary over time.

We pooled data from cross-sections of various waves of the health surveys undertaken in each of the countries, adjusted to account for sample size differences across waves. We devised separate APC models for the six countries and two outcome measures (overweight and obesity). BMI was measured in England and Korea and self-reported in the rest, but was assessed consistently over time in each of the surveys.

In brief, the APC analysis confirms the importance of period effects (an actual increase in the prevalence of overweight and obesity in all six countries over the periods surveyed) but suggests that the pace of the increase in overweight and obesity may be underestimated in analyses which do not fully account for age and cohort effects.

Factors and dynamics that have characterised recent decades have sharply increased everyone's likelihood of becoming overweight or obese, regardless of their age or birth cohort, reflecting the powerful influences of physical, social and economic environments that favour obesity.

Looking at the results in more detail (Figure 2.4) shows that the underlying probability of obesity of successive birth cohorts was generally declining in the earlier part of the 20th century, until showing signs of an upturn in Canada, France and the United States (and possibly Korea) from the 1960s. This was not observed for overweight, where cohort trends consistently declined apart from Korea.

There are a number of possible explanations for the mostly declining cohort trends identified in our analysis. First, education and socio-economic status have improved substantially since World War II. Both of these factors are associated with lower probabilities of obesity in OECD countries. Individuals born in the earliest cohorts observed in our analysis, dating back to the 1920s and 1930s, are likely to have been exposed to more limited education, especially health education, than those born later. When we accounted for individual education (based on highest qualification achieved) and occupation-based social class, cohort effects were attenuated but still showed a decline. Material living conditions and nutrition are also likely to have been poorer, on average, for the earliest cohorts. The role of material deprivation, particularly food deprivation, during childhood as a factor that may increase the likelihood of obesity in later life is highlighted in a number of studies, and this effect may be stronger in women than in men.

Negatively sloped and relatively small cohort effects suggest that the large increases in overweight and obesity rates observed since the 1980s are attributed primarily to factors and dynamics that have characterised the latter time period, which have sharply increased everyone's likelihood of becoming overweight or obese, regardless of their age or birth cohort. These factors and dynamics reflect the powerful influences of obesogenic environments (aspects

Figure 2.4. **Cohort patterns in obesity and overweight in selected OECD countries**

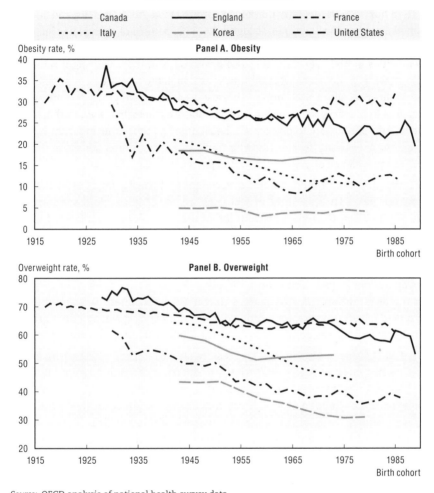

Source: OECD analysis of national health survey data.

StatLink ⬛⬛ http://dx.doi.org/10.1787/888932315678

of physical, social and economic environments that favour obesity), which have been consolidating over the course of the past 20-30 years, and are behind the increasing period effects resulting from the APC analysis.

Projections of obesity rates up to 2020

The distributions of BMI across the national populations of OECD countries have been shifting over time following a typical pattern. This pattern does not reflect a uniform increase in BMI across national populations. Rather, it is consistent with a progressive increase in BMI in a substantial group, determining a gradual transition of such group from the left-hand side of the distribution (normal weight) to the pre-obese section first, and then to the obese section. This pattern has been particularly marked in countries like Australia, England and the United States and is illustrated in Figure 2.5. This pattern of change has led to an increase in the spread of the BMI distribution, which means increasing inequalities in BMI over time. It is also likely to mean that overweight rates will stop growing in the not too distant future, although the proportion of people with the highest levels of BMI among those who are overweight will continue to increase. In practice, the prevalence of pre-obesity will stabilise when those who move from pre-obesity to obesity will be as many as those moving from normal weight to pre-obesity. If those moving "out" were even more than those moving "in", the prevalence of pre-obesity would decrease.

We projected trends in adult overweight and obesity (age 15-74) over the next ten years in a number of OECD countries (Figure 2.6), based on the assumption that the entire distribution of BMI in national populations would continue to evolve following the patterns observed in the past. The projection model accounts for a possible non linearity of time trends in overweight and obesity rates. However, the resulting projections should be read as extrapolations of past trends into the future. As such, they are implicitly based on the assumption that the factors that have determined the rate changes observed in recent years, including policies adopted by governments to tackle emerging trends, will continue to exert the same influence on future trends.

OECD projections predict a progressive stabilisation or slight shrinkage of pre-obesity rates in many countries (e.g. Australia, England, United States), with a continued increase in obesity rates. Increases in overweight and obesity are expected to happen at a progressively faster pace in countries (e.g. Korea, France) where rates of obesity were historically lower. It is conceivable, although not necessarily proven by the data, that the pattern observed in Australia, Canada, England and the United States is simply a later stage in a progression that Austria, France, Italy, Korea and Spain may experience further down the line, unless key determinants of such progression are dealt with in the near future. In the absence of effective interventions, countries with historically low rates of overweight and obesity, such as Korea, may expect within the next ten years to reach the same proportions of pre-obese population (BMI between 25 and 30) as countries that currently rank near the top of the BMI league table, such as England.

Obesity is more common in older age groups, within the age range examined, and appears to be growing at slightly faster rates than in younger age groups in several countries. However, changes in the age structures of national populations in the OECD area are unlikely to have contributed in a major way to past increases in overweight and obesity, or to contribute to expected future increases.

Figure 2.5. **Changes over time in the BMI distribution in Australia and England**

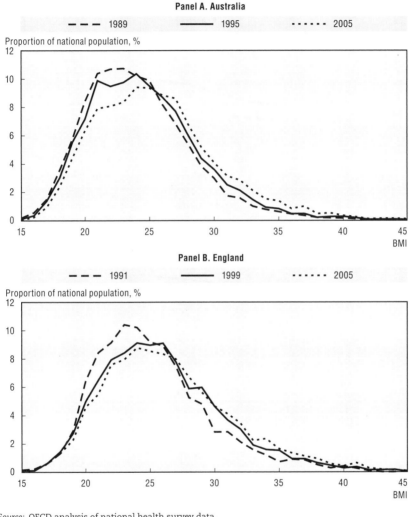

Panel A. Australia

– – – 1989   ——— 1995   ······ 2005

Proportion of national population, %

Panel B. England

– – – 1991   ——— 1999   ······ 2005

Proportion of national population, %

Source: OECD analysis of national health survey data.

StatLink ⟶ http://dx.doi.org/10.1787/888932315697

Similar projections were made for child overweight and obesity (age 3-17) over the next ten years in England, France, Korea and the United States (Figure 2.7). The same assumptions as for adults were made,[3] however, given a higher degree of uncertainty concerning expected future changes in child obesity, two alternative statistical approaches were used to estimate a possible range of variation in future overweight and obesity estimates. Only one approach was used for Korea, because of a more limited availability of past trend data.

Figure 2.6. **Past and projected future rates of obesity and overweight, age 15-74, selected OECD countries**

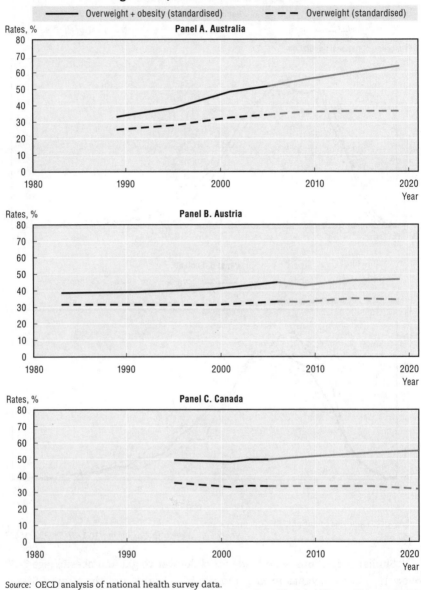

Source: OECD analysis of national health survey data.

StatLink ᴍᴍᴍ᠍ http://dx.doi.org/10.1787/888932315716

Child overweight and obesity increased substantially in England and in the United States between 1990 and the early 2000s, with overweight rates reaching peaks of nearly 40% around 2005. In the most recent years, there have been signs of a stabilisation or even a possible slight retrenchment of overweight and

Figure 2.6. **Past and projected future rates of obesity and overweight, age 15-74, selected OECD countries** *(cont.)*

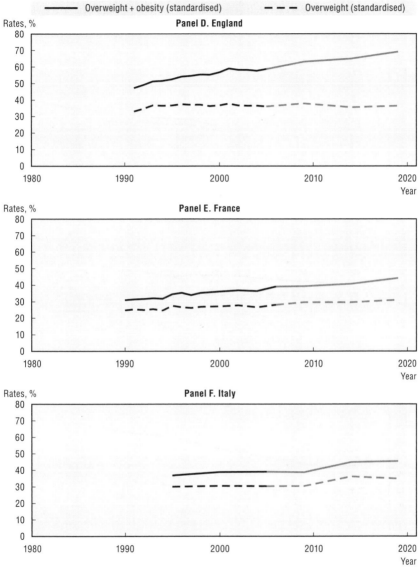

Source: OECD analysis of national health survey data.

StatLink 📊 *http://dx.doi.org/10.1787/888932315716*

obesity in the above two countries. OECD projections suggest that these trends may push overweight rates further up or down by up to 7-8% relative to current rates. The range of variation in projections is slightly smaller for obesity rates, but with rates more likely to increase in the United States.

Figure 2.6. **Past and projected future rates of obesity and overweight, age 15-74, selected OECD countries** (cont.)

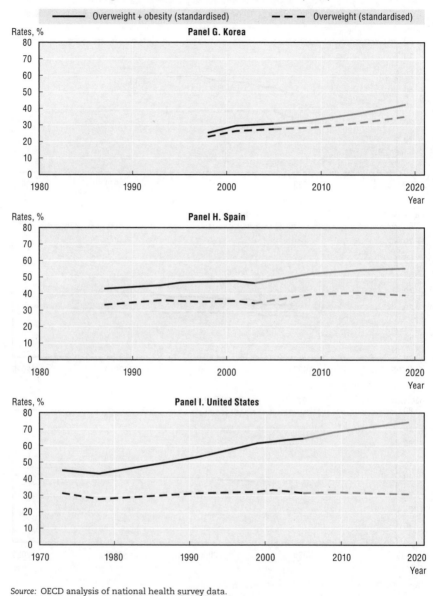

Source: OECD analysis of national health survey data.

StatLink ᴭᴵ᠍᠍ᴮ http://dx.doi.org/10.1787/888932315716

Trends in child obesity are different in France, where rates have been consistently lower than in the previous two countries and relatively stable over the past 15 years.[4] Thus, the range of variation in projections is substantially

Figure 2.7. **Past and projected future rates of child obesity and overweight, age 3-17, in four OECD countries**

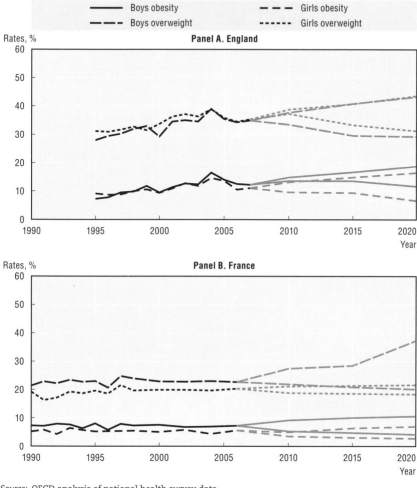

Legend:
——— Boys obesity   — — — Girls obesity
— — — Boys overweight   ······· Girls overweight

Panel A. England

Panel B. France

Source: OECD analysis of national health survey data.

StatLink 🔗 *http://dx.doi.org/10.1787/888932315735*

smaller than for England and the United States, although the possibility of a relatively large increase in overweight in boys over the next ten years cannot be ruled out, based on existing evidence. The two data points available for Korea reveal high rates of obesity and overweight, mainly in boys. Projections show a likely slight decrease of overweight and a stabilisation of child obesity.

Figure 2.7. **Past and projected future rates of child obesity and overweight, age 3-17, in four OECD countries** (*cont.*)

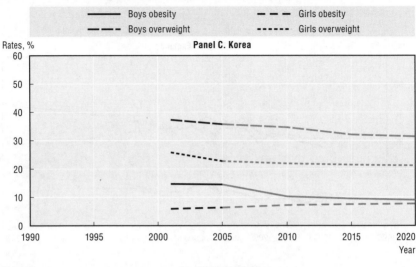

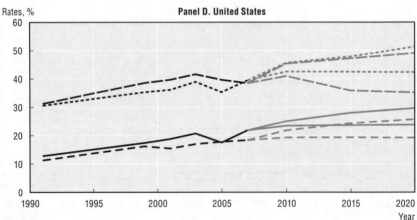

Source: OECD analysis of national health survey data.

StatLink 🔗 http://dx.doi.org/10.1787/888932315735

Key messages

- Obesity has risen to epidemic proportions in the OECD area during the past 30 years. Rates are still somewhat lower in major non-OECD countries, but growing at a similarly fast pace as in higher income countries, especially in urban areas.

- Over 50% of the population is currently overweight in almost half of OECD countries. Rates are highest in the United States and Mexico, where about one in three adults is obese. In Europe, rates are highest in the United

Kingdom, where one in four adults is obese. On the other hand, rates are up to ten times lower in Asian OECD countries.

- Height, weight and body mass have been increasing gradually at least since the 18th century, contributing to a steady progress in life expectancy. The rapid acceleration in BMI growth over the past 30 years will likely slow down further progress in longevity.

- The obesity epidemic has largely been determined by factors and dynamics that have characterised the last 30 years, which have created obesogenic environments. Improved education and socio-economic conditions have decreased the underlying probability of obesity in successive birth cohorts.

- OECD projections envisage a progressive stabilisation or slight shrinkage of pre-obesity rates in several countries (*e.g.* Australia, England, United States), with a continued increase in obesity rates.

- Increases in overweight and obesity are expected to happen at a progressively faster pace in countries (*e.g.* Korea, France) where rates of obesity have been historically lower.

- Projections of child overweight and obesity are more uncertain, as periods of stabilisation, or even slight shrinkage, have followed previous rate increases in several OECD countries.

Notes

1. The simple formula for the body mass index is weight in kilograms divided by square height in meters.

2. The terms pre-obese/pre-obesity are used here, in line with WHO recommendations, to identify individuals who are overweight but not obese, *i.e.* with a BMI of 25 and above, but lower than 30.

3. The definitions of overweight and obesity applied to children differ from those applied to adults. Instead of the conventional BMI thresholds of, respectively, 25 and 30, age-specific thresholds are used to define overweight and obesity in children, based on current knowledge of the link between BMI and health status. At least two sets of thresholds have been used extensively in the assessment of child obesity, one developed by the International Obesity Task Force (IOTF) (Cole *et al.*, 2000), the second by the World Health Organisation (age 0-5: *www.who.int/childgrowth/standards/bmi_for_age/en/index.html*; age 5-17: *www.who.int/growthref/who2007_bmi_for_age/en/index.html*). When applied to assess the prevalence of overweight and obesity in children, the two sets of thresholds may lead to substantially different estimates. Key differences between the two sets and underlying approaches are discussed in Monasta *et al.* (2010) and in De Onis and Lobstein (forthcoming). The analyses of child overweight and obesity undertaken by the OECD, including analyses of past and projected future trends and analyses of disparities by socio-economic status and by ethnicity, reported in this chapter and in Chapter 3 are all based on WHO thresholds, while the data presented in Tim Lobstein's special contribution which follows Chapter 3 in this book are based on IOTF thresholds.

4. It should be noted that past trends in child obesity calculated by the OECD for France differ from those reported in Tim Lobstein's special contribution which follows Chapter 3. In the latter, overweight rates are shown to have increased substantially during the 1990s. This is due to the use of different data sources, different age groups (3-17 in the OECD analysis, 5-11 in the analysis in T. Lobstein's contribution), and different criteria for defining overweight (see note 3 above).

Bibliography

Baillie, K. (2008), "Health Implications of Transition from a Planned to a Free-market Economy – An Overview", *Obesity Reviews*, Vol. 9, Suppl. 1, pp. 146-150.

Cawley, J. and R.V. Burkhauser (2006), "Beyond BMI: The Value of More Accurate Measures of Fatness and Obesity in Social Science Research", NBER Working Paper No. 12291, available on *www.nber.org/papers/w12291*.

Cole, T.J. (2000), M.C. Bellizzi, K.M. Flegal, W.H. Dietz (2000), "Establishing a Standard Definition for Child Overweight and Obesity Worldwide: International Survey", *British Medical Journal*, Vol. 320, No. 7244, pp. 1240-1243.

De Onis, M. and T. Lobstein (forthcoming), "Defining Obesity Risk Status in the General Childhood Population: Which Cut-offs Should We Use?", *International Journal of Pediatric Obesity*, 17 March, pp. 1-3.

Deaton, A. (2006), "The Great Escape: A Review of Robert Fogel's The Escape from Hunger and Premature Death, 1700-2100", *Journal of Economic Literature*, Vol. XLIV, pp. 106-114, March.

Fogel, R.W. (1994), "Economic Growth, Population Theory, and Physiology: The Bearing of Long-Term Processes on the Making of Economic Policy", *American Economic Review*, Vol. 84, No. 3, pp. 369-395, June.

Komlos, J. (1998), "Shrinking in a Growing Economy? The Mystery of Physical Stature during the Industrial Revolution", *Journal of Economic History*, Vol. 58, No. 3, pp. 779-802.

Lewis, C.E., K.M. McTigue, L.E. Burke, P. Poirier, R.H. Eckel, B.V. Howard, D.B. Allison, S. Kumanyika and F.X. Pi-Sunyer (2009), "Mortality, Health Outcomes, and Body Mass Index in the Overweight Range", *Circulation*, Vol. 119, pp. 3263-3271, 30 June.

Lu, Y. and D. Goldman (2010), "The Effects of Relative Food Prices on Obesity – Evidence from China: 1991-2006", NBER Working Paper No. 15720, Cambridge, MA, February, available on *www.nber.org/papers/w15720*.

Monasta, L., T. Lobstein, T.J. Cole, J. Vignerová and A. Cattaneo (2010), "Defining Overweight and Obesity in Pre-School Children: IOTF Reference or WHO Standard?", *Obesity Reviews*, epublication ahead of print, DOI: *http://dx.doi.org/10.1111/j.1467-789X.2010.00748.x*.

Monteiro, C.A., W.L. Conde and B.M. Popkin (2007), "Income Specific Trends in Obesity in Brazil: 1975-2003", *Am. J. Public Health*, Vol. 97, No. 10, pp. 1808-1812.

Popkin, B. (2009), "The World is Fat: The Fads, Trends, Policies, and Products That Are Fattening the Human Race", Avery, New York.

Prospective Studies Collaboration (2009), "Body-Mass Index and Cause-Specific Mortality in 900 000 Adults: Collaborative Analyses of 57 Prospective Studies", *The Lancet*, Vol. 373, No. 9669, pp. 1083-1096.

Puoane, T., K. Steyn, D. Bradshaw, R. Laubscher, J. Fourie, V. Lambert and N. Mbananga (2002), "Obesity in South Africa: The South African Demographic and Health Survey", *Obesity Research,* Vol. 10, pp. 1038-1048, DOI: *10.1038/oby.2002.141.*

Reas, D.L., J.F. Nygård, E. Svensson, T. Sørensen and I. Sandanger (2007), "Changes in Body Mass Index by Age, Gender, and Socio-Economic Status Among a Cohort of Norwegian Men and Women (1990-2001)", *BMC Public Health,* Vol. 7, No. 269.

Sassi, F., M. Devaux, M. Cecchini and E. Rusticelli (2009), "The Obesity Epidemic: Analysis of Past and Projected Future Trends in Selected OECD Countries", OECD Health Working Paper No. 45, OECD Publishing, Paris.

Steckel, R.H. (1995), "Stature and the Standard of Living", *Journal of Economic Literature,* Vol. XXXIII, No. 4, pp. 1903-1940.

Strand, B.H. and A. Tverdal (2006), "Trends in Educational Inequalities in Cardiovascular Risk Factors: A Longitudinal Study Among 48 000 Middle-aged Norwegian Men and Women", *Eur. J. Epidemiol.,* Vol. 21, No. 10, pp. 731-739.

Wang, Y., H.-J. Chen, S. Shaikh and P. Mathur (2009), "Is Obesity Becoming a Public Health Problem in India? Examine the Shift from Under- to Overnutrition Problems Over Time", *Obesity Reviews,* Vol. 10, pp. 456-474.

WHO Expert Consultation (2004), "Appropriate Body-Mass Index for Asian Populations and Its Implications for Policy and Intervention Strategies", *The Lancet,* Vol. 363, pp. 157-163.

Yang, W., J. Lu, J. Weng, W. Jia, L. Ji, J. Xiao, Z. Shan, J. Liu, H. Tian, Q. Ji, D. Zhu, J. Ge, L. Lin, L. Chen, X. Guo, Z. Zhao, Q. Li, Z. Zhou, G. Shan and J. He for the China National Diabetes and Metabolic Disorders Study Group, (2010), "Prevalence of Diabetes among Men and Women in China", *New England Journal of Medicine,* Vol. 362, No. 12, pp. 1090-1101.

Obesity and the Economics of Prevention
Fit not Fat
© OECD 2010

Chapter 3

The Social Dimensions of Obesity

The social impacts of obesity are addressed in this chapter in terms of the concentration of obesity in certain population groups and of the consequences of obesity on labour market outcomes. The first part of the chapter provides evidence of disparities in obesity along demographic characteristics, such as age and gender, as well as social dimensions, such as education, socio-economic status and ethnicity. Differences in the likelihood of overweight and obesity among groups defined along those dimensions are presented and discussed, and comparisons across OECD countries are made in the size of social disparities in obesity. Evidence is also presented of social disparities by socio-economic status and ethnicity in children, based on data from four OECD countries. The second part of the chapter contains a comprehensive review of the existing evidence of disparities in labour market outcomes between the obese and people of normal weight. The final section presents ample evidence of a disadvantage suffered, particularly by obese women, in employment, earnings and productivity.

Obesity in different social groups

Obesity is not distributed evenly across and within population groups, whether the latter are defined along demographic or social characteristics. Disparities in obesity are linked to different dietary patterns and levels of physical activity at work and during leisure time in different population groups. Disparities along certain dimensions, such as age, have caused less concern than other disparities, *e.g.* those by socio-economic status or ethnicity, which tend to be viewed as undesirable, or even unacceptable, from the point of view of individual and societal ethics. To the extent that differences in obesity are due to social structures rather than biological factors, evidence of disparities is often perceived as a call for action to redress the imbalance and alleviate the burden suffered by the most disadvantaged groups.

A particularly important dimension linked to obesity is education, as this factor can be more easily modified by suitable policies than other factors. Strong evidence of an association between greater education and a lower probability of obesity, which at least some studies identify as a causal effect of education, suggests that policies increasing general school education or supporting the delivery of health and lifestyle education may contribute to tackling the obesity epidemic.

Obesity in men and women

There does not appear to be a uniform gender pattern in obesity across countries. Worldwide, obesity rates tend to be higher in women than in men, other things being equal, and the same is true, on average, in the OECD area. However, this is not the case in all countries. Men display higher non-standardised obesity rates in half of OECD countries (with Greece, Ireland, Norway, Germany and Korea showing proportionally larger disadvantages for men), as shown in Chapter 2, Figure 2.1. Male obesity rates have also been growing faster than female rates in most OECD countries, although the latter have been growing marginally faster in countries such as Denmark, Canada and Italy in recent years.

Unlike obesity, pre-obesity is overwhelmingly more prevalent in men than in women in all OECD countries. Trends over time show pre-obesity rates increasing at a faster pace in women than men in countries such as Australia, Switzerland, United States or United Kingdom, while the opposite is true in countries such as Finland, Japan or Spain.

pregnancy

A number of possible explanations have been proposed for the higher prevalence of obesity in women in many countries. In a study based on data from the United States, Chou et al. (2003) identified women as one of a number of groups, along with low-wage earners and ethnic minorities, in which declining real incomes, coupled with increasing numbers of hours devoted to work, have been associated with escalating obesity rates since the 1970s. A suggestion has also been made, supported by some biological evidence, that women who suffer nutritional deprivation in childhood are prone to becoming obese in adult life, whereas this effect does not appear to be present in men (Case and Menendez, 2007).

Gender differences in obesity are important *per se*, because they may suggest possible pathways through which obesity is generated. However, the gender dimension is perhaps even more important because of its significant interactions with other individual characteristics, such as socio-economic condition or ethnicity. Evidence from a number of countries shows that socio-economic disparities in obesity are wider in women than in men (Wardle et al., 2002; Branca et al., 2007), as illustrated further on in this chapter. In some countries disparities can be observed only in women (Wardle et al., 2002). Women in certain ethnic minority groups are substantially more likely to be obese than other women, even after controlling for differences in socio-economic conditions, while this is not true for men in the same minority groups. Such interactions underscore the complexity of some of the causal mechanisms that shape body characteristics in modern societies.

Obesity at different ages

Evidence from a range of countries shows that the relationship between body mass index and age generally follows an inverse U-shaped pattern. Weight tends to increase slightly but progressively as individuals age, until it reaches a peak and begins to drop, while height remains relatively constant in adulthood. The age at which population rates of obesity start to decline varies in different countries, but is generally around the fifth decade of life (Figure 3.1), once period and cohort effects are accounted for, based on the analysis described in Chapter 2, while descriptive statistics tend to show an increase in obesity rates up to age 65-75 before rates start to decline. However, there is a degree of uncertainty as to whether the pattern shown by most of the available statistics reflects a true relationship between age and BMI or overweight and obesity rates. As mortality rates are higher in the obese, especially at older ages, it is plausible that the descending portion of the obesity-by-age curve is at least in part driven by that, although low BMI is also associated with chronic disease and higher mortality in old age and it is difficult to estimate whose higher mortality influences the obesity-by-age curve the most.

Figure 3.1. **Obesity and overweight by age in six OECD countries**

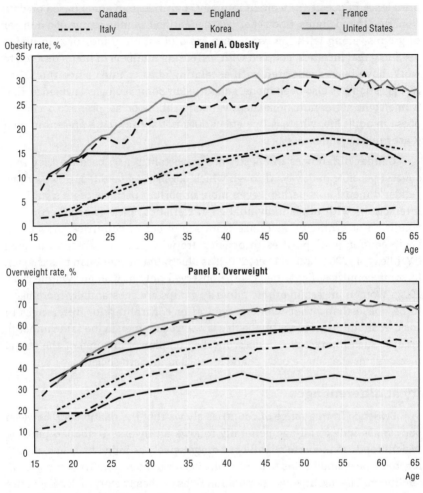

Source: OECD analysis of national health survey data.

StatLink ⬛️⬛️ http://dx.doi.org/10.1787/888932315754

The relationship between age and obesity is not just a reflection of individual biological characteristics, of course, it is also the reflection of changes in health related behaviours over the life course, which may partly be driven by environmental influences to which individuals are exposed at different stages during the course of their lives.

Obesity and socio-economic condition

A complex relationship exists between socio-economic condition and obesity. At the population level, the relationship changes direction as countries increase their wealth. In low-income countries obesity is generally more prevalent among the better off, while disadvantaged groups are increasingly affected as countries grow richer. Many studies have shown an overall socio-economic gradient in obesity in modern industrialised societies. Rates tend to decrease progressively with increasing socio-economic status, whether the latter is measured by income, education, or occupation-based social class. However, the socio-economic gradient in obesity does not appear to be as steep as that observed in general health status and in the prevalence of a number of chronic diseases (Lobstein *et al.*, 2007). This finding may be linked to substantial gender differences in the relationship between socio-economic condition and obesity. In fact, the overall socio-economic gradient in obesity observed in many countries is an average of a strong gradient in women and a substantially milder gradient in men, or even the lack of one (see additional results on selected OECD countries in Figures A.1 and A.2 in Annex A). This difference has been reported in a number of studies, but hypotheses about possible explanations remain largely unexplored.

A study looking at differences between men and women in terms of the relationship between socio-economic factors and obesity found that income, rather than education, had a greater effect on BMI and waist circumference in men, whereas higher levels of education were more important for women (Yoon *et al.*, 2006).

Men and women in poor socio-economic conditions differ in their lifestyle choices. For instance, rates of smoking, or alcohol abuse, are higher among men at the bottom of the social ladder, and there is at least some evidence that both of these behaviours are inversely related to obesity. Obese women are more heavily penalised on labour markets than obese men (*e.g.* Morris, 2006), both in terms of employment and wages, as further discussed below in this chapter. Another channel through which disparities develop is marriage and partner selection, and there is evidence that obesity reduces the probability of marriage in women (Conley and Glauber, 2007). Similarly, evidence from a longitudinal study has shown that overweight women are more likely to be unmarried, have lower education and lower incomes, while these effects are weaker in men (Gortmaker *et al.*, 1993). Men and women in poor socio-economic circumstances may also differ with regard to their patterns of physical activity. Low-paid jobs typically reserved to men tend to be more physically demanding than those more often taken up by women. Finally, the link between malnutrition in childhood and obesity in adulthood may be an additional reason for gender differences since Case and Menendez (2007) showed on South African data that women who were nutritionally deprived as children are significantly more likely to be obese as adults, while men who were deprived as children face no greater risk.

The implications of the gender difference in socio-economic gradients are of course important. Among other things, the higher prevalence of obesity in women belonging to disadvantaged socio-economic groups means that these women are more likely to give birth and raise children who will themselves be overweight or obese, and in turn will have fewer chances of moving up the social ladder, perpetuating the link between obesity and socio-economic disadvantage. A number of studies provide evidence of mother-to-child transmission of obesity (*e.g.* Whitaker *et al.*, 1997). Acting on the mechanisms that make individuals who are poorly educated and in disadvantaged socio-economic circumstances so vulnerable to obesity, and those at the other end of the socio-economic spectrum much more able to handle obesogenic environments, is of great importance not just as a way of redressing existing inequalities, but also because of its potential effect on overall social welfare.

In the remainder of this section, we provide an in-depth discussion of the link between obesity and education, based on existing evidence and new analyses undertaken by the OECD. In addition, we present an international comparison of social disparities in obesity in a range of OECD countries based on comparable measures of education, household income or occupation-based social class.

Obesity and education

The number of years spent in formal school education is the single most important factor associated with good health (Grossman and Kaestner, 1997). Those with more years of schooling are less likely to smoke, abuse alcohol, to be overweight or obese or to use illegal drugs. They are also more likely to exercise and to obtain preventive care such as flu shots, vaccines, mammograms, pap smears and colonoscopies (Cutler and Lleras-Muney, 2006). A study of twins showed that one additional year of education may decrease the probability of being overweight by 2% to 4% (Webbink *et al.*, 2008).

OECD analyses of health survey data from Australia, Canada, England and Korea show a broadly linear relationship between the number of years spent in full-time education and the probability of obesity, with most educated individuals displaying lower rates of the condition (the only exception being men in Korea, who are slightly more likely to be obese if well educated). This suggests that the strength of the link between education and obesity is approximately constant throughout the education spectrum (Figure 3.2), although evidence based on data from the United States seems to point to a non-linear relationship, with increasing effects of additional years of schooling (Cutler and Lleras-Muney, 2006). Complementary analyses on selected OECD countries are available in Annex A (Figures A.3 and A.4).

The education gradient in obesity is stronger in women than in men. Differences between genders are minor in Australia and Canada, more

Figure 3.2. **Obesity by education level in four OECD countries**

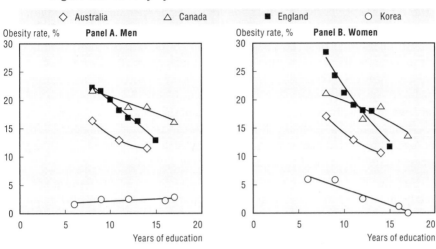

Source: OECD analysis of national health survey data.

StatLink 📊 http://dx.doi.org/10.1787/888932315773

pronounced in England and major in Korea, where the education gradients in obesity observed in men and women are in opposite directions. The scale of differences in obesity between the most and the least educated has not meaningfully changed since the early 1990s. However, there is at least some evidence that over longer periods of time more educated individuals have been less likely to be become obese than their less educated counterparts, suggesting that education has a longer term influence on obesity.

Generalising from the broader literature on education and health, the link between education and obesity revealed by many studies may reflect a true causal effect of education on the probability of becoming obese, but it may also reflect a reverse causal link, indicating that children who are obese terminate their school education earlier than normal-weight children. However, it is also possible that no causal link exists either way, and the correlation between education and obesity is due to unobserved factors affecting both obesity and education in opposite directions, such as family background, genetic traits or other differences in individual characteristics like ability to delay gratification.

The three pathways above are not mutually exclusive, of course, and some combination of the three is likely to provide the most plausible explanation of the strong correlations consistently found across countries between education and obesity. Although there is evidence to support the hypothesis that the direction of causality is from more schooling to better health (Grossman, 2000), when overall health status or longevity are the outcomes of interest, there are few studies shedding light on the causal nature of the relationship between education and obesity specifically. A study of twins suggested that education does have a causal effect on health, but it found no evidence that lifestyle factors such as smoking and obesity contribute to the health/education gradient (Lundborg, 2008). However, recent evidence from the Whitehall II longitudinal study of British civil servants, arguably the most prominent and longest running study of social disparities in health worldwide, suggests that three quarters of the socio-economic gradient in mortality is accounted for by differences in health-related behaviours, with diet (excluding alcohol consumption) and physical activity each accounting for about one-fifth of the difference (Stringhini *et al.*, 2010).

Natural experiments investigating the effects of policy changes that directly affect the number of years of mandatory schooling, can provide an indication of the causal nature of the link between education and obesity. Arendt (2005) used changes in compulsory education laws in Denmark and found inconclusive results regarding the effect of education on BMI. Clark and Royer (2008) focused on an educational reform implemented in England in 1947, which increased the minimum compulsory schooling age in the country from 14 to 15. They found that cohorts affected by the law display only slightly improved long-run health outcomes and their findings did not support a causal link between education and obesity. An OECD analysis of a further one year increase in compulsory schooling age in England in 1973 led to a similar conclusion (Sassi *et al.*, 2009b). However, Spasojevic (2003) using a similar estimation strategy for Sweden found that additional years of education have a causal effect on maintaining a healthy body mass index. Brunello *et al.* (2009a) used compulsory school reforms implemented in European countries after World War II to investigate the causal effect of education on BMI and obesity among European women, and concluded that years of schooling have a protective effect on BMI. Grabner (2009) investigated the effects of changes in state-specific compulsory schooling laws between 1914 and 1978 in the United States, and found a strong effect of additional schooling on BMI (more schooling leading to a lower BMI), which was especially pronounced in females. The OECD also analysed data from France which include information on weight at age 20 to explore a possible reverse causal effect. The analysis showed that those who are obese tend to spend fewer years in full-time education (Figure 3.3), however, the strength of the association between education and obesity is only minimally affected when reduced educational opportunities for those who are obese in young age are accounted for, suggesting that the direction of causality appears to run mostly from education to obesity.

Michael Grossman's demand-for-health model, developed in the 1980s, hypothesised that "schooling raises a person's knowledge about the

Figure 3.3. **Years spent in full-time education according to obesity status at age 20, France, population aged 25-65**

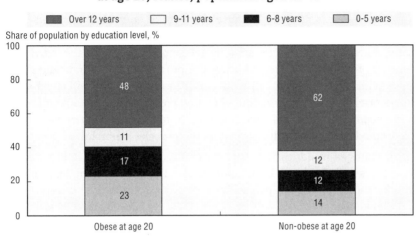

Source: OECD analysis of data from the French Enquête Décennale Santé 2002-03.

StatLink ⦿⦿ http://dx.doi.org/10.1787/888932315792

production relationship and therefore increases his or her ability to select a healthy diet, avoid unhealthy habits and make efficient use of medical care" (Kemna, 1987). Educated individuals make better use of health-related information than those who are less educated. Education provides individuals with better access to information and improved critical thinking skills. Speakman *et al.* (2005) hypothesised that the lack of education about energy contents of foods may contribute to the effects of social class on obesity. Results from their study show that on average, non-obese individuals in the lower social class group have better food knowledge than those who are obese in the same group. However non-obese subjects in all groups overestimate food energy in alcoholic beverages and snack foods indicating poorer knowledge of the energy content of these foods. Lack of information could also affect one's own perception about their body mass. Research has shown that over time more overweight individuals are under-perceiving their body mass compared to people of normal weight (Haas, 2008). It is possible that more highly educated people have the knowledge to develop healthy lifestyles and have more awareness of the health risks associated with being obese (Yoon, 2006). The more educated are more likely to choose healthy lifestyles; however, it has been shown that the highly educated choose healthier behaviours than individuals who are highly knowledgeable about the consequences of those behaviours (Kenkel, 1991). This could indicate that the effect of education on obesity is driven by different mechanisms, and not just by information and knowledge about healthy lifestyles. Examples of the latter include an improved ability to handle information, a clearer perception of the risks associated with lifestyle choices, as well as an improved self-control and consistency of preferences over time.

However, it is not just the absolute level of education achieved by an individual that matters, but also how such level of education compares with that of other individuals in the same social context. The higher the individual's education relative to others, the lower the probability of the individual being obese. The latter effect may be due to different levels of perceived stress experienced by individuals in different social positions, and by different coping mechanisms. Access to resources required to maintain a healthy weight may also be driven by an individual's position in the social hierarchy.

If changes in education can be expected to influence health-related behaviours and obesity rates in a population, this might strengthen the case for educational policies to be used as part of a public health strategy. Cutler and Lleras-Muney (2006), with reference to the broader health effects of education, argued that if a causal link were proven, education subsidies might be desirable. These would promote higher levels of education for a larger share of the population and correspondingly improve population health. Education policies directed at disadvantaged groups might reduce some of the existing health disparities (Grossman and Kaestner, 1997). Health education programmes aimed at promoting healthy lifestyles might in principle generate similar effects to those associated with school education by providing relevant information. However, if "people in lower social strata already know what foods have high energy contents, but fail to act on this information" health promotion will mostly help those who have a higher level of education (Speakman et al., 2005).

Whether through formal schooling or health promotion campaigns, education may play a role in tackling overweight and obesity. Education policies aimed at increasing formal schooling include a flexible range of policies, which may be targeted at specific age and socio-economic groups. We showed that the strength of the link between education and obesity is approximately constant throughout the education spectrum, which means that similar gains could be achieved in terms of reduction of obesity rates by increasing educational attainment for early school leavers as well as for those who spend the longest in full time education. However, policies targeting early school leavers would likely improve equity by focusing on individuals who are more likely to belong to disadvantaged socio-economic groups. Similar results could be achieved by improving access to education, e.g. through financial incentives, for disadvantaged groups.

International comparison of social disparities in obesity

Only few studies provide an international perspective on social disparities in obesity, while most focus on disparities within countries using measures and approaches which are not always comparable. The most important finding which has emerged consistently in existing international comparisons is the difference in social gradients in obesity between men and women. Gradients are relatively steep in women, but mild or even absent in men. This is true when socio-economic status is assessed on the basis of

---

Box 3.1. **Social disparities in child obesity**

Social disparities in obesity exist among children as well as adults. The latest WHO collaborative survey Health Behaviour in School-aged Children (HBSC) in 2005/06 showed that family affluence is significantly associated with overweight and obesity in around half of the 41 countries covered by the survey. Children from less affluent families are more likely to be obese or overweight, especially in western Europe (WHO, 2008).

The OECD used individual-level data from four countries (England, France, Korea and the United States) to assess the extent of social disparities in child overweight and obesity. A social gradient, more marked for obesity than overweight, was found in all countries except Korea. Social condition was assessed in relation to household income in the United States and Korea, and occupation-based social class of the head of household in England and France. The figure below illustrates differences in the likelihood of overweight and obesity for children in different social groups, after controlling for age differences between groups.

Unlike in adults, there are no major gender differences in social gradients in child obesity. Boys in disadvantaged socio-economic circumstances suffer approximately the same degree of disadvantage as girls in disadvantaged circumstances in England, France and the United States. These findings are broadly consistent with those of previous studies based on data from the same countries (Guignon, 2008, Stamatakis *et al.*, 2010; Wang and Zhang, 2006; Ogden *et al.*, 2010). Previous reports showed increasing social disparities in England over time, and decreasing disparities in the United States. Further differences in social gradients emerge when these are analysed in sub-groups of children of different ages.

On Korean data, the OECD analysis shows that children in lower income households are not more likely to be overweight or obese than those in higher income households. On the contrary, consistently with what was observed in adults, there is an inverse social gradient in boys, with children in higher income households significantly more likely to be overweight or obese.

Box 3.1. **Social disparities in child obesity** (*cont.*)

Figure Box 3.1. **Social disparities in child overweight and obesity**
Panel A. England

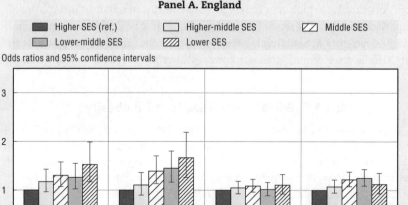

Note: Socio-economic status (SES) measured by occupation-based social class of the head of household.
Source: OECD analysis of data from the Health Survey for England 1995 to 2007.
StatLink ᴍsᴘ http://dx.doi.org/10.1787/888932315925

Panel B. France

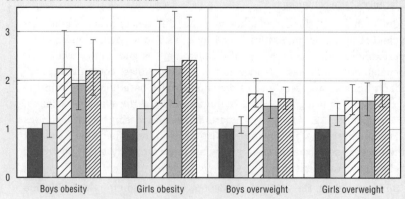

Note: SES measured by occupation-based social class of the head of household.
Source: OECD analysis of data from the survey Santé et Protection Sociale, 1992 to 2006.
StatLink ᴍsᴘ http://dx.doi.org/10.1787/888932315925

Box 3.1. **Social disparities in child obesity** *(cont.)*

Figure Box 3.1. **Social disparities in child overweight and obesity** *(cont.)*

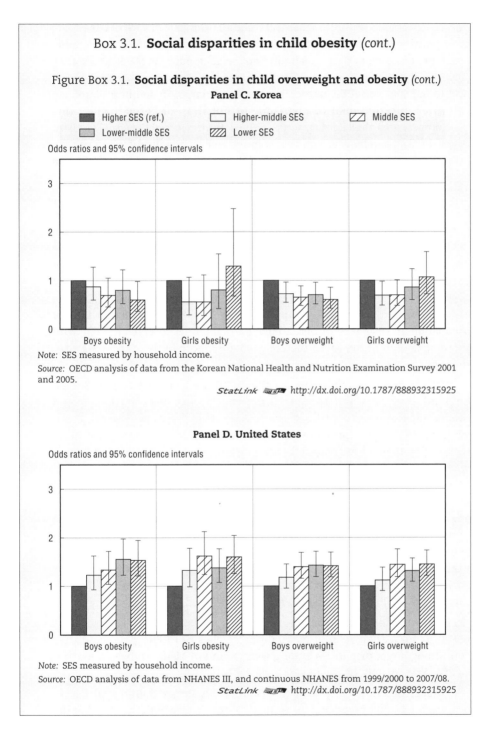

Panel C. Korea

- ■ Higher SES (ref.)
- □ Higher-middle SES
- ▨ Middle SES
- ▨ Lower-middle SES
- ▨ Lower SES

Odds ratios and 95% confidence intervals

Note: SES measured by household income.

Source: OECD analysis of data from the Korean National Health and Nutrition Examination Survey 2001 and 2005.

StatLink ᵐᵍ▸ *http://dx.doi.org/10.1787/888932315925*

Panel D. United States

Odds ratios and 95% confidence intervals

Note: SES measured by household income.

Source: OECD analysis of data from NHANES III, and continuous NHANES from 1999/2000 to 2007/08.

StatLink ᵐᵍ▸ *http://dx.doi.org/10.1787/888932315925*

household income, as Garcia Villar and Quintana-Domeque (2009) did in a study of disparities in BMI in nine European countries, but also when educational attainment is used to distinguish different social groups, as Mackenbach *et al.* (2008) did in a broad study of health disparities in 22 European countries, which also found that social disparities in obesity are larger in southern European countries. International comparisons of nutrition patterns in the same geographical area shed light on some of the determinants of the social gradient in obesity, as a similar gradient, by income as well as by education, can be seen in healthy nutrition patterns, and especially in the consumption of fruit and vegetables (De Irala-Estevez *et al.*, 2000).

A new analysis of socio-economic disparities in obesity undertaken by the OECD shows significant disparities in all of the OECD countries examined, but also wide variations across countries in the size of those disparities. The OECD analysis provides support to previous reports indicating that disparities are larger in women than in men. Women at the highest end of the socio-economic spectrum display consistently lower rates of obesity and overweight in all of the countries examined. This is not always true for men, especially when disparities are measured by household income or type of occupation. In several countries, an inverse gradient is observed in men, with those at the top of the social hierarchy slightly more likely to be obese than those at the bottom.

Of the countries examined in the OECD analysis, the United States, England, Australia and Hungary have the largest rates of obesity and overweight. However, countries where the largest relative social disparities exist are not necessarily those where obesity and overweight rates are highest. Least educated women are at greatest disadvantage in Korea, Spain, Italy and France, where their chances of being overweight or obese are many times higher than those of their most educated counterparts. Conversely, disparities are smallest in England and Australia, where women at the two extremes of the education spectrum differ in their overweight and obesity rates by a factor of less than two. Disparities in obesity by education among men are largest in France, Sweden, Austria, Spain and Italy, but still substantially smaller than among women, and are relatively minor in other countries. Disparities in obesity by socio-economic status follow a similar pattern, and are largest in France, Austria and Spain for men and in France, Sweden and Spain for women.

OECD findings are consistent with those published by Mackenbach *et al.* (2008) on education-related inequalities in obesity in European countries confirming larger disparities among women and in Mediterranean countries such as France, Italy, Spain and Portugal.

Disparities in obesity tend to be noticeably larger than disparities in overweight, both for men and for women. This is in line with the fact that the

Figure 3.4. **Disparities in obesity and overweight by education level,
selected OECD countries**

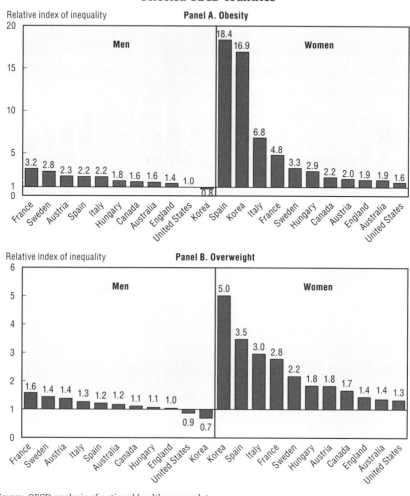

Source: OECD analysis of national health survey data.

StatLink ⓘⓢ http://dx.doi.org/10.1787/888932315811

highest levels of BMI are often observed among the poorly educated and more generally among those in disadvantaged socio-economic circumstances.

The OECD analysis also looked at how social disparities in overweight and obesity evolved during the past 15 years, showing that disparities remained remarkably stable over time. Only in few instances relatively small changes were detected. Disparities in overweight decreased slightly in men in England and Korea, while they increased slightly in Italy. Likewise, a modest decline was observed in disparities in obesity among women in France and England.

Figure 3.5. **Disparities in obesity and overweight by household income or occupation-based social class, selected OECD countries**

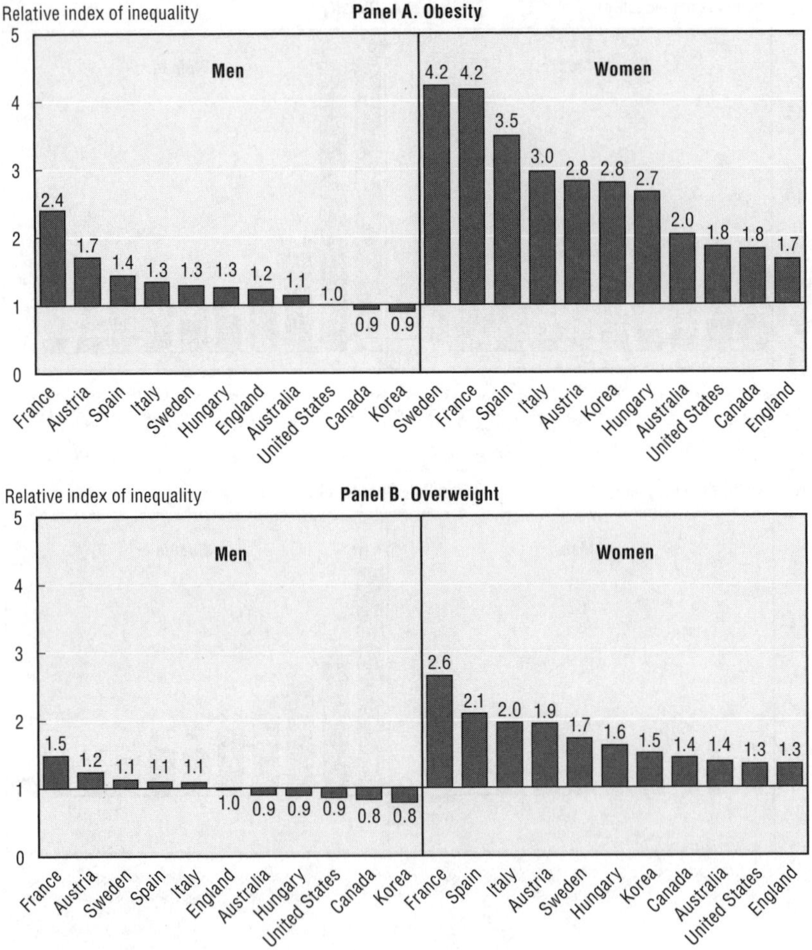

Relative index of inequality — **Panel A. Obesity**

Men: France 2.4, Austria 1.7, Spain 1.4, Italy 1.3, Sweden 1.3, Hungary 1.3, England 1.2, Australia 1.1, United States 1.0, Canada 0.9, Korea 0.9

Women: Sweden 4.2, France 4.2, Spain 3.5, Italy 3.0, Austria 2.8, Korea 2.8, Hungary 2.7, Australia 2.0, United States 1.8, Canada 1.8, England 1.7

Relative index of inequality — **Panel B. Overweight**

Men: France 1.5, Austria 1.2, Sweden 1.1, Spain 1.1, Italy 1.1, England 1.0, Australia 0.9, Hungary 0.9, United States 0.9, Canada 0.8, Korea 0.8

Women: France 2.6, Spain 2.1, Italy 2.0, Austria 1.9, Sweden 1.7, Hungary 1.6, Korea 1.5, Canada 1.4, Australia 1.4, United States 1.3, England 1.3

Source: OECD analyses of national health survey data.
StatLink ᗢᑒ http://dx.doi.org/10.1787/888932315830

Figures 3.4 and 3.5 illustrate the findings of the OECD analysis using the relative index of inequality, which provides a measure of how many times more likely to be overweight or obese are those at the lower end of the socio-economic spectrum relative to those at the upper end. As in some of the analyses reported in Chapter 2, BMI data are measured in certain countries and self-reported in others. Self-reports have been shown to underestimate true BMI in some national surveys, but what is shown here is differences in BMI status across social groups, which are likely to be affected by self-report bias to a smaller degree. In addition, it should be noted that the socio-economic condition variable is based on household income in four countries (Australia, Canada, Korea and the United States) while it is occupation-based in the others. All of the former four countries display a positive relationship between the socio-economic variable and overweight in men, which is not the case when socio-economic condition is measured by occupation. Similarly, a positive relationship for obesity is observed in Canada and Korea.

Obesity in different racial and ethnic groups

Ethnic origin and migrant status are important dimensions along which variations in health and health-related behaviours have been shown in a wide range of empirical studies. Such variations exist also in relation to overweight and obesity, even after accounting for the socio-economic characteristics often associated with ethnic minority and migrant status. Not all minority groups, however, display higher than average rates of overweight and obesity. Moreover, as evidence from the United States and England shows, when minorities do have higher obesity rates these may be unevenly distributed across gender groups, with minority women displaying substantially higher than average obesity rates and minority men broadly in line with the average. Figures 3.6 and 3.7 illustrate differences in overweight and obesity rates in different racial and ethnic groups in the United States and in England. Essentially, it is black women in England and black and Hispanic women in the United States who have larger than average obesity rates, while obesity rates are highest in white men in both countries.

Figure 3.6. **Obesity and overweight by ethnic group in England (adults)**

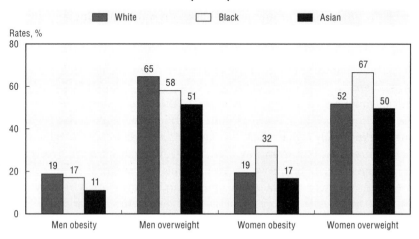

Source: OECD analysis of Health Survey for England (HSE) data 1995-2007.

StatLink http://dx.doi.org/10.1787/888932315849

Figure 3.7. **Obesity and overweight by ethnic group in the United States (adults)**

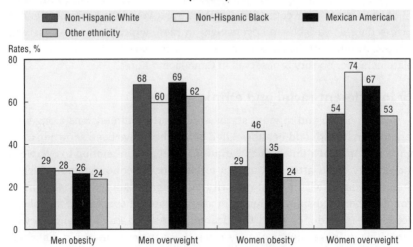

Source: OECD analysis of National Health and Nutrition Examination Survey (NHANES) data 1999-2008.
StatLink ⟨⟨⟨ http://dx.doi.org/10.1787/888932315868

However, a mechanistic application of the BMI thresholds used for populations of Caucasian background to ethnic minorities, particularly those of African, Caribbean or Asian origin, may be misleading, as the levels of BMI at which the risk of chronic diseases starts to increase substantially may be lower than those measured in individuals of Caucasian background.

Cutler and Lleras-Muney (2006) found that the education gradient in obesity was steeper in whites than in ethnic minorities in the United States. An OECD analysis by ethnic group based on data from England showed substantially milder education gradients in obesity for minority men, relative to white men, but similar gradients in women of different ethnic backgrounds.

Ethnic minority children are at greater disadvantage than adults in England and in the United States. Black and Asian children in England and African-American and Hispanic children in the United States are at least as likely to be overweight or obese as white children between the ages of 3 and 17. Rates are especially high in black boys and girls in England, with roughly 40% of them overweight. But even more Mexican-American boys are overweight, almost one in two in the above age group, while overweight rates are over 40% in African-American and Mexican-American girls and obesity rates are 50% larger in African-American girls than in white girls (Figures 3.8 and 3.9).

Figure 3.8. **Obesity and overweight by ethnic group in England (children 3-17)**

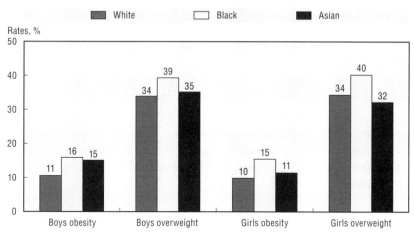

Note: Rates are adjusted for age and socio-economic differences among ethnic groups.
Source: OECD analysis of Health Survey for England (HSE) data 1995-2007.

StatLink ᵐˢᵖ http://dx.doi.org/10.1787/888932315887

Figure 3.9. **Obesity and overweight by ethnic group in the United States (children 3-17)**

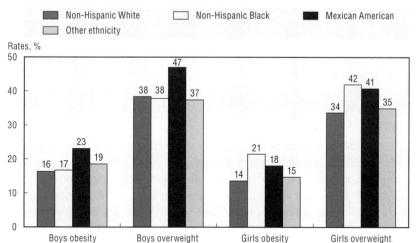

Note: Rates are adjusted for age and socio-economic differences among ethnic groups.
Source: OECD analysis of National Health and Nutrition Examination Survey (NHANES) 1999-2008.

StatLink ᵐˢᵖ http://dx.doi.org/10.1787/888932315906

Does obesity affect employment, wages and productivity?

The evidence of disparities in obesity among people with different levels of income or different types of occupation discussed previously in this chapter suggests that those, especially women, who live in disadvantaged socio-economic circumstances are more likely to be or become obese. We discussed a number of possible mechanisms that may explain this link. However, a number of studies have gathered evidence of the same link taking the opposite perspective, *i.e.* exploring whether those who are obese are more likely to be unemployed or be in lower paid jobs than normal-weight people. This approach rests on the assumption that the causal link is from obesity to adverse labour market outcomes, which may be supported by a number of possible mechanisms ranging from decreased productivity to stigma and discrimination.

As in the case of obesity and education, the relationship between obesity and wages, or labour market outcomes, is likely to be driven by causal effects in both directions reinforcing each other to produce a marked and persisting social gradient. Once again, however, the gradient is clear in women but much less so in men.

Obesity and employment

An obese person is less likely to have a job than a normal-weight person. The obese have fewer chances of success when they seek employment and they tend to spend longer periods of time unemployed. The probability of regaining employment after a period of unemployment is similarly lower for those with a higher BMI. There is some evidence that the obese are especially disadvantaged in finding employment in occupations involving direct personal contact with customers (Rooth, 2007). The obese are also more likely to be inactive (unemployed and not actively seeking employment) (Cawley and Danziger, 2005; Klarenbach *et al.*, 2006) either because they are in poor health and unable to work, they are discouraged by their lack of success in obtaining employment, or they lack the incentives to pursue a condition (employment) that they may find more distressing and less enjoyable than people of normal weight do, on average.

A number of studies provide evidence of a clear link between obesity and employment both in men and in women, and reach the conclusion that the association reflects a causal effect of obesity on labour market outcomes (*e.g.* Morris, 2007; Tunceli *et al.*, 2006). Other studies have reached different conclusions, finding either a weak link between obesity and employment, type or sector of occupation (Garcia Villar and Quintana-Domeque, 2006), or no link at all (Cawley, 2000). On the whole, however, the balance of evidence points to a negative influence of obesity on employment, especially, but not exclusively, for women.

Psychologists and sociologists have tried to ascertain whether the negative influence of obesity on employment is the result of systematic discrimination by prospective employers. Roehling (1999) reviewed the findings of 17 separate "laboratory" studies on obesity-related discrimination in employment dating from 1979. In these experiments, subjects were asked to make hiring and promotion decisions on hypothetical candidates where the only difference was a verbal or graphic manipulation of the candidate's weight. Those studies consistently found discrimination on the basis of weight in all aspects of employment (including selection, placement, compensation, promotion, and discharge).

But discrimination is a complex phenomenon, which does not always, or not exclusively, reflect prejudicial attitudes. A number of authors have preferred to use the concept of "statistical discrimination" (*e.g.* Lundborg *et al.*, 2010) to reflect attitudes based on (statistically founded) expectations concerning the skills, physical fitness and productivity of obese men and women. Obesity, in this case, becomes a marker of diminished individual potential in the labour market.

Obesity affects employment to different degrees in different racial and ethnic groups. This has been studied mostly in the United States (Cawley, 2000; Cawley and Danziger, 2005) where white women who are severely obese are substantially more likely than average to be out of work (42.2% *vs.* 31%), while the same condition makes virtually no difference among African-American women. Obesity is more common, therefore possibly less stigmatised, among African-American women, and it is not associated with decreased self-esteem in African-American women as much as it is in white women (Averett and Korenman, 1996).

Obesity and wages

What happens to those obese people who do succeed in their search for employment? They simply end up earning less than their colleagues, even when they have equivalent positions and discharge the same tasks. The evidence is perhaps even stronger than on the link between obesity and employment. A comprehensive review undertaken by the OECD found that all of the 18 studies that looked at the impact of obesity on wages in women in various countries identified a negative association between obesity and wages, although not all of those studies found evidence that the effect is causal and statistically significant. Of the 15 studies retrieved that focused on men, 12 reported a negative effect of obesity on wages, while three reported a slightly positive impact. Wage penalties are generally larger in women, although at least one study (Brunello and d'Hombres, 2007) reported larger penalties in men. A recent study of 450 000 men in Sweden found an exceptionally large 18% wage penalty associated with obesity (Lundborg *et al.*, 2010), although most studies identified pay gaps in the order of 10%.

Obesity affects wages in the private sector but not, or at least not to the same degree, in the public sector, as shown by a study of workers in Denmark

(Greve, 2008). There is also evidence from Finland that obese women with higher levels of education and those in higher occupational positions suffer the largest wage disadvantage relative to their normal-weight peers, while the gap is substantially smaller among less educated women and manual workers (Sarlio-Lähteenkorva *et al.*, 2004). Based on evidence from the United States, racial and ethnic differences mirror those reported above for employment, with obese white women suffering substantial disadvantage in wages, while African-American and Hispanic women are virtually unaffected (Cawley, 2004; Cawley and Danziger, 2005).

As for the impact of obesity on employment, the role of discrimination in the link between obesity and wages has been the subject of much debate. Discrimination may be associated with lower expected or actual productivity on the job, increased sickness absence and need for medical care, which may be particularly burdensome for employers who are directly responsible for providing health insurance. On the other hand, part of the wage penalty associated with obesity must be caused by the employment disparities discussed above in this chapter. The obese who struggle in the labour market – who may have lower educational qualifications, lower skills and poorer general health – will likely settle for lower paid jobs than their normal-weight counterparts.

Obesity and labour productivity

A further aspect of the impact of obesity on labour markets is differences in productivity between obese and non-obese workers. Differences emerge in relation to absenteeism (sickness absence), but also in relation to the degree of productivity and performance at work (presenteeism). The obese are also more likely to claim disability benefits and to become unable to work for extended periods of time, or even permanently.

Evidence from several countries documents differences in absence from work due to sickness among workers with different BMI levels. Some of the earliest estimates available from the United States suggest that overweight and obese workers, men and women, have twice as many days of sick leave as lower weight workers (Burton *et al.*, 1998). The same study also found a gradient in sick leave with increasing BMI levels. Later studies provided more detailed measures of this gradient, showing that the increase in days off work due to sickness is larger in women than in men (Finkelstein *et al.*, 2005; Cawley *et al.*, 2007) and that the increase in sick leave starts at higher BMI levels in men (from severe obesity) than in women (Finklestein *et al.*, 2005). Differences in sick leave between obese and non-obese workers are present in the public, as well as in the private, sectors (Bungum *et al.*, 2003). Similar evidence of increased sick leave in obese men and women is available from Belgium (Moens *et al.*, 1999; Moreau *et al.*, 2004), and a statistically significant relationship between obesity and absenteeism was found in female workers in Denmark, Finland, Portugal and Spain, based on data from the European Community Household Panel survey (Sanz De-Galdeano, 2007). In men, obesity leads to increased absenteeism in some types of occupations more than in others. A study based in the United States shows that absenteeism increases with BMI in professional and sales workers, while only morbid obesity is associated with a greater probability of missed work among managers, office workers and equipment operators (Cawley *et al.*, 2007).

Health problems associated with obesity may lead to temporary or permanent disability. Formal definitions of what is recognised as disability and criteria for awarding state benefits to the disabled vary across countries, but obesity is an increasingly important cause of disability throughout the OECD area. In the United States, the odds of short-term disability episodes are increased by 76% in the obese, and by 26% in those who are overweight but not obese (Arena *et al.*, 2006). The recent growth in obesity rates is a leading cause of increases in disability, accounting for about one third of increases in 30- to 45-year-olds (Bhattacharya *et al.*, 2008). In Sweden, a J-shaped relationship was found between BMI and receipt of disability pensions in the working-age population, with the underweight more likely to receive a pension than the overweight (but not obese), but the obese substantially more likely to receive a pension than anyone else, about 2.8 times more likely than a normal-weight person (Månsson *et al.*, 1996). In Finland, BMI is a similarly strong predictor of early work disability, with obese women twice as likely to be in receipt of a work invalidity pension and obese men 1.5 times as likely as their normal-weight counterparts (Rissanen *et al.*, 1990).

Presenteeism is far more difficult to measure than absenteeism or disability. A small number of studies have attempted to quantify reduced productivity for obese workers in the manufacturing sector, mainly through monetary valuations of the impact of self-reported reduced performance on the job due to health reasons. Moderately and severely obese manufacturing workers experience greater difficulties with job-related physical tasks and in completing work demands on time than normal-weight workers. Existing estimates suggest that the loss of productivity associated with presenteeism is even larger than that associated with absenteeism, accounting for up to two thirds of the monetary value of total productivity losses (Ricci and Chee, 2005; Gates *et al.*, 2008). In addition, absences from work may not cost employers the full value of the time employees spend off work to the extent that absences result in unpaid leave or other workers compensate for those who are absent.

Although studies of the impact of obesity on productivity and work disability have more often explored correlations rather than the causal nature of the links involved, there is sufficient evidence to conclude that obesity is at least a marker for increased absence from work due to illness and for decreased productivity on the job. Far from justifying discrimination against the obese in employer's decisions about hiring, promotion and pay, this sets the issue firmly into the public health and social policy agenda. Brunello *et al.* (2009b) identify wage differentials as a clear market failure associated with obesity. The need for government intervention to protect the obese in labour markets and ensure they enjoy the same opportunities as anyone else in terms of employment, type of job, sector of occupation and pay naturally follows the evidence presented in this chapter.

Key messages

- Analyses of national health survey data from more than one third of OECD countries show important social disparities in overweight and obesity in women and lesser or no disparities in men.

- Social disparities within countries are larger in obesity than in overweight, but when comparisons across countries are made, the size of disparities is not related to countries' overall obesity rates.

- With few exceptions, social disparities in obesity remained remarkably stable over the past 15 years.

- Social disparities are also present in children in three out of the four countries examined, but no major differences between genders are observed in degrees of disparity. The gap in obesity between children who belong to ethnic minorities and white children in England and in the United States is larger than that observed in adults.

- Disparities in labour market outcomes between the obese and people of normal weight, which are particularly strong in women, likely contribute to the social gradient in overweight and obesity.

- The obese are less likely to be part of the labour force and to be in employment. Discrimination in hiring decisions, partly due to expectations of lower productivity, contributes to the employment gap. White women are especially disadvantaged in this respect.

- The obese are likely to earn less than people of normal weight. Wage penalties of up to 18% have been associated with obesity in existing research. Again, obese women are penalised more than men.

- The obese tend to have more days of absence from work, a lower productivity on the job and a greater access to disability benefits than people of normal weight, which sets obesity firmly on the social policy agenda.

- The need for government intervention to protect the obese in labour markets and ensure they enjoy the same opportunities as anyone else in terms of employment, type of job, sector of occupation and pay naturally follows the evidence presented in this chapter.

Bibliography

Arena, V.C., K.R. Padiyar, W.N. Burton and J.J. Schwerha (2006), "The Impact of Body Mass Index on Short-term Disability in the Workplace", *J. Occup. Environ. Med.*, Vol. 48, No. 11, pp. 1118-1124, November.

Arendt, J.N. (2005), "Does Education Cause Better Health? A Panel Data Analysis Using School Reforms for Identification", *Economics of Education Review*, Vol. 24, No. 2, pp. 149-160.

Averett, S. and S. Korenman (1996), "The Economic Reality of the Beauty Myth", *Journal of Human Resources*, Vol. 31, pp. 304-330.

Bhattacharya, J., K. Choudhry and D.N. Lakdawalla (2008), "Chronic Disease and Trends in Severe Disability in Working Age Populations", *Medical Care*, Vol. 46, No. 1, pp. 92-100.

Branca, F., H. Nikogosian and T. Lobstein (eds.) (2007), "The Challenge of Obesity in the WHO European Region and the Strategies for Response", WHO Regional Office for Europe, Copenhagen.

Brunello, G. and B. d'Hombres (2007), "Does Body Weight Affect Wages: Evidence from Europe", *Economics and Human Biology*, Vol. 5, pp. 1-19.

Brunello, G., D. Fabbri and M. Fort (2009a), "Years of Schooling, Human Capital and the Body Mass Index of European Females", IZA Discussion Paper No. 4667, Bonn.

Brunello G., P.C. Michaud and A. Sanz-de-Galdeano (2009b), "The Rise of Obesity in Europe: An Economic Perspective", *Economic Policy*, CEPR, CES, MSH, Vol. 24, pp. 551-596.

Bungum, T., M. Satterwhite, A.W. Jackson and J.R. Morrow (2003), "The Relationship of Body Mass Index, Medical Costs, and Job Absenteeism", *Am. J. Health Behav.*, Vol. 27, No. 4, pp. 456-462.

Burton, W.N., C.Y. Chen, A.B. Schultz and D.W. Edington (1998), "The Economic Costs Associated with Body Mass Index in a Workplace", *J. Occup. Env. Med.*, Vol. 40, No. 9, pp. 786-792, September.

Case, A. and A. Menendez (2007), "Sex Differences in Obesity Rates in Poor Countries: Evidence from South Africa", NBER Working Paper No. 13541, Cambridge, MA, available at *www.nber.org/papers/w13541*.

Cawley, J. (2000), "An Instrumental Variables Approach to Measuring the Effect of Obesity on Employment Disability", *Health Services Research*, Vol. 35, pp. 1159-1179.

Cawley, J. (2004), "The Impact of Obesity on Wages", *J. Hum. Resour.*, Vol. 39, No. 2, pp. 451-474.

Cawley, J. and S. Danziger (2005), "Morbid Obesity and the Transition from Welfare to Work", *J. Policy Anal. Manage*, Vol. 24, No. 4, pp. 727-743.

Cawley, J., J.A. Rizzo and K. Haas (2007), "Occupation-Specific Absenteeism Costs Associated with Obesity and Morbid Obesity", *J. Occup. Environ. Med.*, Vol. 49, No. 12, pp. 1317-1324.

Chou, S., M. Grossman and H. Saffer (2003), "An Economic Analysis of Adult Obesity: Results from the Behavioral Risk Factor Surveillance System", *Journal of Health Economics*, Vol. 23, pp. 565-587.

Clark, D. and H. Royer (2008), "The Effect of Education on Adult Mortality and Health: Evidence from the United Kingdom", available at *www.frbsf.org/economics/conferences/0806/royer.pdf*.

Conley, D. and R. Glauber (2007), "Gender, Body Mass, and Socioeconomic Status: New Evidence from the PSID", *Advances in Health Economics and Health Services Research*, Vol. 17, pp. 253-275.

Cutler, D. and A. Lleras-Muney (2006), "Education and Health: Evaluating Theories and Evidence", NBER Working Paper No. 12352, Cambridge, MA, available at *www.nber.org/papers/w12352*.

De Irala-Estévez, J., M. Groth, L. Johansson, U. Oltersdorf, R. Prättälä and M.A. Martínez-González (2000), "A Systematic Review of Socio-Economic Differences in Food Habits in Europe: Consumption of Fruit and Vegetables", *European Journal of Clinical Nutrition*, Vol. 54, pp. 706-714.

Finkelstein, E., C. Fiebelkorn and G. Wang (2005), "The Costs of Obesity Among Full-Time Employees", *Am. J. Health Promot.*, Vol. 20, No. 1, pp. 45-51, Sep.-Oct.

Garcia Villar, J. and C. Quintana-Domeque (2006), "Obesity, Employment and Wages in Europe", in K. Bolin and J. Cawley (eds.), *Advances in Health Economics and Health Services Research*, Elsevier, Amsterdam, pp. 189-219.

Garcia Villar, J and C. Quintana-Domeque (2009), "Income and Body Mass Index in Europe", *Econ. Hum. Biol.*, Vol. 7, No. 1, pp. 73-83.

Gates, D.M., P. Succop, B.J. Brehm, G.L. Gillespie and B.D. Sommers (2008), "Obesity and Presenteeism: The Impact of Body Mass Index on Workplace Productivity", *Journal of Occupational and Environmental Medicine*, Vol. 50, No. 1, pp. 39-45.

Gortmaker, S.L., A. Must, J.M. Perrin, A.M. Sobol and W.H. Dietz (1993), "Social and Economic Consequences of Overweight among Adolescents and Young Adults", *New England Journal of Medicine*, Vol. 329, pp. 1008-1012.

Grabner, M. (2009), "The Causal Effect of Education on Obesity: Evidence from Compulsory Schooling Laws", 12 November, available at SSRN, available at *http://ssrn.com/abstract=1505075*.

Greve, J. (2008), "Obesity and Labor Market Outcomes in Denmark", *Economics and Human Biology*, Vol. 6, pp. 350-362.

Grossman, M. (2000), "The Human Capital Model", in A.J. Culyer and J.P. Newhouse (eds.), *Handbook of Health Economics*, Vol. 1A, Elsevier, Amsterdam, pp. 347-408.

Grossman, M. and R. Kaestner (1997), "Effects of Education on Health", in J.R. Behrman and N. Stacey (eds.), *The Social Benefits of Education*, University of Michigan Press, Ann Arbor, MI, pp. 69-123.

Guignon, N. (2008), "La santé des enfants scolarisés en CM2 en 2004-2005. Premiers résultats", *Études et Résultats*, Publication DREES No. 632, Paris, April.

Haas, M. (2008), "Weigh Too Fat", UTS Speaks, Public Lecture 22 May 2008, available at *www.chere.uts.edu.au/pdf/utspeaks_haas.pdf*.

Kemna, H. (1987), "Working Conditions and the Relationship between Schooling and Health", *Journal of Health Economics*, Vol. 6, pp. 189-210.

Kenkel, D.S. (1991), "Health Behavior, Health Knowledge, and Schooling", *Journal of Political Economy*, Vol. 99, No. 2, pp. 287-305.

Klarenbach, S., R. Padwal, A. Chuck and P. Jacobs (2006), "Population-Based Analysis of Obesity and Labour Force Participation", *Obesity*, Vol. 14, pp. 920-927.

Lobstein, T. and R. Jackson Leach (2007), "Tackling Obesities: Future Choices – International Comparisons of Obesity Trends, Determinants and Responses – Evidence Review", Foresight, Government Office of the Chief Scientist, available at *www.foresight.gov.uk*.

Lundborg, P. (2008), "The Health Returns to Education – What Can We Learn from Twins?", Tinbergen Institute Discussion Paper No. TI 08-027/3, available at SSRN: *http://ssrn.com/abstract=1113685*.

Lundborg, P., P. Nystedt and D. Rooth (2010), "No Country for Fat Men? Obesity, Earnings, Skills, and Health among 450,000 Swedish Men", IZA Discussion Paper No. 4775, available at *www.ed.lu.se/papers/iza_lundborg.pdf*.

Mackenbach, J.P., I. Stirbu, A.R. Roskam, M.M. Schaap, G. Menvielle, M. Leinsalu and A.E. Kunst, for the European Union Working Group on Socioeconomic Inequalities in Health (2008), "Socioeconomic Inequalities in Health in 22 European Countries", *New England Journal of Medicine*, Vol. 358, No. 23, pp. 2468-2481.

Månsson, N.O., K.F. Eriksson, B. Israelsson, J. Ranstam, A. Melander and L. Råstam (1996), "Body Mass Index and Disability Pension in Middle-Aged Men – Non-Linear Relations", *Int. J. Epidemiol.*, Vol. 25, No. 1, pp. 80-85.

Moens, G., L.V. Gaal, E. Muls, B. Viaene and P. Jacques (1999), "Body Mass Index and Health Among the Working Population, Epidemiological Data from Belgium", *European Journal of Public Health*, Vol. 9, No. 2, pp. 119-123.

Moreau, M., F. Valente, R. Mak, E. Pelfrene, P. de Smet, G. De Backer and M. Kornitzer (2004), "Obesity, Body Fat Distribution and Incidence of Sick Leave in the Belgian Workforce: The Belstress Study", *Int J. Obes. Relat. Metab. Disord.*, Vol. 28, No. 4, pp. 574-582, April.

Morris, S. (2006), "Body Mass Index and Occupational Attainment", *Journal of Health Economics*, Vol. 25, pp. 347-364.

Morris, S. (2007), "The Impact of Obesity on Employment", *Labour Economics*, Vol. 14, pp. 413-433.

Ogden, C.L., M.D. Carroll, L.R. Curtin, M.M. Lamb and K.M. Flegal (2010), "Prevalence of High Body Mass Index in US Children and Adolescents, 2007-2008", *JAMA*, Vol. 303, No. 3, pp. 242-249.

Ricci, J.A. and E. Chee (2005), "Lost Productive Time Associated with Excess Weight in the US Workforce", *J. Occup. Environ. Med.*, Vol. 47, No. 12, pp. 1227-1234.

Rissanen, A., M. Heliovaara, P. Knekt, A. Reunanen, A. Aromaa and J. Maatela (1990), "Risk of Disability and Mortality Due to Overweight in a Finnish Population", *British Medical Journal*, Vol. 301, No. 6756, pp. 835-837.

Roehling, M.V. (1999), "Weight-Based Discrimination in Employment: Psychological and Legal Aspects", *Personnel Psychology*, Vol. 52, pp. 969-1017.

Rooth, D.O. (2007), "Evidence of Unequal Treatment in Hiring against Obese Applicants: A Field Experiment", IZA Discussion Paper No. 2775, Bonn, available at *ftp://repec.iza.org/RePEc/Discussionpaper/dp2775.pdf*.

Sanz de Galdeano, A. (2007), "An Economic Analysis of Obesity in Europe: Health, Medical Care and Absenteeism Costs", Working Paper No. 2007-38, FEDEA,

Fundacíon de Estudios de Economía Aplicada, Madrid, available at *www.fedea.es/pub/Papers/2008/dt2007-38.pdf.*

Sarlio-Lähteenkorva, S., K. Silventoinen and E. Lahelma (2004), "Relative Weight and Income at Different Levels of Socioeconomic Status", *Am. J. Public Health*, Vol. 94, No. 3, pp. 468-472, March.

Sassi, F., M. Devaux, M. Cecchini and E. Rusticelli (2009a), "The Obesity Epidemic: Analysis of Past and Projected Future Trends in Selected OECD Countries", OECD Health Working Paper No. 45, OECD Publishing, Paris.

Sassi, F., M. Devaux, J. Church, M. Cecchini and F. Borgonovi (2009b), "Education and Obesity in Four OECD Countries", OECD Health Working Paper No. 46, OECD Publishing, Paris.

Spasojevic, J. (2003), "Effects of Education on Adult Health in Sweden: Results from a Natural Experiment", PhD Dissertation., Graduate Center, City University of New York.

Speakman, J.R., H. Walker, L. Walker and D.M. Jackson (2005), "Associations between BMI, Social Strata and the Estimated Energy Content of Foods", *International Journal of Obesity*, Vol. 29, No. 10, pp. 1281-1288.

Stamatakis, E., J. Wardle and T.J. Cole (2010), "Childhood Obesity and Overweight Prevalence Trends in England: Evidence for Growing Socioeconomics Disparities", *International Journal of Obesity*, Vol. 34, pp. 41-47.

Stringhini, S., S. Sabia, M. Shipley, E. Brunner, H. Nabi, M. Kivimaki and A. Singh-Manoux (2010), "Association of Socioeconomic Position with Health Behaviors and Mortality", *JAMA*, Vol. 303, No. 12, pp. 1159-1166.

Tunceli, K., K. Li and L.K. Williams (2006), "Long-Term Effects of Obesity on Employment and Work Limitations Among US Adults, 1986 to 1999", *Obesity (Silver Spring)*, Vol. 14, No. 9, pp. 1637-1646, September.

Wang, Y. and Q. Zhang (2006), "Are American Children and Adolescents of Low Socioeconomic Status at Increased Risk of Obesity? Changes in the Association between Overweight and Family Income between 1971 and 2002", *Am. J. Clin. Nutr.*, Vol. 84, No. 4, pp. 707-716.

Wardle, J., J. Waller and M.J. Jarvis (2002), "Sex Differences in the Association of Socioeconomic Status with Obesity", *American Journal of Public Health*, Vol. 92, pp. 1299-1304.

Webbink, D., N.G. Martin and P.M. Visscher (2008), "Does Education Reduce the Probability of Being Overweight?", CPB Discussion Paper No. 102, CPB Netherlands Bureau for Economic Policy Analysis.

Whitaker, R.C., J.A. Wright, M.S. Pepe, K.D. Seidel and W.H. Dietz (1997), "Predicting Obesity in Young Adulthood from Childhood and Parental Obesity", *New England Journal of Medicine*, Vol. 337, No. 13, pp. 869-873.

WHO (2008), "Inequalities in Young People's Health, HBSC International Report from the 2005/2006 Survey", in C. Currie, S. Nic Gabhainn, E. Godeau, C. Roberts, R. Smith, D. Currie, W. Picket, M. Richter, A. Morgan and V. Barnekow (eds.), *Health Outcomes*, Chapter 2, Section 2.

Yoon, Y.S., S.W. Oh and H.S. Park (2006), "Socio-Economic Status in Relation to Obesity and Abdominal Obesity in Korean Adults: A Focus on Sex Differences", *Obesity (Silver Spring)*, Vol. 14, No. 5, pp. 909-919.

Special Focus II.
The Size and Risks
of the International Epidemic of Child Obesity

by

Tim Lobstein, International Association for the Study of Obesity,
and Science Policy Research Unit, University of Sussex

Evidence for an epidemic

In many developed economies child obesity levels doubled between the 1960s and the 1980s, and have doubled again since then (Lobstein *et al.*, 2004). By 2005, one third of all US children were affected by excess body weight, and children in other developed economies have been following the US pattern. Even in emerging and less developed economies, child obesity prevalence levels are also rising (Wang and Lobstein, 2006), especially in urban areas where the need for physical activity is lower and the opportunities for sedentary behaviour and access to energy-dense foods and beverages far greater. As child obesity is strongly predictive of adult obesity and of chronic disease, the child obesity epidemic has been described as "a massive tsunami" (Ludwig, 2005), and "a health time-bomb" (Chief Medical Officer, 2003).

Figure SFII.1 shows estimates of excess body weight prevalence in specified countries. The figures are based on BMI measures. The definitions of overweight and obesity in children are adjusted to take account of their natural growth during childhood, as well as differences between boys and girls in their growth patterns. The BMI thresholds used to identify overweight and obese children are those developed by the IOTF (see note 3 in Chapter 2 for further details).

Researchers should be aware that there are various ways of defining and categorising excess adiposity in children, and care should be taken when comparing published prevalence figures for overweight and obesity to ensure they are truly comparable. Overweight usually refers to children with some excess adiposity and at risk of becoming more overweight, while obese refers to children with greater excess adiposity and at immediate risk of developing

Figure SFII.1. **Estimated prevalence of child overweight in OECD member states and associated countries**

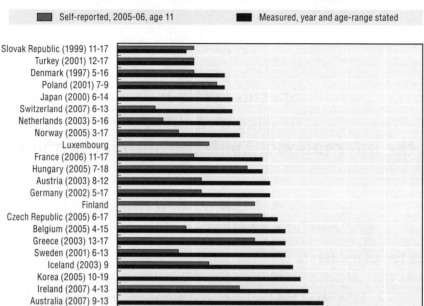

* The statistical data for Israel are supplied by and under the responsibility of the relevant Israeli authorities. The use of such data by the OECD is without prejudice to the status of the Golan Heights, East Jerusalem and Israeli settlements in the West Bank under the terms of international law.

Source: Figures from World Health Organisation Health Behaviour in School Children (HBSC) 2005-06 survey (self-reported weight and height of 11-year-old children), and from latest available national surveys of children in which weight and height were measured.

StatLink ᛃᛃᛃ http://dx.doi.org/10.1787/888932315944

additional health problems. However, the use of the descriptive terms may differ, and some reports give the prevalence value for all "overweight" children including those that are obese, while others give the prevalence for overweight children excluding those that are obese. Readers should also note that prevalence levels using reference curves from the United States sometimes refer to "at risk of overweight" and "overweight" for the top two categories of adiposity, and sometimes to "overweight" and "obese".

Policy makers working in this area are likely to be struck by a lack of high-quality information on the extent and trends in the problem of child obesity. The surveillance of child obesity prevalence has been remarkably poor, despite the importance of the issue to the children involved and to the future health of the population. Only in very few countries have children's heights and weights been routinely monitored, with data on their overweight status collated, analysed and reported consistently.

Even where data are available, they need to be examined carefully. Firstly, the source of the data may be from surveys of children in which height and weight were physically measured, or the survey may use questionnaires and the estimates of weight and height may be self-reported (or reported by parents). Self-reported data tends to underestimate the prevalence of obesity, as individuals tend to self-report weights that are below actual level, and heights that are above actual level, especially among more overweight respondents. Secondly, data may be from nationally representative surveys or they may be from smaller surveys undertaken in the more accessible (often urban) areas which do not represent national populations. Thirdly, when comparing two surveys across a period of time, surveys need to be properly comparable in terms of the data collection methods and the analytic definitions, and also in terms of sample characteristics, such as the children's ages and their ethnic and socio-demographic mix at the time of the survey.

The rapid rise in the numbers of children affected is particularly prominent in western Europe, Australia and North America. Figure SFII.2 shows trends for England, France and United States, with an indication that the epidemic may have reached a turning point, at least in these countries.

In 2004, it was estimated that, for the world as a whole, some 10% of school-age children (aged 5-17) were estimated as overweight (including obese) including some 2-3% who were obese (Wang and Lobstein, 2006). This global average reflects a wide range of prevalence levels in different regions and countries, with the prevalence of overweight in Africa and Asia averaging well below 5% and in the Americas and Europe above 20%. Projections for the year 2010 are shown in Table SFII.1.

Figure SFII.2. **Trends in prevalence of overweight among children in England, France and United States (obese only)**

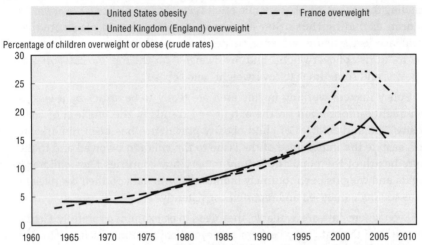

Note: The definitions of overweight and obesity differ between countries. See note 4 in Chapter 2 for an explanation of differences in trends for France between this analysis and the analysis reported in Chapter 2.

Source: Wang and Lobstein (2006) and updates (see www.iaso.org).

StatLink ⛰️ http://dx.doi.org/10.1787/888932315963

Table SFII.1. **Estimated prevalence of excess body weight in school-age children in 2010**

Region[1]	Obese (%)	Overweight (including obese) (%)
Americas	15	46
Middle East and North Africa	12	42
Europe and former USSR	10	38
West Pacific	7	27
South East Asia	5	23
Africa	< 1	< 5

1. Countries in each region are according to the World Health Organisation.
Source: Wang and Lobstein (2006).

Health consequences

The extraordinary rise in child obesity is of concern for several reasons. Excess weight in childhood raises the risk of excess weight in adulthood and with it the risk of earlier onset of obesity-related chronic disease. The persistence, or tracking, of obesity from childhood and adolescence to adulthood has been well documented in longitudinal (cohort) studies (Power et al., 1997). Evidence from a longitudinal study of children, the Bogalusa Heart Study, suggest that children who have overweight onset before age 8 years are at significantly increased risk of obesity in adulthood (Freedman et al., 2005a).

Comparing racial groups, tracking of adiposity was stronger for black compared with white youths, especially for females (Freedman *et al.*, 2005b). In the United States, Whitaker *et al.* (1997) demonstrated that if a child was obese during childhood, the chance of being obese in young adulthood ranged from 8% for 1- or 2-year-olds without obese parents to 79% for 10-14-year-olds with at least one obese parent. The raised risk of obesity if one's parents were obese has been observed in many studies, although the contribution of genetics, family lifestyle, local environment or other factors have not been fully determined (Lytle, 2009).

In addition to raising the risk of obesity in adulthood, overweight children themselves may carry early signs of chronic disease without being aware they have a problem, exacerbating the likely disease outcome. Raised blood pressure, raised markers for cardiovascular risk, raised indicators of diabetes risk, early stages of fatty liver disease and similar co-morbidities of child obesity are essentially silent and neither the child nor their family may be aware of the need to take preventive measures to reduce later disease risk. The high level of co-morbidity (over 20% of obese children are likely to carry one or more markers of co-morbid risk) has significant implications for the development of paediatric services in countries where child obesity is highly prevalent, or likely to become so (Lobstein and Jackson-Leach, 2006).

The health service aspects of childhood ill-health associated with obesity were investigated by Wang and Dietz. Using hospital discharge diagnoses from 1997 through 1999 compared with two decades earlier, they found increases in the number and severity of obesity-related disorders in childhood, and time spent as an inpatient was longer for children with obesity (Wang and Dietz, 2002).

Lastly, it should not be forgotten that an obese child may also suffer psychosocial problems, including low self-esteem and reduced social networking (Daniel, 2006). Obese children are at risk of social stigma and exclusion, and subsequent greater risk of early school drop-out, lower academic achievement, early school drop-out, reduced employment stability and lower earnings (Gortmaker *et al.*, 1993).

Socio-economic patterns

In more developed economies child obesity prevalence levels have risen particularly strongly among lower income households and minority ethnic groups, while in less developed economies child obesity levels have risen most rapidly in urban areas and among higher income households. Thus the social gradient, which shows higher levels of obesity among poorer families, found in much of the developed world (Robertson *et al.*, 2007; Lobstein *et al.*, 2004) is reversed in the emerging economies, where child obesity appears to be closely linked to the availability and affordability of mass-produced energy-dense foods such as soft drinks, snacks, confectionery and fast food, perhaps combined with the availability and affordability of sedentary entertainments such as television, video gaming and internet services.

There is some evidence that child obesity (and obesity levels in adults too) is associated with the degree of social inequality prevailing in a country. Several measures of inequality (such as the Gini index and the proportion of the population in poverty) are correlated with child obesity prevalence levels in Europe (Robertson *et al.*, 2007) and adult obesity (and diabetes) is correlated with Gini index scores across OECD countries (Pickett *et al.*, 2005).

Most recent trends

Since 2006, there have been a number of reports suggesting that the upwards trends in the prevalence of overweight and obesity among children may be easing in some countries. In France, where the prevalence of overweight (including obesity) had climbed steadily in the 1990s to over 18% of school-age children by 2000, a survey in 2007 found the prevalence had fallen to under 16%. The difference was not significant but the trend was remarkable as being a possible indication that the problem had "peaked" and that the trends might be reversed. Notably, the strong inverse relationship between family socio-economic status and child overweight prevalence which was apparent in the 2000 survey continued to be apparent in the 2007 survey.

In both the United Kingdom (England) a downturn in the prevalence levels has been noted, although the size is not of statistical significance. A similar suggestion has been made for Australia, where the upward trend may have eased with little further upward movement in the last decade (Olds *et al.*, 2009). This information was mis-interpreted by the popular press to suggest that child obesity was "a myth".

Data from the United States indicated that there was no significant increase between major national surveys (NHANES) conducted in 2003-04 and in 2005-06, using locally-defined criteria for overweight (Ogden *et al.*, 2008). Among lower income, pre-school children, a non-significant increase from 14.5 to 14.6% obesity prevalence was found between 2003 and 2008 (Sharma *et al.*, 2009). In Switzerland, one report suggested that overweight prevalence had significantly decreased between 2002 and 2007 (Aeberli *et al.*, 2008). In Sweden, several local surveys have indicated a decline in overweight prevalence among girls and a stabilisation of prevalence among boys, in the period 1999-2004 (Sundblom *et al.*, 2008; Sjöberg *et al.*, 2008).

The reasons for this apparent easing of the epidemic are not clear, and factors suggested in one country may not be relevant in another. French policies to improve school food and limit the availability of snack foods on school premises, plus national restrictions on advertising of food products and other local and national measures have been cited to explain the French prevalence data. Local food and activity programmes in Sweden are cited as possible causes, against a background of strong controls on marketing to children. Dietary changes such as a reduction in the consumption of trans fats have been suggested, and this might be expected to lead to a parallel decline in adult obesity rates. Other possible explanations include a change in maternal diets during pregnancy, a change in maternal smoking patterns in pregnancy or a change in infant feeding patterns (such as an increase in breastfeeding or improvements in formula feed composition). An additional possibility is that the increasing media attention to the issue of obesity has increased awareness and increased the reluctance of overweight children (and their parents) to participate in the recent surveys, compared with those conducted earlier in previous years.

Concluding comment

That the world has seen a remarkable increase in the prevalence of child overweight and obesity is beyond doubt. The health implications for children in terms of subsequent risk of chronic disease and immediate risk of a range of disorders, including social and psychological problems, are beyond the scope of this chapter, but are urgent issues that need to be examined, and for which national health services need to be prepared.

There is now some evidence that the extraordinary rise in child obesity may be easing in some countries, although there is only very little evidence of rates actually declining. If the upward trends are easing, then the causes of this change need to be examined and the policy implications extracted.

Bibliography

Aeberli, I., R.S. Amman, M. Knabenhans and M.B. Zimmermann (2008), "The National Prevalence of Overweight in School-Age Children in Switzerland Has Decreased Between 2002 and 2007", *Int. J. Obes.*, Vol. 32, S214.

Chief Medical Officer (2003), *Annual Report of the Chief Medical Officer 2002*, UK Department of Health, London.

Daniels, S.R. (2006), "The Consequences of Childhood Overweight and Obesity", *The Future of Children (Princeton-Brookings)*, Vol. 16, No. 1, Spring, pp. 47-67.

Freedman, D.S., L.K. Khan, M.K. Serdula, W.H. Dietz, S.R. Srinivasan and G.S. Berenson (2005a), "Racial Differences in the Tracking of Childhood BMI to Adulthood", *Obes. Res.*, Vol. 13, pp. 928-935.

Freedman, D.S., L.K. Khan, M.K. Serdula, W.H. Dietz, S.R. Srinivasan and G.S. Berenson (2005b), "The Relation of Childhood BMI to Adult Adiposity: The Bogalusa Heart Study", *Pediatrics*, Vol. 115, pp. 22-27.

Gortmaker, S.L. *et al.* (1993), "Social and Economic Consequences of Overweight in Adolescence and Young Adulthood", *New England Journal of Medicine*, Vol. 329, pp. 1008-1012.

Lobstein, T. and R. Jackson-Leach (2006), "Estimated Burden of Paediatric Obesity and Co-morbidities in Europe. Part 2. Numbers of Children with Indicators of Obesity-Related Disease", *Int. J. Pediatr. Obes.*, Vol. 1, No. 1, pp. 33-41.

Lobstein, T., L. Baur and R. Uauy (2004), "IASO International Obesity Task Force. Obesity in Children and Young People: A Crisis in Public Health", *Obes. Rev.*, Vol. 5, Supplement 1, pp. 4-104.

Ludwig, D. (2008), "Children's Hospital, Boston", cited by D. DeNoon in *"Will Obesity Shorten the American Lifespan?"*, *Medcsape Today*, 16 March, accessed 11 June 2008 at *www.medscape.com/viewarticle/527397.*

Lytle, L.A. (2009), "Examining the Etiology of Childhood Obesity: The IDEA Study", *Am. J. Community Psychol.*, epub 17 Oct. 2009.

Ogden, C.L., M.D. Carrol and K.M. Flegal (2008), "High Body Mass Index for Age among US Children and Adolescents, 2003-2006", *JAMA*, Vol. 299, No. 20, pp. 2401-2405.

Olds, T., K. Ferrar, G. Tomkinson and C. Maher (2009), "Childhood Obesity: The End of the Epidemic?", *Australasian Epidemiologist*, Vol. 16, No. 1,pp. 16-19.

Pickett, K.E., S. Kelly, E. Brunner, T. Lobstein and R.G. Wilkinson (2005), "Wider Income Gaps, Wider Waistbands? An Ecological Study of Obesity and Income Inequality", *J. Epidemiol. Community Health,* Vol. 59, No. 8, August, pp. 670-674.

Robertson, A. T. Lobstein and C. Knai (2007), "Obesity and Socio-Economic Groups in Europe: Evidence Review and Implications for Action", Report prepared for the European Commission funded by contract SANCO/2005/C4-NUTRITION-03, 2007, available at *http://ec.europa.eu/health/ph_determinants/life_style/nutrition/documents/ev20081028_rep_en.pdf.*

Salanave, B., S. Peneau, M.F. Rolland-Cachera, S. Hercberg and K. Castetbon (2009), "Stabilization of Overweight Prevalence in French Children between 2000 and 2007", *Int. J. Pediatr. Obes.*, Vol. 4, pp. 66-72.

Sharma, A.J., L.M. Grummer-Strawn, K. Dalenius, D. Galuska, M. Anandappa, E. Borland, H. Mackintosh and R. Smith (2009), "Obesity Prevalence among Low-Income, Preschool-aged Children, United States, 1998-2008", *MMWR Weekly*, Vol. 58, No. 28, pp. 769-773, accessed 20 August 2009 at *www.cdc.gov/mmwr/preview/mmwrhtml/mm5828a1.htm.*

Sjöberg, A., L. Lissner, K. Albertsson-Wikland and S. Mårild (2008), "Recent Anthropometric Trends among Swedish School Children: Evidence for Decreasing Prevalence of Overweight in Girls", *Acta Paediatr.*, Vol. 97, No. 1, pp. 118-123.

Sundblom, E., M. Petzold, F. Rasmussen, E. Callmer and L. Lissner (2008). "Childhood Overweight and Obesity Prevalences Levelling Off in Stockholm but Socioeconomic Differences Persist", *Int. J. Obes.*, Vol. 32, No. 10, pp. 1525-1530.

Wang, G. and W.H. Dietz (2002), "Economic Burden of Obesity in Youths Aged 6 to 17 Years: 1979-1999", *Pediatrics*, Vol. 109, e81.

Wang, Y. and T. Lobstein (2006), "Worldwide Trends in Childhood Overweight and Obesity", *Int. J. Pediatr. Obes.*, Vol. 1, pp. 11-25.

Whitaker, R., J. Wright, M. Pepe, K. Seidel and W.H. Dietz (1997), "Predicting Obesity in Young Adulthood from Childhood and Parental Obesity", *N. Engl. J. Med.*, Vol. 337, pp. 869-873.

Chapter 4

How Does Obesity Spread?

The obesity epidemic is the result of multiple, complex and interacting dynamics, which have progressively converged to produce lasting changes in people's lifestyles. Remarkable changes in the supply, availability and prices of food in the second half of the 20th century, in line with major changes in food production technologies and marketing approaches, decreased physical activity at work, and changes in labour markets and conditions heavily influenced lifestyles and contributed to the obesity epidemic. This chapter explores some of the key determinants of health and their role in the obesity epidemic. The question is addressed of whether the changes that fuelled obesity and chronic diseases are simply the outcome of efficient market dynamics, or the effect of market and rationality failures preventing individuals from achieving more desirable outcomes. Social multiplier effects (the clustering and spread of overweight and obesity within households and social networks) are shown to be especially relevant to the formulation of effective policies to tackle obesity.

The determinants of health and disease

It is not uncommon for lifestyles to be viewed as independent from other determinants of health, and purely the result of free choice, in line with a traditional (personal) health care approach to disease prevention. This view tends to reinforce a culture of "victim-blaming" (Evans and Stoddart, 1994) that stigmatises those who take up unhealthy behaviours. The policy response that naturally follows calls for individuals to take responsibility for their own health and ensures the provision of suitable health care to those who reach high levels of risk or develop chronic diseases. If, on the other hand, lifestyles are viewed as individual responses to environmental influences, the focus of policy will shifts towards the environmental factors that determine individual behaviours.

A number of attempts have been made in recent years to conceptualise the roles and reciprocal influences of different groups of health determinants. As discussed in Chapter 2, dramatic improvements have been recorded over the past few centuries in health status and longevity (Fogel, 1994). Research has highlighted some of the factors that have contributed to such improvements, like increasing standards of living, education, access to clean water and sanitation, access to health care (Frank and Mustard, 1995). A large part of the work on health determinants originated from efforts to understand and tackle persisting health disparities (Mackenbach, 2006), particularly among socio-economic groups, as the focus of such research has often been on the determinants of differences in health among population groups.

Biology, environments and choices

The "Lalonde report" (Government of Canada, 1974) is often cited as an early attempt to frame the determinants of population health in a broader policy perspective than that associated with a medically-dominated paradigm. The report, inspired by Thomas McKeown's work published in the 1970s, characterises the "health field" as encompassing environmental and lifestyle factors, as well as human biology.

Dahlgren and Whitehead (1991) developed a model of the determinants of health inequalities centred on the individual and on his/her biological characteristics, with various "layers of influence", or groups of factors influencing health. The layers include: individual lifestyle factors; social and community influences; living and working conditions; general socio-economic, cultural and environmental conditions. Each of these layers has a

116

direct influence on individual health, but interactions between layers contribute significantly to shaping the impact of each group of determinants. The existence of a socio-economic gradient in all layers of determinants supports the view that the layers are closely interconnected. Understanding the relationships between layers of influence is as important as understanding the direct impact of each layer on individual health.

Wilkinson and Marmot (2003) identified ten areas in which solid evidence exists of the role of aspects of the social environment on health, elsewhere developed into a more extensive inventory of social determinants of health and evidence of their impact (Marmot and Wilkinson, 2006). The World Health Organisation established a Commission on the Social Determinants of Health in 2005 to emphasise the role of socio-economic influences in shaping recent dramatic changes in population health patterns and trends at the global level. The conceptual framework developed for the work of the Commission is built upon a model of the influences of two main groups of determinants: structural determinants, such as socio-economic and the political contexts, social structures and socio-economic position; and intermediary determinants, which mediate the effect of the former, including biological and behavioural factors, living and working conditions, psychosocial factors and health system determinants (Solar and Irwin, 2007).

In a policy perspective, it is important to know whether links between specific determinants and health are of a causal nature, in order to be able to design effective interventions. Good evidence of a causal link exists for education as a determinant of health status (Arendt, 2005), longevity (Lleras-Muney, 2005), and health-related behaviours such as smoking and obesity (Kenkel *et al.*, 2006; Gilman *et al.*, 2008). In turn, lifestyles were shown to be causally related to chronic diseases. For instance, both active and passive smoking, as well as environmental factors, were shown to cause lung cancer (Alberg *et al.*, 2005; Taylor *et al.*, 2007). Aspects of diet and drinking patterns were found to cause various types of cancers (Key *et al.*, 2004) and to be causally associated with risk factors such as hypertension (John *et al.*, 2002). However, other associations between lifestyles and chronic diseases have not yet been proven to be causal. For instance, the association of smoking with diabetes (Willi *et al.*, 2007), or the negative association of fruit and vegetable intake with coronary heart disease (Dauchet *et al.*, 2006). Environmental factors such as food production technologies, restaurant density, the price of restaurant meals, and the density of urban developments have a causal influence on obesity (Cutler *et al.*, 2003; Plantinga and Bernell, 2005; Rashad, 2006).

The importance of interactions between determinants

A large part of the research undertaken in recent years on the determinants of health focused on gathering evidence of the role of individual determinants and groups of determinants (Lurie *et al.*, 2003). However, an increasing number of contributions emphasise the importance of the relationships among groups of determinants, and the fact that certain determinants mediate or modulate the influence of other determinants. Extensive interactions between determinants are also recognised in the work of the WHO Commission on the Social Determinants of Health, particularly between structural and intermediary determinants. Using different terminologies but the same basic idea, other models identify primary health determinants, including socio-economic and demographic factors, and secondary determinants, including a range of biological and psychosocial mediators of the effect of primary determinants (*e.g.* Kosteniuk and Dickinson, 2003).

Understanding interactions between individual health-related behaviours and the range of determinants that contribute to shaping such behaviours is a fundamental step in the design of effective interventions. Cutler and Glaeser (2005) observe that individual characteristics alone are unlikely to explain the uptake of health-related behaviours. If the opposite were true, individuals with certain characteristics, *e.g.* poor self-control, would tend to engage in different risky behaviours at the same time. On the contrary, the correlation of risky behaviours in individuals appears to be very low: smokers are unlikely to be also heavy drinkers (correlation 12.9%); obesity has virtually no correlation with smoking or heavy drinking; the uptake of medical preventive services like flu shots or screening is negatively, but very weakly, correlated with risky behaviours such as smoking, drinking, or having a high BMI. Cutler and Glaeser find empirical support for the hypothesis that certain "situational influences" are likely to trigger specific lifestyle choices in those who are exposed to such influences, with an intensity of response that may be modulated by individual characteristics. One such situational influence that the same authors explore in some depth is changes in food production technology, which are partly responsible for dietary changes and for the rise of obesity rates, particularly in individuals and families whose time available for meal preparation and cooking has become increasingly limited (Cutler *et al.*, 2003). This work lends support to the hypothesis that health-related behaviours are primarily determined by interactions between individual characteristics and specific environmental influences, rather than by the former alone.

If lifestyle choices are the result of environmental influences interacting with individual characteristics, then the socio-economic gradient in lifestyles and related health outcomes is likely to reflect differences between individuals in the degree of control they have over their own environment. Research conducted in the United Kingdom since the 1970s on the relationship between socio-economic position and health (Marmot, 2004) underscores the importance of the ability of individuals to gain control over their own environment as a crucial determinant of the same individuals' health and health-related behaviours. Evidence is becoming available of the role of work-related stress in the relationship between socio-economic position and health. Stress was shown to be causally associated, for instance, with unhealthy lifestyles, the metabolic syndrome and coronary heart disease (Chandola *et al.*, 2008). However, the direction of the causal relationship remains uncertain. Are individuals predisposed (genetically or by other means) to achieving a better control over their own environment also able to reach more privileged socio-economic positions as well as a better health status through healthier lifestyle choices, or does a privileged socio-economic position confer better control and healthier lifestyles?

A certain degree of inertia in the relationship between socio-economic condition and health has been observed, as changes in the former do not always appear to translate swiftly into corresponding changes in the latter. The health effects of social mobility, discussed below, provide an example of such inertia. However, a larger scale phenomenon can be observed in cross-national comparisons showing very strong correlations between income and health in cross-sectional analyses, which become substantially weaker, or even disappear, when changes over time are considered. This may lead to the conclusion that factors such as technology transfer and health systems may determine the speed at which changes in wealth translate into changes in health at the national level (Deaton, 2004). A knowledge-based phenomenon similar to technology transfer might also act at the individual level, possibly based on education and ability to use information effectively, determining the speed at which changes in socio-economic position translate into changes in health. These observations further emphasise the importance of interactions between socio-economic condition and other determinants of health.

Determinants of health over the life course and across generations

The importance of adopting a life-course approach in assessing the determinants of health and disease has been widely acknowledged (Kuh and Ben Shlomo, 2004) based on a large body of evidence indicating that many key determinants of health produce their effects over the course of many years, across different life stages and sometimes even across generations. Health is the result of the accumulation of influences to which an individual is exposed since conception, and of the interactions of such exposures with individual biological characteristics.

The clustering of exposures to factors potentially leading to chronic diseases that is observed in cross-sectional studies in certain population groups (*e.g.* association of many aspects of disadvantage, from occupational hazards to inadequate housing, from poor education to low income, in the same individuals) can also be observed in a life-course perspective (Blane, 2006). Exposures to the same factors in earlier stages of life tend to correlate highly with similar exposures in later stages. Social mobility may mitigate the health effects of such exposures over time. Perhaps the most accredited model of life-course effects is the "accumulation model", which essentially views the accumulation of exposures, and the interactions between such exposures, as responsible for the long-term health of individuals. This model has found some empirical support in relation to obesity. Research as part of the British Whitehall II study (Heraclides and Brunner, 2009) shows that the likelihood of obesity among adults increases with the accumulation of social disadvantage. Alternative models have also found empirical support. Some of the latter view exposures at critical stages of life as primary health determinants, others focus on the correlation of exposures at different stages in the life course, while viewing current exposures as primarily responsible for current health status (Blane, 2006; Hallqvist, 2004). The impact of social mobility has also been studied using different models. The evidence appears to indicate that social mobility tends to produce a convergence of health status towards the mean, i.e. socially mobile individuals depart from the typical health status of the group they leave but do not fully achieve the levels characteristic of the group they join. A resultant, immediately observable, effect is a reduction in health inequalities (Blane et al., 1999b). A similar pattern has been observed in health-related behaviours (Karvonen et al., 1999). Evidence from the Whitehall II study shows that downward social mobility is associated with a higher likelihood of obesity, but upward mobility does not appear to decrease the chances of becoming obese (Heraclides and Brunner, 2009). The relationship between social mobility and obesity has also been studied in young men in Sweden from the opposite perspective (whether obesity affects social mobility). Obesity was found to be a significant obstacle to upward social mobility, while it was often associated with downward mobility (Karnehed et al., 2008).

However, health-related behaviours do not appear to be subject to life-course influences to the same degree as health status. Behaviours such as diet, physical activity and smoking correlate more strongly with current exposures to known determinants of those behaviours than with earlier exposures, with few exceptions, mainly in relation to diet (Blane et al., 1996).

Education plays a particularly significant role in determining intergenerational health effects as well as intergenerational social mobility (Blane et al., 1999a). Individuals belonging to disadvantaged socio-economic groups may be locked over time into pathways of disadvantage (their parents' educational attainment determines their own, and their own in turn determines their offspring's). This suggests that policies aimed at improving health and social outcomes by increasing educational opportunities for individuals with a background of disadvantage and lesser parental education have a potential for contributing to a prevention strategy.

The main driving forces behind the epidemic

A vast literature exists on the individual and environmental factors that have contributed to the obesity epidemic. A wealth of empirical analyses have been produced, many of which have shown important and statistically significant influences on individual behaviours and BMI. This literature is reviewed elsewhere (*e.g.* Branca *et al.*, 2007) pointing to a wide range of interconnected factors over the life course of individuals, from genetic background to early nutrition, to education, to exposure to obesogenic environments affecting many aspects of the lives of individuals. The knowledge that can be distilled from this literature leads to identifying three main groups of factors that have contributed to fuelling obesity in the last part of the 20th century and beyond: factors related with the supply of lifestyle commodities, particularly food; government policies in various sectors which have not always taken into consideration potential unwanted effects on individual lifestyles and health; and changes in labour markets and working conditions.

The mass production of food has changed both the quality and availability of food over time, with major effects on food prices and convenience of consumption from technological innovation (*e.g.* Cutler *et al.*, 2003). Falling relative prices of food contributed to up to 40% of the increase in BMI over the period 1976 to 1994 in the United States, according to some estimates (Lakdawalla and Philipson, 2002). Convenience also played a major role, in combination with falling prices, with the spread and concentration of fast food restaurants, for instance, being blamed in several studies as one of the factors contributing to obesity (Chou *et al.*, 2004; Rashad, 2006). The use of increasingly sophisticated marketing techniques is naturally associated with an increased supply of food, and is likely to have further contributed to the obesity epidemic (*e.g.* Nestle, 2006). These effects are consistent with the patterns observed in the distribution of obesity among population groups, with more vulnerable individuals and families, and those whose time available for meal preparation and cooking has become increasingly limited, being more exposed to the influences of supply-side changes.

A number of government policies are likely to have had unintended adverse effects on obesity and health in OECD countries by providing incentives to individuals, or even forcing them, to make certain lifestyle choices. For instance, agricultural policies adopted in many OECD countries, mostly based on fiscal measures such as subsidies to producers, may have raised the relative prices of healthy foods, such as fruit and vegetables, and lowered the relative price of less healthy foods, such as fats and sugar (*e.g.* Schäfer Elinder, 2005). International trade policies may have played a similar role in certain cases (*e.g.* Labonte and Sanger, 2006). Town planning, the design of the built environment and traffic regulation may discourage active transport (such as walking and cycling) in favour of inactive (vehicular) transport. Recent research has been focusing, in particular on the contribution of urban sprawl on the spread of obesity (*e.g.* Plantinga and Bernell, 2005).

Changes in production technologies are among the most important contributors to reduced physical activity over recent decades, leading to a massive decrease in the number of those working in agriculture and, in certain manufacturing sectors, and a corresponding increase in sedentary jobs, particularly in the service sector (Lakdawalla and Philipson, 2002). Increased participation of women in the labour force, increasing levels of stress and job insecurity, longer working hours for some jobs have also been found to be associated with increasing levels of obesity.

Market failures in lifestyle choices

An economic approach to prevention involves interpreting individual lifestyles as the result of choices regarding the consumption of commodities such as food and physical activity or leisure time. These choices are subject to many external influences and constraints, and are driven by opportunity costs and other incentives. The dynamics through which lifestyles are shaped are broadly interpreted in economics as market mechanisms, whether or not monetary exchanges are involved. The health determinants that influence lifestyles, discussed earlier in this chapter, are in turn the result of similar dynamics.

Sometimes markers fail to operate efficiently. If those failures could be avoided, social welfare would be increased. Information failures may contribute to the adoption of unhealthy behaviours and lifestyles through an inadequate knowledge or understanding of the long-term consequences of such behaviours. Externalities may lead to the social costs and benefits of certain forms of consumption not being fully reflected in their private costs and benefits to individual consumers. A biased perception of the importance of future risks may prevent individuals from making choices in their own best interest now.

Several economists have reviewed potential market failures in relation to chronic diseases and prevention (*e.g.* Kenkel, 2000; and Suhrcke *et al.*, 2006), and some have focused specifically on diet, physical activity and obesity (*e.g.* Cawley, 2004; Brunello *et al.*, 2008). Where market failures exist and have a significant impact, the benefits potentially deriving from tackling the inefficiencies they cause may sometimes justify some form of corrective action, either by governments or other actors, provided such actions are viable and effective.

Externalities: Health expenditure and productivity

Passive smoking is a typical externality, as it has been shown to cause negative health effects on individuals other than the smoker. Such effects would not be reflected in the price of cigarettes if this were negotiated in a free market between smokers and tobacco manufacturers. Negative externalities, such as passive smoking, lead to a consumption that is greater than socially desirable, because consumers do not pay the full price that would cover external effects. Conversely, positive externalities lead to underconsumption. In many cases, external effects can be "internalised", so that production and consumption may be brought back in line with social costs and benefits. Internalising externalities requires measures like transfers, taxes or subsidies, which may be imposed on, or offered to, consumers or suppliers of the commodity that generates the externality.

It is difficult to identify externalities immediately associated with diet, physical activity and obesity, similar to passive smoking, violent and disorderly behaviour associated with alcohol abuse, or traffic accidents resulting from reckless driving. But externalities may also be deferred, as the link between lifestyle choices and chronic diseases typically operates in the long term. Once chronic diseases emerge, and in some cases even before they emerge (*e.g.* when important risk factors emerge such as hypertension), the individuals affected will become less productive, possibly entirely unproductive, they will make a more intensive use of medical and social services, which may be collectively funded (through fiscal revenues or insurance), they may require care by members of the family and friends. Conversely, a reduced life expectancy may mean a less prolonged use of publicly funded medical and social services at the end of life, as well as reduced pension payments, which are not themselves externalities, but would translate into a less onerous fiscal burden and therefore less distortional effects on the overall economy. All of these phenomena involve externalities (negative and positive) on society at large, family and friends, ultimately associated with the lifestyle choices originally made by the individual.

But, do the externalities described here apply to obesity? Two externalities, in particular, deserve consideration: the fiscal, or insurance, externality, particularly in relation to the demand for collectively funded health care by the obese; and labour market externalities.

The discussion of health care costs associated with obesity in Chapter 1 suggests that costs increase steeply with BMI. This has provided some support to the widespread claim that obesity is associated with insurance externalities (individuals sharing the same risk pool will bear higher costs). However, as Brunello *et al.* (2008) emphasise: "A necessary condition for the externality to occur is that the obese incur higher lifetime costs than the non-obese." There is no conclusive evidence that lifetime health care costs are indeed higher for the obese. The evidence presented in Chapter 1 shows conflicting results from different studies. Even though Brunello and his co-authors reach the conclusion that lifetime costs are higher for the obese, both in the United Stated (8% higher than for the non-obese) and in Europe (12% higher), considering the likely degree of moral hazard associated with those differences their analysis leads to the conclusion that the size of the insurance externality associated with obesity is too small to warrant attention by policy makers. This is in line with empirical evidence produced by Bhattacharya and Sood (2005), who estimated an externality in the order of USD 150 per capita, and with the arguments put forward by Philipson and Posner (2008).

Externalities may also be associated with the labour market outcomes of obesity, discussed extensively in Chapter 3. In particular, differences in productivity between the obese and people of normal weight, often associated with a larger recourse to disability benefits, represent an important source of negative externalities, although the size of these externalities depends on the characteristics of the relevant labour markets and has not been quantified in existing research. Further productive inefficiencies associated with obesity are those related to disadvantage in wages and employment opportunities suffered by the obese, especially women, of which ample evidence has been presented in Chapter 3.

Suhrcke (2006) emphasises the distinction between externalities that occur within the household (but some externalities within an individual's broader social network could be viewed in the same way) and externalities imposed on other subjects or society at large. The former, defined as "quasi-externalities", may be assimilated to either private or fully external effects. This is mostly a value judgement, and it is not for the economist to determine among what effects quasi-externalities should be accounted for, as long as they are not ignored. In the final section of this chapter we shall discuss some of the effects of obesity within households and social networks, that we shall call social multiplier effects, which may be regarded as externalities.

The classical tools to address externalities are taxes and subsidies. These may improve the efficiency of market exchanges, but will also produce distributional changes. For instance, if a government imposes a tax on a form of consumption that generates negative externalities, it may or may not be possible, or desirable, for the same government to redistribute the tax revenues raised to those who suffer the consequences of the negative externality (which will be diminished by the tax, but not eliminated altogether). Similarly, if a commodity that produces positive externalities is subsidised, it may not be possible to fund the subsidy by charging those who enjoy the positive external effects. From a mere efficiency standpoint, what matters is just that welfare gains exceed any losses, but societies are not indifferent to the distribution of those gains and losses, therefore governments will have to take this into account in assessing the desirability of a policy to address externalities.

Information failures

Information is a critical factor for markets to operate efficiently. In order to make rational and efficient choices, consumers have to be fully informed about the characteristics and quality of the goods they consume, about the benefits (and harms) they will derive from consumption, and about the opportunity costs they will incur. In the case of health-related behaviours, information on the nature and the size of the associated health risks may be lacking or difficult to use. It may be lacking because it does not exist (*e.g.* information on the long-term health effects of the consumption of genetically modified crops); because it is concealed or communicated in a misleading form by parties that have a vested interest (*e.g.* information on the health effects of smoking withheld by the tobacco industry in the recent past); or because it is complex and not easily accessible to the lay person (*e.g.* information on the health risks involved in the consumption of different types of fats).

The importance of information in forming health-related beliefs, a first step towards influencing lifestyle choices, is shown, for instance, by Cutler and Glaeser (2006) in their analysis of the determinants of higher smoking rates in Europe compared to the United States. The authors reach the conclusion that beliefs were changed in the United States when "substantial information about the harms of smoking" was made available to the public, while the same information appears to have been communicated less effectively in Europe.

Information clearly plays an important role in dietary choices and choices about physical activity, as discussed in Donald Kenkel's special focus contribution which follows this chapter, although many would argue that most individuals today possess the basic knowledge required for them to broadly discriminate between more and less healthy options. However, there is evidence that interventions based on the provision of information in various forms, from nutritional labelling to health education campaigns, from health claims in advertising to the dissemination of nutritional guidelines, has at least some impact on individual dietary choices (see, for instance, the evidence discussed in Chapter 6), suggesting that there is still scope for improving the information-base upon which individuals make their dietary choices.

In a policy perspective, the question is whether information failures may warrant some form of corrective action. Brunello *et al.* (2008), as well as Philipson and Posner (2008), do not find that existing evidence of information failures in relation to obesity would justify, *per se*, government action. Cawley (2004) insists on the "public good" nature of information, which suggests that information would be underprovided in a market setting and justifies governments' involvement in its provision. However, in relation to the issue of information on calories he concludes that "lack of information [...] may not be resolved by simply providing more information, but may require finding ways to present information so that consumers may process it more quickly and easily", which suggests that possible failures may concern individual ability to process information, rather than information itself (Cawley, 2004).

The direct provision of information by governments (*e.g.* health education campaigns to improve diets or increase physical activity) or the regulation of information (*e.g.* limits on advertising, guidelines on food labelling) are usually justified by limited or imperfect information on the part of the consumer. However, Glaeser (2006) and others do not appear to support the provision of information by governments (classified as "soft paternalism") in the generality of cases. One of the main reasons for this conclusion is that governments are not always equipped for delivering complex communication strategies, and in some cases their action may be influenced by the very interests it attempts to counter. When information failures cannot be fixed, for instance because communication of information is difficult, governments may still attempt to compensate for the effects of imperfect information by influencing behaviours through appropriate incentives (*e.g.* fiscal incentives like taxes and subsidies).

Additional insights from behavioural economics

A relatively recent stream of economic research supported by a growing body of empirical evidence, which goes under the name of behavioural economics, sheds light on additional potential failures affecting lifestyle choices. Behavioural research shows that the assumption of perfect rationality of the individuals and organisations involved in market transactions does not always reflect the behaviours of those agents. Failures of rationality may affect the way choices are made, the information upon which choices are based or the preferences that guide those choices. The first aspect includes, for instance, the use of heuristics, or rules of thumb, in decision making. The second includes a biased perception of the information available, because the way information is presented (framing) influences choices and because of cognitive errors in the interpretation of information. The third aspect includes inconsistent preferences for outcomes expected at different points in time, or for gains and losses.

Time preferences and self-control

Understanding the way in which people discount future costs and benefits in making their lifestyle choices is critical to the design of effective policies to counter the possible long-term ill-health effects of particular behaviours. A large body of empirical literature about time preferences in relation to a variety of outcomes, including health (reviewed by Lipscomb *et al.*, 1996), suggests that there are no particular reasons for the future health risks associated with certain lifestyle choices to be discounted at particularly high, or particularly low rates. Some characteristics of those choices, such as the relatively small size of the perceived health risks involved, will make people discount future risks more heavily. But other characteristics of the same choices will have the opposite effect.

However, empirical evidence from behavioural economics research suggests that health-related behaviours often reflect a wholly different approach to discounting future health risks, termed hyperbolic discounting. This refers to an accelerated form of discounting, which heavily penalises future outcomes in present judgements, in a way that makes time preferences inconsistent. In lay terms, this may be identified as a self-control problem. Take, for instance, an obese person who is perfectly aware of the long term health risks associated with her condition. She may decide that such risks are offset by the pleasure she derives from her dietary habits and sedentary lifestyle at present, therefore she will choose to postpone quitting her habits. Procrastination, as discussed in Chapter 1, is a key feature of hyperbolic discounting. She perceives this as a postponement because she feels that after some time (say, in one year) she will no longer value pleasure from her current lifestyle more highly than the long term health risks associated with it. She is convinced that a year later she will be prepared to change some of her dietary and activity behaviours. However, after one year she will find herself discounting future health risks more heavily than she previously thought she would do, and she will still feel that the pleasures of her lifestyle offsets future health risks. Inconsistency in time preferences is reflected by the discrepancy between the way the individual originally thought she would discount future outcomes and they way she actually discounted them one year later. The result is a likely indefinite postponement of the decision to quit current habits. At least some evidence of hyperbolic discounting has been found in relation to obesity: "Time inconsistent preferences regarding weight is a very common problem among teenagers, since the majority of them end up failing to reduce their BMI after having declared to be trying to lose weight" (Brunello *et al.*, 2008).

Possible solutions to present-biased preferences have been discussed in a broad literature. For instance, Glaeser (2006) argues that there is limited scope for paternalistic government intervention to counter self-control problems, as this would require "tricky social welfare decisions", or a judgement of whether individuals' future self, or long term preferences, should be given priority over their present self, or short term preferences. Such problems, in Glaeser's view, are best addressed by increasing the availability of "technologies or contracts that facilitate private self-control". An example could be the fiscal deductibility of private expenditures on devices that may facilitate self-control (*e.g.* nutrition advice, organised physical activities, etc.).

Addictive and habitual behaviours

Certain behaviours reflect sequences of repeated acts of consumption which are not independent of each other. This may happen because the commodity consumed generates a form of chemical dependence that makes it difficult for individuals to quit consuming it, as is the case with heroin, or because of psychological mechanisms that encourage the reiteration of consumption. The term "habit" is generally used in relation to the latter mechanisms, while the term "addiction" is applied more widely, both in relation to drugs or tobacco smoking (which involves a certain degree of dependence on nicotine) and in relation to consumption that does not involve chemical dependence (*e.g.* gambling addiction). However, it is the non-independence of acts of consumption that may cause concern about individuals' ability to maximise their welfare, rather than the nature of the underlying mechanisms, which often co-exist to varying degrees. The presence of a chemical dependence may strengthen the justification for intervention, but some forms of psychological addiction may also be extremely powerful and potentially damaging.

Once an individual has first engaged in a certain form of addictive consumption, overcoming the disincentives involved in that original choice (*e.g.* the opportunity cost, or price, of the commodity consumed), they will tend to continue that consumption and they will need much greater disincentives to be able to quit than those they faced when they started. Lack of self-control and inconsistent time preferences may be seen to produce similar effects. Individuals perceive consumption as desirable at the present time, while thinking that sometime in the future they may find it no longer desirable and they will quit. However, their current and future preferences change as time passes and those individuals tend to continue their consumption and further procrastinate quitting.

Habit forming behaviour is consolidated behaviour in which individuals engage over a prolonged period of time and from which they find it difficult to wean themselves. A recent report on obesity published by a United Kingdom government agency emphasises two psychological mechanisms characterising habitual behaviour that represent obstacles to behaviour change (Maio *et al.*, 2007). The first is defined as "tunnel vision" and refers to a reduced motivation to seek and use information that may lead to a better understanding of the consequences of the behaviour in question, and to a tendency to discount the value of new information that is received, particularly when it highlights risks associated with the habitual behaviour. The second aspect is that people who engage in habitual behaviour act on the implicit assumption that if they found the behaviour desirable when they first adopted it, it must also be desirable for them to continue to engage in the same behaviour. Factors like those described here are likely to prevent markets from working efficiently and may lead to sub-optimal outcomes for consumers. Of course consumers take up habits because they find it convenient to do so. In a short-term perspective, it may be efficient to avoid re-examining the desirability of a certain form of consumption every time consumption is repeated, but in doing so consumers may overlook longer term consequences of that consumption which may well offset any short-term efficiency gains. Economic models of "rational addiction", originally proposed by Becker and Murphy (1988), find support in empirical evidence (e.g. as discussed by Chaloupka and Warner, 2000, in relation to smoking). These models assume that consumers engaging in addictive, or habitual, behaviours are rationally aware of the short term as well as the long term consequences of those behaviours and make judgements on their desirability based on both the short term and the long term opportunity costs involved.

The issue of whether specific foods, or ingredients, may have addictive effects is still contentious (for instance, see Avena et al., 2008, and Benton, 2010, on the controversy concerning the addictive properties of sugar). While the role of habitual behaviours, combined with strong environmental pressures, in the maintenance of unhealthy eating habits is a potentially important determinant of the obesity epidemic, the existing evidence-base is far too small to conceive any actions specifically aimed at tackling this effect or to justify broader interventions.

The social multiplier effect: Clustering of obesity within households, peer groups and social networks

When acts of consumption made by an individual over time are not independent of each other we may have addictive or habitual behaviour, as discussed in the previous section. When acts of consumption made by different individuals are not independent of each other, as in the presence of social influences and peer pressures, we likely have externalities (positive or negative). When an individual's decision to adopt a certain behaviour affects the likelihood that other individuals related to the first will adopt the same behaviour, it is possible that the behaviour in question will spread to a larger extent than is desirable (in the case of negative externalities) or to a smaller extent (in the case of positive externalities). For instance, if adults' eating behaviour influences that of their children, and if we assume that adults will make their food choices freely, on the basis of their own preferences alone, and they are fully aware of the health consequences of those choices, an inefficiently large number of adults will adopt less healthy eating behaviours (which cause negative externalities on their children), and an inefficiently small number will adopt healthier behaviours (causing positive externalities).

Individual behaviours are subject to powerful social influences that contribute to shaping individual preferences. Social influences interact with market behaviours to create what Becker and Murphy (2000) defined as "social markets". A recent important study, based on a unique dataset, provided an empirical demonstration of the impact that social networks of family and friends may have on an individual's chances of becoming obese (Christakis and Fowler, 2007). Individuals whose friends (including those living in remote locations) or relatives had been gaining weight were substantially more likely to become themselves obese.* Social influences and peer pressures are not necessarily market failures, but they can contribute to spreading unhealthy lifestyles in certain population groups and in certain communities. Whether or not social influences are to be considered deviations from perfectly rational choice, they are likely to pose an externality problem. The presence of social influences raises issues not only about the design of efficient ways to tackle unhealthy lifestyles, but also about the impact of any interventions on the distribution of health.

Much of the existing research on the clustering of obesity, particularly within families, has been conducted within a "nature vs. nurture" framework trying to distinguish the role of common genetic backgrounds from the role of shared environmental exposures and behavioural responses. Studies of twins and adopted children have offered the best chances to shed light on this conundrum of interacting effects. The former have tried to compare body weight and BMI in monozygotic and dizygotic twins, while the latter have compared correlations between children and natural parents with those between children and adoptive parents. The most recent review of these types of studies (Silventoinen et al., 2010) reaches the conclusion that both genetic factors and shared exposures contribute to obesity. For instance, correlations in BMI between children and adoptive parents of between 0.10 and 0.16 are observed, some of which are statistically significant. Although these correlations are weaker than those observed between children and their natural parents, they are sufficient to show that shared exposures and behavioural responses do play a part in the spread of obesity. In addition, many of the existing studies are fairly old, dating as far back as the 1960s and 1970s, when the obesity epidemic was yet to materialise. It is plausible that increasing environmental pressures and rapid changes in behaviours in more recent years have augmented the effects observed in earlier studies.

---

* After the publication of Christakis and Fowler's study, a note by Cohen-Cole and Fletcher (2008) in the *Journal of Health Economics* disputed the conclusions of the former study on the grounds that it did not properly account for shared contextual (environmental) effects. In their rejoinder, however, Fowler and Christakis (2008) dismissed the criticism received.

The OECD could conduct analyses of the spread of obesity within families in a select group of countries for which individual data were available at the household level. The relationship between parental and child (age 3-17) overweight and obesity was examined in England, France and Korea. The likelihood of being obese and overweight was assessed after adjusting for demographic and socio-economic characteristics such as age, gender, and socio-economic condition of the household. OECD findings highlighted a significantly higher likelihood for children to be overweight or obese if at least one of their parents, in turn, is overweight or obese. Figure 4.1 shows that the odds of a boy being obese when at least one of the parents is obese are almost three times higher in England compared to boys having both parents with normal BMI, and almost 3.5 times higher for girls. The strength of these correlations is even stronger in France and Korea.

In order to explore the potential role of behavioural influences in explaining the clustering of obesity, we compared correlations in BMI between spouses with those between mothers and their children, assuming the former would be purely driven by shared exposures and behavioural responses, while the latter would also be driven by shared genetic backgrounds. Figure 4.2 shows that the correlations between mothers and their children are stronger than those observed between spouses, but not by a large margin, in England, France and Italy. Korea is an exception in this analysis, because the correlation observed between spouses is very low. A recent study based on data from Germany (Clark and Etilé, 2010) suggests that the relatively strong correlation in BMI between spouses is mostly the result of partner selection, which may contribute to explaining the findings for Korea. It is also interesting to note that the correlations observed in this analysis are larger than those reported in older studies, which suggests that the clustering of obesity within families increased as the obesity epidemic progressed.

If the correlation in BMI were mainly the result of partner selection, concerns about its role in the spread of obesity would be somewhat attenuated. However, further OECD analyses of correlations in BMI between spousal couples of different ages, which shows that the strength of these correlations increases with couples' age (assumed to reflect the length of time spouses lived together) in three out of four countries examined (Figure 4.3), suggests that behavioural influences play a part in these correlations, as well as partner selection mechanisms. Of course, it is also possible that correlations increasing with age reflect the influence of period or cohort effects on such correlations, but it was not possible to ascertain this with the available data.

Further evidence of the importance of behavioural influences comes from studies of peer-group influences conducted among teenagers. In particular, two studies, both based on the US National Longitudinal Study of Adolescent Health, reach the conclusion that adolescents' weight is correlated with that

Figure 4.1. **Child obesity and overweight by parents' obesity status**

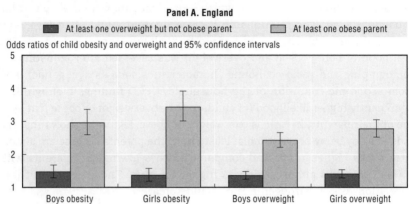

Panel A. England

■ At least one overweight but not obese parent   ☐ At least one obese parent

Odds ratios of child obesity and overweight and 95% confidence intervals

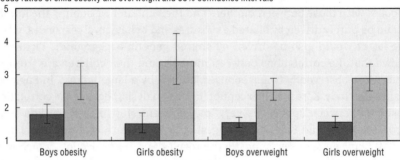

Panel B. France

Odds ratios of child obesity and overweight and 95% confidence intervals

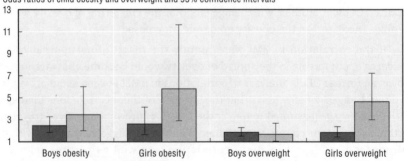

Panel C. Korea

Odds ratios of child obesity and overweight and 95% confidence intervals

Note: Odds ratios are relative to children with normal-weight parents.

Source: OECD analyses of data from: Health Survey for England 1995-2007, French survey Santé et Protection Sociale 1992-2006 and Korean National Health and Nutrition Examination Survey 2001 and 2005.

StatLink 🖹🖵 http://dx.doi.org/10.1787/888932315982

Figure 4.2. **BMI correlation between spouses and between mothers and children**

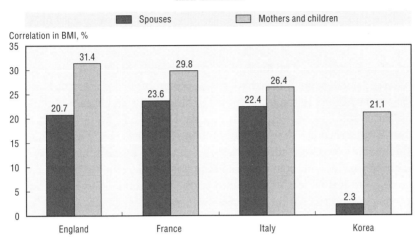

Source: OECD analyses of data from: Health Survey for England 1995-2007; French survey Enquête Santé et Protection Sociale 1995-2006; Italian survey Condizioni di Salute 1994-95, 2000 and 2005; Korean National Health and Nutrition Examination Survey 1998, 2001 and 2005.

StatLink 🔗 *http://dx.doi.org/10.1787/888932316001*

Figure 4.3. **BMI Correlation in couples of different ages**

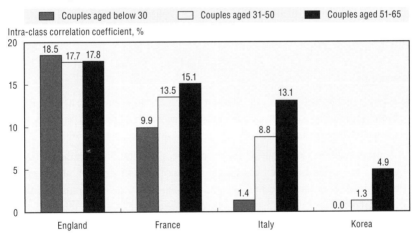

Source: OECD analyses of data from: Health Survey for England 1995-2007; French survey Enquête Santé et Protection Sociale 1995-2006; Italian survey Condizioni di Salute 1994-95, 2000 and 2005; Korean National Health and Nutrition Examination Survey 1998, 2001 and 2005.

StatLink 🔗 *http://dx.doi.org/10.1787/888932316020*

of friends and other adolescents in their peer group (Renna *et al.*, 2008; Trogdon *et al.*, 2008).

The clustering of overweight and obesity within households, social networks, and possibly other levels of aggregation, provides important insights on the trends in obesity observed in recent years and on possible ways of tackling them. The findings of OECD analyses confirm the existence of what has been described elsewhere as a social multiplier effect, which is likely to have contributed to the rapid spread of overweight and obesity throughout the OECD area. In economic terms, this effect may be described as an externality, indicating that individual lifestyle choices are likely to have an influence on other individuals' lifestyles. The impact on other individuals' health may be less direct in this case than, for instance, in the case of passive smoking, but it is no less important. A strong indication emerges that actions targeting individuals within their social context are likely to be more effective (Bahr *et al.*, 2009). A number of countries are increasingly promoting interventions involving peer groups (*e.g.* school-based, or workplace interventions) or family members (*e.g.* children and parents). These interventions may better exploit the social multiplier effect, turning it into a positive externality generating favourable influences on health behaviours among members of families and social networks. In addition to providing better chances of interventions being effective in changing behaviours, exploiting the social multiplier effect in the way just described may produce faster reductions in overweight and obesity rates than interventions targeting individuals out of their social context.

Key messages

- Understanding the pathways through which chronic diseases are generated requires an assessment of individual determinants of those diseases as well as interactions among them.

- A central role is played by lifestyle choices, for their direct influence on health and because they mediate some of the effects of other health determinants. Lifestyles are closely associated with a significant portion of the morbidity and mortality from chronic diseases.

- An individual's health status is the result of recent as well as distant exposures to the action of risk factors and health determinants. A life-course approach is required to identify the mechanisms that should be acted upon in the prevention of chronic diseases.

- Market failures and imperfect rationality may prevent markets from ensuring efficient and equitable outcomes.

- Existing evidence suggests that externalities deriving from higher health care expenditures for the obese, collectively funded through insurance or tax-funded systems are unlikely to be large enough to require specific government intervention.

- A more important source of externalities is associated with the spread of obesity within families and social networks, which reveals important social multiplier effects. The latter can be exploited in the design of policies to counter the obesity epidemic.

- Information failures are unlikely to play a major role in the current spread of obesity, but there is a clear role for governments in ensuring an adequate provision of information, especially to vulnerable groups, such children and those in disadvantaged socio-economic circumstances.

- Inconsistencies in time preferences, leading to poor self-control in health-related consumption, and a biased perception of risk make obesity more likely, but the scope for intervention to address these failures is unclear.

- The targeting of specific market failures in the design of prevention policies may be justified when these failures have a sufficiently large impact to warrant government intervention and when failures are amenable to correction through appropriate policies.

Bibliography

Alberg, A.J., M.V. Brock, J.M. Samet (2005), "Epidemiology of Lung Cancer: Looking to the Future", *Journal of Clinical Oncololgy*, Vol. 23, No. 14, pp. 3175-3185.

Arendt, J.N. (2005), "Does Education Cause Better Health? A Panel Data Analysis Using School Reforms for Identification", *Economics of Education Review*, Vol. 24, pp. 149-160.

Avena, N.M., P. Rada and B.G. Hoebel (2008), "Evidence for Sugar Addiction: Behavioral and Neurochemical Effects of Intermittent, Excessive Sugar Intake", *Neuroscience and Biobehavioral Reviews*, Vol. 32, No. 1, pp. 20-39.

Bahr, D.B., R.C. Browning, H.R. Wyatt and J.O. Hill (2009), "Exploiting Social Networks to Mitigate the Obesity Epidemic", *Obesity*, Vol. 17, No. 4, pp. 723-728.

Becker, G.S. and K.M. Murphy (1988), "A Theory of Rational Addiction", *Journal of Political Economy*, Vol. 96, No. 4, pp. 675-700.

Becker, G.S. and K.M. Murphy (2000), *Social Economics: Market Behaviour in a Social Environment*, Harvard University Press, Cambridge, MA.

Benton, D. (2010), "The Plausibility of Sugar Addiction and its Role in Obesity and Eating Disorders", *Clinical Nutrition*, Vol. 29, No. 3, pp. 288-303.

Bhattacharya, J. and N. Sood (2005), "Health Insurance and the Obesity Externality", NBER Working Paper No. 11529, National Bureau of Economic Research, Cambridge, MA.

Blane, D. (2006), "The Life Course, the Social Gradient, and Health", in M. Marmot and R.G. Wilkinson (eds.), *Social Determinants of Health*, 2nd edition, Oxford University Press, Oxford, UK.

Blane, D., G. Davey Smith and C. Hart (1999a), "Some Social and Physical Correlates of Intergenerational Social Mobility: Evidence from the West of Scotland Collaborative Study", *Sociology*, Vol. 33, pp. 169-183.

Blane, D., S. Harding and M. Rosato (1999b), "Does Social Mobility Affect the Size of the socioeconomic Mortality Differential? Evidence from the Office of National Statistics Longitudinal Study", *Journal of the Royal Statistical Society*, Vol. 162, pp. 59-70.

Blane, D., *et al.* (1996), "Association of Cardiovascular Disease Risk Factors with Socioeconomic Position During Childhood and During Adulthood", *British Medical Journal*, Vol. 313, No. 7070, pp. 1434-1438.

Branca, F., H. Nikogosian and T. Lobstein (eds.) (2007), *The Challenge of Obesity in the WHO European Region and the Strategies for Response*, WHO Regional Office for Europe, Copenhagen.

Brunello, G., P.C. Michaud and A. Sanz-de-Galdeano (2008), "The Rise in Obesity Across the Atlantic: An Economic Perspective", IZA Discussion Paper No. 3529, Bonn.

Cawley, J. (2004), "An Economic Framework for Understanding Physical Activity and Eating Behaviors", *American Journal of Preventive Medicine*, Vol. 27, No. 3S, pp. 117-125.

Chaloupka, F.J. and K.E. Warner (2000), "The Economics of Smoking", in A.J. Culyer and J.P. Newhouse (eds.), *Handbook of Health Economics*, Oxford, North Holland.

Chandola, T. *et al.* (2008), "Work Stress and Coronary Heart Disease: What Are the Mechanisms?", *European Heart Journal*, DOI: http://dx.doi.org/10.1093/eurheartj/ehm584.

Chou, S.Y., M. Grossman and H. Saffer (2004), "An Economic Analysis of Adult Obesity: Results from the Behavioral Risk Factor Surveillance System", *Journal of Health Economics*, Vol. 23, No. 3, pp. 565-587.

Christakis, N.A. and J.H. Fowler (2007), "The Spread of Obesity in a Large Social Network over 32 Years", *New England Journal of Medicine*, Vol. 357, No. 4, pp. 370-379.

Clark, A.E. and F. Etilé (2010), "Happy House: Spousal Weight and Individual Well-being", Paris School of Economics Working Paper No. 2010-07, Paris.

Cohen-Cole, E. and J.M. Fletcher (2008), "Is Obesity Contagious? Social Networks *vs.* Environmental Factors in the Obesity Epidemic", *Journal of Health Economics*, Vol. 27, pp. 1382-1387.

Cutler, D.M. and E.L. Glaeser (2005), "What Explains Differences in Smoking, Drinking and Other Health-Related Behaviors?", NBER Working Paper, No. 11100, Cambridge, MA.

Cutler, D.M. and E.L. Glaeser (2006), "Why Do Europeans Smoke more than Americans?", NBER Working Paper No. 12124, National Bureau of Economic Research, Cambrdige, MA.

Cutler, D.M., E.L. Glaeser, J.M. Shapiro (2003), "Why Have Americans Become More Obese?", *Journal of Economic Perspectives*, Vol. 17, No. 3, pp. 93-118.

Dahlgren, G. and M. Whitehead (1991), *Policies and Strategies to Promote Social Equity in Health*, Institute for Futures Studies, Stockholm.

Dauchet, L. *et al.* (2006), "Fruit and Vegetable Consumption and Risk of Coronary Heart Disease: A Meta-Analysis of Cohort Studies", *Journal of Nutrition*, Vol. 136, No. 10, pp. 2588-2593.

Deaton, A. (2004), "Globalization and Health", in S.M. Collins and C. Graham (eds.), *Brookings Trade Forum: Globalization, Poverty, and Inequality*, Brookings Institution Press, Washington DC.

Evans R.G. and G.L. Stoddart (1994), "Producing Health, Consuming Health Care", in R.G. Evans, M.L. Barer and T.R. Marmor (eds.), *Why are Some People Healthy and Others Not? The Determinants of Health of Populations*, Aldine de Gruyter, New York.

Fogel, R.W. (1994), "Economic Growth, Population Theory, and Physiology: The Bearing of Long-Term Processes on the Making of Economic Policy", *American Economic Review*, Vol. 84, No. 3, pp. 369-395.

Fowler, J.H. and N.A. Christakis (2008), "Estimating Peer Effects on Health in Social Networks: A Response to Cohen-Cole and Fletcher; Trogdon, Nonnemaker, Pais", *Journal of Health Economics*, Vol. 27, No. 5, pp. 1400-1405.

Frank, J.W. and J.F. Mustard (1994), "The Determinants of Health from a Historical Perspective". *Daedalus, Journal of the American Academy of Arts and Sciences*, Vol. 123, No. 4, pp. 1-19.

Gilman, S.E. *et al.* (2008), "Educational Attainment and Cigarette Smoking: A Causal Association?", *International Journal of Epidemiology*, IJE Advance Access published online on 6 January 2008, DOI: *http://dx.doi.org/10.1093/ije/dym250*.

Glaeser, E. (2006), "Paternalism and Psychology", *University of Chicago Law Review*, Vol. 73, pp. 133-156.

Government of Canada (1974), *A New Perspective on the Health of Canadians*, Department of National Health and Welfare, Ottawa.

Hallqvist, J. *et al.* (2004), "Can We Disentangle Life Course Processes of Accumulation, Critical Period and Social Mobility? An Analysis of Disadvantaged Socio-Economic Positions and Myocardial Infarction in the Stockholm Heart Epidemiology Program", *Social Science and Medicine*, Vol. 58, No. 8, pp. 1555-1562.

Heraclides, A. and E. Brunner (2009), "Social Mobility and Social Accumulation Across the Life-course in Relation to Adult Overweight and Obesity: The Whitehall II study", *Journal of Epidemiology and Community Health*, Published Online First: 7 September 2009, DOI: *http://dx.doi.org/10.1136/jech.2009.087692*.

John, J.H. *et al.* (2002), "Effects of Fruit and Vegetable Consumption on Plasma Antioxidant Concentrations and Blood Pressure: A Randomised Controlled trial", *The Lancet*, Vol. 359, No. 9322, pp. 1969-1974.

Karnehed, N.E.K., F. Rasmussen, T. Hemmingsson and P. Tynelius (2008), "Obesity in Young Adulthood is Related to Social Mobility Among Swedish Men", *Obesity*, Vol. 16 3, pp. 654-658.

Karvonen, S., A.H. Rimpela and M.K. Rimpela (1999), "Social Mobility and Health Related Behaviours in Young People", *Journal of Epidemiology and Community Health*, Vol. 53, pp. 211-217.

Kenkel, D.S. (2000), "Prevention", in A.J. Culyer and J.P. Newhouse (eds.) *Handbook of Health Economics*, Oxford, North Holland.

Kenkel, D.S., D. Lillard and A. Mathios (2006), "The Roles of High School Completion and GED Receipt in Smoking and Obesity", *Journal of Labor Economics*, Vol. 24, No. 3, pp. 635-660.

Key, T.J. *et al.* (2004), "Diet, Nutrition and the Prevention of Cancer", *Public Health Nutrition*, Vol. 7, No. 1A, pp. 187-200.

Kosteniuk, J. and H.D. Dickinson (2003), "Tracing the Social Gradient in the Health of Canadians: Primary and Secondary Determinants", *Social Science and Medicine*, Vol. 57, pp. 263-276.

Kuh, D. and Y. Ben Shlomo (2004) (eds.), *A Life Course Approach to Chronic Disease Epidemiology*, 2nd edition, Oxford University Press, Oxford, UK.

Lakdawalla, D. and T.J. Philipson (2002), "The Growth of Obesity and Technological Change: A Theoretical and Empirical Examination", NBER Working Paper No. W8946, National Bureau for Economic Research, Cambridge, MA.

Labonte, R. and M. Sanger (2006), "Glossary of the World Trade Organisation and Public Health: Part 1", *Journal of Epidemiology and Community Health*, Vol. 60, pp. 655-661.

Lipscomb, J., M.C. Weinstein and G.W. Torrance (1996), "Time Preference", Chapter 7 in M.R. Gold, J.E. Siegel, L.B. Russell and M.C. Weinstein (eds.), *Cost Effectiveness in Health and Medicine*, Oxford University Press, New York.

Lleras-Muney, A. (2005), "The Relationship Between Education and Adult Mortality in the United States", *Review of Economic Studies*, Vol. 72, pp. 189-221.

Lurie, N., C. McLaughlin and J.S. House (2003), "In Pursuit of the Social Determinants of Health: The Evolution of Health Services Research", *Health Services Research*, Vol. 38 (6 Pt 2), pp. 1641-1643.

Mackenbach, J.P. (2006), *Health Inequalities: Europe in Profile*, European Commission, Brussels, Belgium.

Maio, G.R. *et al.* (2007), *Tackling Obesities: Future Choices – Lifestyle Change – Evidence Review*, Foresight, Department of Innovation Universities and Skills, London.

Marmot, M. (2004), *The Status Syndrome*, Bloomsbury, London and Henry Holt, New York.

Marmot, M. and R.G. Wilkinson (eds.) (2006), *Social Determinants of Health*, 2nd edition, Oxford University Press, Oxford, UK.

Nestle, M. (2006), "Food Marketing and Childhood Obesity – A Matter of Policy", *New England Journal of Medicine*, Vol. 354, No. 24, pp. 2527-2529.

Philipson, T.J. and R.A. Posner (2008), "Is the Obesity Epidemic a Public Health Problem? A Review of Zoltan J. Acs and Alan Lyles's Obesity, Business and Public Policy", *Journal of Economic Literature*, Vol. 46, No. 4, pp. 974-982.

Plantinga, A.J. and S. Bernell (2007), "The Association Between Urban Sprawl and Obesity: Is it a Two-Way Street?", *Journal of Regional Science*, Vol. 47, No. 5, pp. 857-879.

Rashad, I. (2006), "Structural Estimation of Caloric Intake, Exercise, Smoking, and Obesity", *Quarterly Review of Economics and Finance*, Vol. 46, No. 2, pp. 268-283.

Renna, F., I.B. Grafova and N. Thakur (2008), "The Effect of Friends on Adolescent Body Weight", *Economics and Human Biology*, Vol. 6, No. 3, pp. 377-387.

Schäfer Elinder, L. (2005), "Obesity, Hunger, and Agriculture: The Damaging Role of Subsidies", *BMJ*, Vol. 331, pp. 1333-1336.

Silventoinen, K., B. Rokholm, J. Kaprio and T.I.A. Sørensen (2010), "The Genetic and Environmental Influences on Childhood Obesity: A Systematic Review of Twin and Adoption Studies", *International Journal of Obesity*, Vol. 34, pp. 29-40.

Solar, O. and A. Irwin (2007), *A Conceptual Framework for Action on the Social Determinants of Health*, Commission on Social Determinants of Health, Discussion Paper, World Health Organisation, Geneva.

Suhrcke, M. *et al.* (2006), *Chronic Disease: An Economic Perspective*, Oxford Health Alliance, London.

Taylor, R., F. Najafi and A. Dobson (2007), "Meta-Analysis of Studies of Passive Smoking and Lung Cancer: Effects of Study Type and Continent", *International Journal of Epidemiology*, Vol. 36, No. 5, pp. 1048-1059.

Trogdon, J.G., J. Nonnemaker and J. Pais (2008), "Peer Effects in Adolescent Overweight", *Journal of Health Economics*, Vol. 27, No. 5, pp. 1388-1399.

Wilkinson, R.G. and M. Marmot (2003), *Social Determinants of Health: The Solid Facts*, 2nd edition, WHO Regional Office for Europe, Copenhagen.

Willi, C. *et al.* (2007), "Active Smoking and the Risk of Type 2 Diabetes: A Systematic Review and Meta-Analysis", *Journal of the American Medical Association*, Vol. 298, No. 22, pp. 2654-2664.

Special Focus III.
Are Health Behaviors Driven by Information?

by

Donald Kenkel, Cornell University

Some people might choose unhealthy behaviors because they lack complete information about the health consequences of their choices. If so, the provision of information should be an effective approach, and might be a cost-effective approach, to encourage healthier behaviors and promote public health. Empirical health economics research on the role of health information provides several instructive lessons.

Perhaps the most compelling lesson that information can lead to healthier behaviours comes from tobacco control. Over the last half of the 20th century, adult smoking prevalence fell dramatically in the United States and many other OECD countries. In the United States, the prevalence of adult smoking fell from nearly 50% in the 1940s to its current rate of around 20%. Just after scientific research on the health hazards of smoking began to be published in scientific journals in the 1950s, less than half (about 44%) of the US public agreed that smoking was a cause of lung cancer. Today, virtually all consumers recognise the links between smoking and lung cancer, heart disease, and other serious illnesses (Kenkel and Chen, 2000; Cheng *et al.*, 2009).

A series of econometric studies provide quantitative estimates of the causal impact of changes in health information on smoking (Hamilton, 1972; Lewit *et al.*, 1981; Schneider *et al.*, 1981; Blaine and Reed, 1994). These studies exploit information "shocks", including the 1964 Surgeon General's Report on smoking and health and the anti-smoking messages broadcast on US television during the Fairness Doctrine era (1968-70). Kenkel and Chen (2000) review additional studies that suggest that similar information shocks also reduced smoking in a number of other countries.

Smoking is not the only example of strong consumer responses to new health information. Although over the last few decades the United States has experienced increases in overweight and obesity, there have also been important dietary improvements. Health economics research suggests that at least part of these healthier dietary behaviors can again be traced back to improved consumer information. In the mid-1980s, the US regulatory environment changed, making it easier for firms to advertise the link between diet and disease. In a series of studies Ippolito and Mathios (1990, 1995, 1996) explore the impact of the resulting health information shocks. In the cereals market, producer claims about the health benefits of adding dietary fiber appear to have been an important information source for consumers, leading to substantial increases in fiber consumption (Ippolito and Mathios, 1990). Similarly, individual food consumption data and food production data show that consumption of fats, saturated fats, and cholesterol fell from 1977 to 1985, but fell more rapidly between 1985 and 1990 after producer health claims became more common (Ippolito and Mathios, 1995, 1996).

The US Department of Health and Human Services (2000, pp. 12-19) notes that as dietary fat consumption fell, average (age-adjusted) blood cholesterol levels in adults dropped from 213 mg/dL in 1978 to 203 mg/dL in 1991. Improvements in diet and increased use of cholesterollowering medications continued through the 1990s and 2000s, and the United States has already met the goal set for population cholesterol levels in the Healthy People 2010 initiative (US Department of Health and Human Services, 2000, pp. 12-14).

Another lesson from health economics research is that private profits and public health can sometimes go hand-in-hand. Efforts by the tobacco industry to provide misleading information have attracted a great deal of attention both from researchers and regulators. Some critics tend to place food industry advertisements in the same light as tobacco industry advertisements. However, manufacturers also have strong profit incentives to introduce and advertise healthy products. Ippolito and Mathios (1995) report that after the ban on health claims in food advertisements was lifted, the introduction of high fiber cereals jumped from about 1.5 per year to almost 7 per year.

Avery *et al.* (2007) study the private sector market for products such as nicotine gum that help smokers quit. In recent years the pharmaceutical industry has spent between USD 100 to USD 200 million annually advertising smoking cessation products. The potential public health benefits of this advertising have not been overlooked. For example, in 1996 the American Cancer Society's Great American Smoke Out included an advertising campaign that was jointly sponsored with a manufacturer of a cessation product. Avery *et al.* (2007) estimate that when smokers see more magazine advertisements for smoking cessation products, they are more likely to attempt and succeed in quitting. Looking towards the future, Cawley (2004, p. 123) points out: "The enormous profit incentive to develop reduced calorie foods and efficient and enjoyable exercise equipment is a reason for optimism that private markets can help consumers achieve their goals with respect to exercise, nutrition, and weight."

Research on health disparities provides another, and somewhat more complicated, set of lessons about information and health behaviors. The strong gradient between schooling and health behaviors provides more evidence that health information plays an important role. While the empirical association between schooling and health is well-documented, establishing the nature of the link has been more difficult and controversial. A set of recent studies that use schooling reforms as instrumental variables provide new evidence that more schooling causes better health (for a review, see Grossman, 2006). One of the causal channels appears to be through consumer information.

Cutler and Lleras-Muney (2009) estimate that differences in health information account for about 10% of the schooling gradient with smoking and drinking, confirming the earlier estimates of Kenkel (1991). Even though information differences do not explain the majority of the link between schooling and health behaviors, this line of research corroborates research on the impact of information shocks on health behaviors. If people with different levels of schooling learn about and react to information shocks differently, it is not surprising that cross-sectional differences in health behaviors persist for some time after the initial shocks.

The cross-sectional differences or disparities in health behaviors associated with schooling complicate the lessons to be learned. In recent years social scientists have realised that health disparities can be an unintended consequence of scientific progress. In an influential paper, Link and Phelan (1995) urge medical sociologists and social epidemiologists to study social conditions that are the fundamental causes of disease. By their terminology, a defining feature of fundamental causes is that they "involve access to resources that can be used to avoid risks or to minimise the consequences of diseases…", where resources are defined broadly and include knowledge. Link and Phelan further note that: "An additional condition that must obtain for fundamental causes to emerge is change over time in the diseases afflicting humans, the risks of those diseases, knowledge about risks, or the effectiveness of treatments for diseases."

As scientific advances provide new information about health behaviors, it may be difficult to avoid at least temporary increases in health disparities. A more puzzling, and more troubling, pattern is when disparities persist or even widen long after the initial information shocks. For example, 50 years after research on the health consequences of smoking began to emerge, the schooling-smoking gradient is stronger than ever (Cheng et al., 2009).

Some public health advocates suggest that the history of tobacco control provides important lessons to reduce the prevalence of overweight and obesity. There are clear parallels between these behaviors. For example, both smoking and overweight/obesity are among the leading causes of serious chronic diseases and death. Both behaviors show marked disparities associated with schooling and other aspects of socio-economic status. Yet there are also important differences between these unhealthy behaviors.

Compared to smoking and tobacco control, weight-related behaviors involve a more complex information problem and require more subtle policy response. For smoking the message is fairly simple – smoking kills – and in most countries cigarette packages are required to carry a warning label to that effect. Tobacco control advocates at least imagine a world where no one smokes. For maintaining proper weight, the basic message is almost as simple – do not eat too much or exercise too little – and most consumers understand this basic information. It is not rocket science. However, implementing the dietary advice requires more detailed information about the caloric and nutrient values of foods. And the public health ideal is not a world where no one eats, but a world where diets are moderate and balanced by exercise.

The United States and many other countries require food packages to carry labels with nutrition information. Research suggests that the labels required by the US Nutrition Labeling and Education Act (NLEA) had both intended and unintended consequences. While in his study of the salad dressing market Mathios (2000) finds evidence that the NLEA helped improve dietary choices, in his study of the cooking oils market Mathios (1998) finds evidence that the NLEA may have had the unintended consequence of increasing consumption of saturated fat. Variyam and Cawley (2006) findings suggest that overall the NLEA helped certain population groups to control their weight.

The last lesson from economics is basic but bears repeating: Policies that maximise health do not necessarily maximise individual utility or social welfare. Whether it is possible to be "fat and healthy" is a question for medical science, not economics. The economic approach to human behavior calls attention to another question, however: Is it possible to be "fat and happy"? Given the tradeoffs involved, it does not seem unreasonable that some perfectly well informed consumers will decide that some healthier dietary behaviors aren't worth it.

Bibliography

Avery, R., D.S. Kenkel, D.R. Lillard and A.D. Mathios (2007b), "Private Profits and Public Health: Does Advertising Smoking Cessation Products Encourage Smokers to Quit?", *Journal of Political Economy*, Vol. 115, No. 3, pp. 447-481.

Blaine, T.W. and M.R. Reed (1994), "US Cigarette Smoking and Health Warnings: New Evidence from Post World War II Data", *Journal of Agricultural and Applied Economics*, Vol. 26, No. 2, pp. 535-544.

Cawley, J. (2004), "An Economic Framework for Understanding Physical Activity and Eating Behaviors", *American Journal of Preventive Medicine*, Vol. 27, No. 3S, pp. 117-125.

Cheng, K.W., D.S. Kenkel and F. Liu (2009), "The Evolution of the Schooling-Smoking Gradient", Working Paper, Department of Policy Analysis and Management, Cornell University.

Cutler, D. and A. Lleras-Muney (2009), "Understanding Differences in Health Behaviors by Education", *Journal of Health Economics*, forthcoming.

Grossman, M. (2006), "Education and Nonmarket Outcomes," in E. Hanushek and F. Welch (eds.), *Handbook of the Economics of Education*, Amsterdam: North-Holland, an imprint of Elsevier Science.

Hamilton, J.L. (1972), "The Demand for Cigarettes: Advertising, the Health Scare, and the Cigarette Advertising Ban", *Review of Economics and Statistics*, Vol. 54, pp. 401-411.

Ippolito, P. and A. Mathios (1990), "Information, Advertising and Health: A Study of the Cereal Market?", *Rand Journal of Economics*, Vol. 21, No. 3, pp. 459-480.

Ippolito, P. and A. Mathios (1995), "Information and Advertising: The Case of Fat Consumption in the United States?", *American Economic Review: Papers and Proceedings*, Vol. 85, No. 2, pp. 91-95.

Ippolito, P. and A. Mathios (1996). *Information and Advertising Policy: A Study of Fat and Cholesterol Consumption in the United States, 1977-1990*, Bureau of Economics Staff Report, Federal Trade Commission, Washington DC.

Kenkel, D.S. (1991), "Health Behavior, Health Knowledge, and Schooling", *Journal of Political Economy*, Vol. 99, No. 2, pp. 287-305.

Kenkel, D.S. and L. Chen (2000), "Consumer Information and Tobacco Use", in P. Jha and F.J. Chaloupka (eds.), *Tobacco Control in Developing Countries*. Oxford University Press, pp. 177-214.

Lewit, E., D. Coate and M. Grossman (1981), "The Effects of Government Regulation on Teenage Smoking", *Journal of Law and Economics*, Vol. 24, No. 3, pp. 545-569.

Link, B.G. and J. Phelan (1995), "Social Conditions as Fundamental Causes of Disease", *Journal of Health and Social Behavior* (Extra Issue), pp. 80-94.

Mathios, A. (1998), "The Importance of Nutrition Labeling and Health Claim Regulations on Product Choice: An Analysis of the Cooking Oil Market", *Agricultural and Resource Economics Review*, Vol. 27, No. 2.

Mathios, A. (2000), "The Impact of Mandatory Disclosure Laws on Product Choices: An Analysis of the Salad Dressing Market", *Journal of Law and Economics*, Vol. 43, No. 2, pp. 651-678.

Schneider, L., B. Klein and K.M. Murphy (1981), "Governmental Regulation of Cigarette Health Information", *Journal of Law and Economics*, Vol. 24, No. 3, pp. 575-612.

US Department of Health and Human Services (2000), *Healthy People 2010*, 2nd ed. with *Understanding and Improving Health and Objectives for Improving Health*, 2 Vols., US Government Printing Office, Washington DC, November.

US Department of Health and Human Services (2007), *Mid Course Review: Healthy People 2010*, US Government Printing Office, Washington DC.

Variyam, J. and J. Cawley (2006), "Nutrition Labels and Obesity", NBER Working Paper No. 11956, Cambridge, MA.

Chapter 5

Tackling Obesity:
The Roles of Governments and Markets

In most contemporary societies, we look to governments to protect and even increase public welfare. Whether through regulation, taxes, or education, or some combination of these, governments can play a significant part in affecting the choices we make and the outcomes that result from those choices. Governments in the OECD area have taken a broad range of actions in recent years to improve nutrition and physical activity, reacting to a growing concern about increasing obesity rates, particularly in vulnerable population groups. This chapter examines these actions and analyses the scope for, and potential consequences of, government intervention in the context of obesity prevention. It also looks at the response of the private sector to challenges related to food and physical activity in the current epidemic of obesity.

What can governments do to improve the quality of our choices?

If people made their lifestyle choices, such as what foods to consume or what physical activities to undertake on a purely rational basis, they would likely maximise their welfare, balancing immediate satisfaction and convenience with future well-being. In such an ideal world, individuals would choose among competitively priced products relative to their needs and desires. Presumably they would also exercise in sufficient amounts to balance their intake of calories and keep their bodies healthy. Individual rational choices would produce healthier individuals and consequently healthier societies.

However, people do not always behave rationally. Neither are markets as efficient, fair, and conducive to healthy outcomes as some would like to see them. In most contemporary societies, we look to governments to protect and even increase public welfare. Whether through regulation, taxes, or education, or some combination of these, governments can play a significant part in affecting the choices we make and the outcomes that result from those choices. But the desirability of government action is not judged simply on the basis of its measurable impact on social welfare. Government intervention involves at least some interference with individual choice, whether it is intended to modify the context in which choices are made, or the way these are made. The degree to which such interference may be acceptable varies greatly across and within countries. Action aimed at steering individual choice towards improved outcomes is often considered paternalistic and met with resistance.

Part of the policy maker's job is to determine what degree of interference with individual choice a preventive intervention will entail and whether that interference is justified. Government programmes may involve at least four types of actions in the context of obesity prevention: *a)* actions aimed at improving the breadth or the attractiveness of choice options, relative to a free market situation; *b)* actions to modify preferences based on characteristics of choice options other than price; *c)* actions to increase the price of selected choice options; and *d)* banning of selected choice options. The four types of actions will be illustrated in the remainder of this section.

Increasing choice

Increasing choice is the least intrusive form of government intervention, because it does not actually limit the opportunities that individuals enjoy.

Rather, individual choices may be influenced either by expanding the range of choices or by decreasing the price of certain choices considered beneficial. A public investment in a new form of transportation not normally provided through a market mechanism, *e.g.* a programme to make public bicycles available for temporary use in an urban setting, is an example of the former type of intervention. A programme of subsidies to make public transportation more convenient and less expensive, so as to increase its use is an example of the latter. Actions of these types are only mildly intrusive. Nevertheless, they do modify the set of available choice options, and they aim at achieving outcomes other than those that would occur without intervention. Furthermore, they do this at a potentially high cost, which must be paid by someone.

Information, education and influencing established preferences

This is the most varied group of actions, as preferences can be influenced in a large number of ways, some of which may prove more intrusive than others. There are at least two broad types of actions in this category. The first type includes actions aimed at shaping tastes and preferences when these are being formed, especially during childhood. These are typically educational interventions that start from the very early years of life with informal education delivered by parents and continue with schooling and other forms of formal education. The effects of these actions on tastes and preferences may be very powerful and long-lasting, shaping lifestyles well into adult life. The second type of actions includes those aimed at influencing established preferences, such as the provision of information, actions based on persuasion, and other less obvious incentives which involve nudging individuals to adopt virtuous behaviours.

The provision of information to consumers is one of the most common ways of influencing choices. When information is lacking, imperfect, or asymmetrically distributed between suppliers and consumers, governments may intervene to redress the information imbalance. Although often seen as a non-intrusive, or non-paternalistic, form of intervention, the provision of information is seldom neutral. The direction in which new information may influence choice depends on the contents, the framing, and the method of delivery of the information. The extent to which any third party, including the state, can be trusted to package all these elements in the best interest of the consumer is often a matter of value judgement. Of course, there are many situations in which obvious information gaps can be filled by delivering relatively simple and uncontroversial messages, but this cannot be assumed to be true in all cases.

Even when information is not lacking, governments or other public interest groups may still wish to reinforce a particular message to persuade consumers and steer their choices towards outcomes that are deemed to be in their best interest. For instance, consumer knowledge of the health risks associated with smoking has increased substantially over the past decades, and only a very small proportion of individuals are currently unaware of such risks (Kenkel, 2007). However, many governments have adopted the policy of printing dire health warnings on cigarette packs, the main purpose of which is not to provide information that is lacking, but to persuade consumers to limit their consumption by reinforcing a known message. Similarly, an intervention may be aimed at countering other parties' influence and persuasion attempts if the latter are not deemed to be in the best interest of consumers. This may be achieved by regulating, or banning, other parties' actions, as in the case of advertising regulation. For instance, a widely advocated strategy to prevent child obesity involves heavy regulation or outright banning of television advertising of food products during times when children represent a significant part of the audience.

Preferences may also be influenced in more subtle ways than through the direct provision of information. An important example is what has been described as setting the default option by advocates of "libertarian paternalism" (e.g. Sunstein and Thaler, 2003). The underlying principle is that individual preferences driving an act of choice tend to be influenced by how the default option is configured. An example of the default option is the routine association of a certain side dish to a main course ordered in a restaurant. Customers may be entitled to demand an alternative side dish, but if they did not exercise this faculty they would receive the standard (default) option. Using a healthy option as a default instead of a less healthy one would have a significant effect on the number of customers eventually choosing to consume the healthy option. Actions involving changes in default options may display varying degrees of interference with individual choice and they may be perceived as more or less acceptable by consumers depending on the nature of the choices they aim to influence. For instance, changing the order in which food is arranged in a company cafeteria (Sunstein and Thaler, 2003) in order to steer consumer choices towards healthy options would seem to be a fairly non-intrusive action. However, other actions based on the same basic principle, i.e. changing the default option, may be perceived as much more intrusive. An example is policies making organ donations a default, with individuals being allowed to opt out upon request, have been viewed as most controversial and have been fiercely opposed in many countries, despite evidence which shows these policies may increase organ donations by as much as 25-30% compared to countries where the default is not consenting to donation (Abadie and Gay, 2006).

Actions that aim at influencing choice through information and education are not without costs, although they tend to be less expensive than those intended to expand the choice set. Information is a commodity that needs to be produced and delivered to consumers if it is to influence their choices. The costs involved in making the information available to consumers increase with the degree of complexity of the information required, with the difficulty of reaching the target of the information through efficient communication channels, and with the need to reiterate and reinforce messages. To the extent that information campaigns are publicly funded, taxpayers will pick up the bill and costs will be borne by those who engage in risky behaviours as well as those who do not. Actions aimed at regulating the provision of information and the use of persuasion in a market setting generally involve lower costs, mostly in relation to enforcement, but it should also be noted that such actions may lead to price changes for the consumers and the commodities concerned. For instance, a compulsory food labelling scheme would force food manufacturers to convey information to consumers at a very low cost for the public purse, but manufacturers will bear extra costs and may want to recover these from consumers by raising retail prices. Actions aimed at changing default options also tend to be regulatory actions and tend to have similar cost implications as regulating advertising.

Raising prices on unhealthy choices

Governments can also influence choice by raising prices on unhealthy behaviours. A classical example of this is taxation, in particular the use of indirect taxes and other levies charged on the consumption of goods deemed less healthy. Taxes have the effect of raising prices above some consumers' willingness to pay, leading them to reduce or stop consumption of the undesirable product.

The precise impact of imposing taxes on the consumption of certain commodities is determined by the price elasticity of the demand for such commodities, *i.e.* by the responsiveness of consumers to price changes. An inelastic demand means that the relative change in the quantity consumers will demand is smaller than the relative change in price. An elastic demand means the opposite. The elasticity of the demand for a commodity subject to taxation is important because it determines whether consumers will increase the proportion of their own income they spend on that particular form of consumption (inelastic demand), or decrease it (elastic demand).

It is difficult to predict how consumers will react to the price change induced by taxation. Some may respond by reducing their consumption of healthy goods in order to pay for the more expensive unhealthy goods, thus defeating the purpose of the tax. Others may seek substitutes for the taxed product, which might be as unhealthy as those originally consumed. Depending on the elasticity of the demand for the taxed product, consumers will either end up bearing an extra financial burden, or changing the mix of products they consume in ways that can be difficult to identify. The impact of the tax on government and supplier (*e.g.* food manufacturer) revenues will depend on the elasticity of consumers' demand for the taxed product.*

Taxes on lifestyle commodities, or sin taxes, tend to be controversial. Critics perceive them as undue interference with individual choice. Governments levying such taxes are sometimes seen as "profiting" from unhealthy behaviours. In addition, taxes on consumption are typically regressive, unless consumption is concentrated among the wealthiest, which is certainly not the case for most potentially unhealthy lifestyle commodities, as the consumption of these tends to be concentrated among the less well off. Therefore, tax payments will weigh more heavily on the incomes of the most disadvantaged. In addition to distributional effects, imposing taxes on certain forms of consumption may also generate costs, mainly in relation to enforcement. When prices in a market are kept artificially high by taxation, phenomena like parallel trade and smuggling will flourish, which governments must then regulate or repress.

Banning unhealthy behaviours

The actions that involve the most extreme form of interference with individual choice are those that result in the complete banning of one or more choice options. Actions that make one option compulsory, implicitly banning all other options, are essentially of the same nature. Examples include swimming bans in dangerous waters, or compulsory wearing of bicycle helmets. These actions involve a direct limitation of individual choice and require a strong justification in order to become acceptable. Harm caused to others by an individual's behaviour (an externality, in economic terms) is typically one such justification. Examples include the health consequences of passive smoking, or the violent behaviour that may be associated with drinking alcoholic beverages at sports events. But in some cases a potential for self-harm (as in the case of swimming bans and compulsory helmets) is deemed sufficient to justify banning certain behaviours, especially when it is assumed that individuals are not fully able to assess the potential risks involved in adopting such behaviours. The addictive nature of certain forms of consumption often strengthens the case for adopting such severely restrictive measures.

A ban can selectively hinder certain choices, with the aim of limiting the overall consumption of a commodity or incidence of a given behaviour. This is

---

* Among lifestyle commodities, the demand for cigarettes is known to be broadly inelastic (Gallet and List, 2003) but with variations across social groups (Townsend *et al.*, 1994; Madden, 2007). The demand for alcoholic beverages tends to have an elasticity of about –1 (neither elastic nor inelastic) (Fogarty, 2004; Gallet, 2007). The demand for food, generally, is rather inelastic, but the demand for specific foods may be fairly elastic, because of the likely availability of substitutes.

the case of smoking bans in public places, or traffic speed limits. Selective bans tend to target behaviours in the situations in which these involve the greatest risks to the health of the individual or to the health of others. Alternatively, restrictive measures can aim to completely suppress the marketing or consumption of a commodity. Examples include bans on illicit drugs, or bans of food ingredients deemed dangerous for the health of consumers such as certain preservatives or colouring agents, or, more recently, trans-fatty acids (trans fats).

Whether partial or total, bans are essentially regulatory measures and as such they are less expensive than measures aimed at persuading consumers or expanding their choice sets. At the time of implementing a smoking ban in public places in England, the UK Department of Health estimated that the costs involved for the taxpayer, in terms of advertising the ban, hiring and training additional enforcement officers, and adapting existing premises, such as restaurant rooms, would be in the region of GBP 2 per capita (*Daily Telegraph*, 2007). However, as in the case of taxes, enforcement costs associated with banning certain forms of consumption may not be trivial. Illegal marketing and consumption of banned commodities may develop, possibly in an organised form, especially when there is strong demand for such commodities and when consumption is addictive. The impact of such activities on society, including the costs involved in countering them, if and when relevant, should be factored into any decisions to ban specific forms of consumption. The social impact of the prohibition of harmful drugs is a stark illustration of the costs involved in this type of regulation.

Summing up

Actions that widen choice or make certain options more accessible are generally well accepted, despite the objections of some critics. These actions include support to technologies that help private self-control, such as offering rewards to those who accept to delay gratification. Opportunities for adopting actions of these types find their main limits in their financial costs, modest overall effect.

Persuasion and other non-price devices such as default rules are often advocated as minimally intrusive interventions, which do not harm rational consumers. However, there are risks involved in relying on governments to deliver persuasion effectively and in the best interest of individuals, and it is difficult to monitor whether governments are able to do this.

Taxes and consumption bans are more transparent and contestable, although they may lead to potentially large welfare losses, because they will hit all consumers indiscriminately, including those who have healthy consumption patterns regardless of the tax or ban. In principle, taxes could be designed in a way that would limit their negative impacts on rational consumers (O'Donoghue and Rabin, 2006), although such approaches, as they currently stand, are not sufficiently developed to allow applications in real world settings. Actions involving higher than minimal degrees of interference with individual choice can be considered more appropriate when the consumption of a commodity is invariably unhealthy and bears a large potential for harm; when the costs of an unhealthy choice is perceived as too great; or when the individual making the choice is perceived as needing more intervention, as in the case of children.

Government policies on diet and physical activity in the OECD area

Governments in the OECD area have taken a broad range of actions in recent years to improve nutrition and physical activity, reacting to a growing concern about increasing obesity rates, particularly in vulnerable population groups. The OECD carried out a survey of national policies in 2007-08. The survey was designed to compile an inventory and develop a taxonomy of policies and initiatives aimed at tackling unhealthy diets and sedentary lifestyles. Further objectives of the survey were to identify similarities and differences between country approaches and factors that may explain them, and to gather any evaluations of the effectiveness and costs of existing policies, which may not be in the public domain.

The survey covered all OECD and EU countries. The primary focus of the survey was central government initiatives, although governments were also invited to report on activities at the regional or local levels, and provide examples of the latter, when relevant. Health ministries were mainly targeted by the survey, but they were invited to share the questionnaire with other relevant ministries as appropriate. The survey involved the collection of major policy statements on diet and physical activity in each country, as well as information on up to ten preventive interventions adopted during the past ten years in the countries concerned. In particular, information was sought on whether important interventions had been monitored or evaluated and, if so, whether there was any evidence on the effects of the interventions on behaviour or health status.

Policy objectives and rationales for government intervention

A large number of OECD governments view the rise of overweight and obesity as a major public health concern. Governments are concerned about the health, social and economic consequences of obesity and about their projected future increases, which are deemed to justify at least certain forms of government intervention. Most governments see it as their responsibility to ensure that the conditions in which individuals lead their lives are conducive to good health and recognise that living and working conditions have changed substantially in recent decades, leading to changes in individual lifestyles and population health. However, in most cases the magnitude of the problem is assessed in fairly general terms. Only in a few instances have governments engaged in detailed evaluations of the health and economic consequences of obesity.

There is a widespread recognition in the government documents examined as part of the survey that individuals need improved knowledge and understanding of the health effects of lifestyle choices in order to be able to handle the environmental influences that have been associated with the growing obesity problem. Governments acknowledge that individuals are often exposed to large amounts of potentially confusing information on health and lifestyles from a variety of sources, and assert that it is primarily their responsibility to act as a balanced and authoritative source of information, thus providing clear guidance to individuals who struggle to cope with increasingly powerful environmental influences. Many governments began to develop nutritional standards and guidelines well before obesity had risen to the top of the health policy agenda, and they are now intensifying their efforts to promote a culture of healthy eating and active living.

A further rationale for intervention which appears from a number of government documents is the higher prevalence of obesity in certain vulnerable groups. It is of particular concern to some governments that disadvantaged socio-economic groups and ethnic minorities appear to take up less healthy lifestyles in increasing proportions, and they appear to be less responsive than other groups to interventions aimed at improving lifestyles. There is a strong and established link between obesity and various dimensions of disadvantage, from unemployment to low income, from poor education to social isolation, and many governments view interventions to tackle obesity as part of their efforts to protect the health of vulnerable groups and prevent the widening of health gaps between population groups positioned at the opposite ends of the social scale.

Virtually all OECD governments have set themselves objectives and targets in tackling overweight and obesity. In some cases, such objectives remain very general and do not commit governments to achieving specific results, even in countries that have developed and implemented comprehensive and detailed programmes. In other cases, governments have chosen to identify measurable objectives in terms of nutrition (e.g. fat, carbohydrate, sugar, salt, dietary fibre, fruit and vegetable intake, mostly with reference to WHO recommendations); physical activity (e.g. proportion of adults engaging in at least 30 minutes of vigorous physical activity per day); or obesity (e.g. halting the progression of obesity rates or reversing it by a certain proportion within a given time frame).

What interventions?

A large majority of the initiatives reported by OECD countries are aimed at improving diets, rather than increasing physical activity. The latter objective is more typically pursued at the local level, particularly through community-based initiatives, although several countries have adopted comprehensive health promotion strategies at the national level that do include actions to increase physical activity. In most cases, interventions are led or co-ordinated by health ministries, although they often involve several government departments (education, agriculture, industry, transport, sport) and are often implemented outside the conventional boundaries of the health sector. These initiatives often involve the development, diffusion and promotion of nutrition guidelines. The most common target group is children and a large number of interventions are school-based, aiming at encouraging healthy lifestyles from early ages.

Figure 5.1. **Interventions in OECD and other EU countries by type**

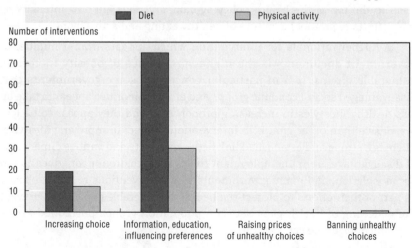

Source: OECD/WHO Europe survey of national policies to tackle unhealthy diets and sedentary lifestyles.

StatLink ⧉ *http://dx.doi.org/10.1787/888932316039*

In relation to the typology of interventions outlined above in this chapter, the policy survey revealed that governments tend to view initiatives that involve the mildest degrees of interference as the most effective on a large scale. No governments reported initiatives in the third group among those they believed had the largest impact, although many OECD governments have been making use of taxes and tax exemptions, particularly in food markets, for some time. No interventions were mentioned in the fourth group either, probably reflecting the

Figure 5.2. **Interventions in OECD and other EU countries by sector**

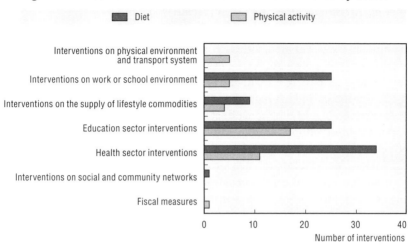

Source: OECD/WHO Europe survey of national policies to tackle unhealthy diets and sedentary lifestyles.

StatLink ᘜᓸ http://dx.doi.org/10.1787/888932316058

consensus that outright bans of specific forms of consumption are unlikely to be appropriate in relation to diet and physical activity.

A large majority of OECD countries have adopted initiatives aimed at school-age children. These entail a variety of measures, often combined for greater impact. Measures include changes in the school environment, sometimes limited to improving school canteen menus, often through re-negotiation of contracts with external caterers. But in many cases they extend to improvements in facilities for physical activity and to changes in the types of food and beverages sold by vending machines and other outlets within schools. Interventions generally involve an educational component as well, entailing the inclusion in school curriculum of health and lifestyle education aimed at improving children's health literacy. It is not uncommon for such initiatives to involve children's families. Additionally, these programmes can be supported by the distribution of discount vouchers or even free food, such as fruit. On the other hand, they rarely involve individualised health checks.

The second most common group of interventions adopted by OECD governments is typically set within the public health function of health systems. These interventions are primarily based on the development and dissemination of nutrition guidelines to a wide variety of population groups, although in some cases they also involve promotion of active transport and active leisure. Accordingly, interventions often make use of a variety of channels to convey health promotion messages, including the mass media, schools, employers, job centres, shops, pharmacies, general practices and other health care facilities, recreation facilities and others.

Regulatory initiatives concerning the market for food products are common in the OECD area, although these have been reported only in a few instances in the policy survey. These include food safety standards, which may be seen as having a relatively limited impact on obesity, but also food labelling schemes and the regulation of nutrition and health claims, which are likely to have a bigger and more direct impact on nutrition choices and obesity. Workplace interventions were also reported in very few instances, probably reflecting the view that employers, and not governments, are primarily responsible for developing such programmes. Finally, a few governments reported interventions on the physical environment (*e.g.* extension of bicycle lanes and green spaces), on the transport system, or partnership with the private sector to improve access to sport and leisure facilities.

In addition to fiscal measures in use in OECD countries (generally omitted from survey responses), at least one country, Japan, and the State of Alabama (United States) have adopted schemes based on financial incentives after the conclusion of the policy survey. The State of Alabama offers a USD 25 health insurance discount to State employees who participate in a wellness programme or show commitment to reduce their levels of risk in relation to BMI, blood pressure cholesterol and glucose. This adds to a similar incentive for non-smokers in the same jurisdiction. In Japan, health insurers have been mandated to screen 56 million people aged 40-74 for the "metabolic syndrome", and to engage those at risk in an effective wellness programme, with financial incentives for its delivery. Incentives of this type have been advocated as a more equitable, and possibly a more effective, alternative to taxes on certain forms of food and beverage consumption, although most existing empirical evidence does not appear to support the claim that financial incentives may contribute to sustainable weight loss (Volpp *et al.*, 2008; Paul-Ebhohimhen and Avenell, 2008; Cawley and Price, 2009).

Private sector responses: Are markets adjusting to the new challenges?

As individuals need to balance energy intake and expenditure in various aspects of their own lives and consumption, the industries in which they are employed and those which supply the commodities they consume can play an important role in helping to prevent overweight and obesity. Industries in which technological innovation and automation of production have more dramatically reduced work-related physical activity may offer incentives and programmes to help employees improve their lifestyles. The sports and exercise industry may provide further opportunities for physical activity during leisure time. The real estate industry may contribute to urban design solutions that facilitate active transport and active leisure opportunities. The food and beverage industry may help consumers maintain a balanced nutrition and an adequate energy supply. The health care industry may provide medical solutions to the problems of overweight and obesity for those cases in which behavioural approaches prove insufficient.

The government documents and statements gathered as part of the OECD policy survey indicate that all governments emphasise the importance of co-operation and partnership with the private sector. A range of stakeholders are mentioned in such documents as natural partners in the development of strategies to improve nutrition and physical activity. However, the precise terms in which such co-operation should take place and the respective roles of the different stakeholders often remain vague.

Business organisations often engage in health promoting production, marketing, and human resource management policies to fulfil the expectations and demands of consumers, government, and society at large. A health and well-being industry has been developing at a very fast pace in recent years, driven by a growing consumer demand. This has provided, for instance, greater opportunities for leisure-time physical activity and healthy nutrition, which may have an impact on obesity. An increased availability and awareness of health-related information, and an increased attention to obesity and its consequences by the mass media, have contributed to changing consumer preferences, to which business organisations have often responded promptly. However, this phenomenon appears to be mostly confined to certain population groups, particularly those with higher levels of education and socio-economic status. More disadvantaged groups continue to display lower levels of leisure-time physical activity (not compensated by work-related physical activity) and less healthy nutrition patterns (Arnade and Gopinath, 2006; Cerin and Leslie, 2008).

A second major force that may lead business organisations to adopt health promoting initiatives and policies is government action, or simply the expectation of government action. Government regulation may produce both direct and indirect effects on markets for health-related commodities, but governments are often reluctant to use regulation because of the complexity of the regulatory process, the enforcement costs involved, and the likelihood to spark a confrontation with the industry. In situations in which an expectation of government regulatory action exists, business organisations may seek to anticipate such actions through self-regulation and co-operation with governments. This has recently been the case, for instance, in the regulation of food advertising to children and in food labelling. In these areas, business organisations have taken initiatives before most governments could implement formal regulatory measures. Industry self-regulation, when pursued within a broader regulatory and monitoring framework set out by, or agreed with governments, presents a number of advantages over government regulation alone, as it may substantially reduce enforcement costs and may avoid conflict with the industry. However, the effectiveness of self-regulation may be hindered when only selected business organisations sign up to the relevant voluntary agreements.

An area of special complexity is product reformulation, especially in the food and beverage industry. In this case, business organisations have to balance consumer demands for taste and convenience with the threats and opportunities involved in different types of government regulation. Demands for taste and convenience may lead to a larger-than-desirable use of certain ingredients which may have negative health consequences, especially if consumed in large quantities, such as salt and sugar for taste, or trans fats for convenience (extended shelf-life). Governments may ban or strictly limit the use of such ingredients, or simply threaten to do this in order to elicit an appropriate response from the industry. However, this form of regulation is not widely applicable in food manufacturing, and governments often prefer to use incentives to encourage business organisations to reformulate less healthy products. Common incentives include those involved in the regulation of nutritional or health claims. Such regulation is often perceived merely as a way to prevent misleading claims but in fact has at least some potential for driving innovation in food manufacturing. Landmark studies by Ippolito and Mathios (1990, 1995, 1996) showed how the decline in fat consumption accelerated, and fibre consumption increased, after the US Food and Drug Administration allowed food manufacturers to make claims about the health benefits of their products in advertising them (in 1985). Regulation can thus generate new market opportunities, which firms are eager to seize by reformulating their products in ways that may justify health claims.

Finally, business organisations may engage in health promoting initiatives to fulfil broader societal expectations, as a form of corporate social responsibility. Societal concerns have increasingly been voiced in recent years by consumer organisations and advocacy groups battling against obesity and unhealthy individual lifestyles. Business organisations, both as employers and as producers and marketers of products and services that have a potential impact on health, have a strong interest in retaining a positive and credible image, particularly when their market success depends crucially on advertising. A number of large employers have therefore taken initiatives to promote healthy lifestyles among their employees, despite limited evidence that such initiatives generate positive returns in terms of reduction of sick leave and higher productivity.

Major players in the food and beverage industry have contributed to health education initiatives or programmes to promote physical activity among children. Coca-Cola and Kraft Foods, for instance, have promoted initiatives such as "Triple Play", an after-school health and wellness programme at Boys and Girls Clubs of America, as well as similar initiatives in various Asian and South American countries. Coca-Cola's "Happy Playtime" initiative reached over 700 schools in 19 Chinese cities. A similar initiative in Brazil, *Prazer de estar bem* was promoted by a group of food and beverage manufacturers in close to 300 schools in the State of São Paulo. Programmes are often run in collaboration with government departments, as the "It's Fun to Be Fit" initiative in the Philippines, or the *Movimiento Bienestar* programmes in a number of Latin American countries. These initiatives likely contribute to brand loyalty and may even increase consumption of the products of the sponsoring firms by those who are exposed to them, although there are instances in which firms grant unbranded sponsorship to events and programmes. There is hardly any independent evidence of what the net effect of these initiatives may be on children's and other people's lifestyles. Some evidence from consumer research shows that listing healthy options, for instance, in restaurant menus, makes indulgent food choices more likely, by triggering a goal-activation mechanism (Wilcox *et al.*, 2009). Whether initiatives like the ones mentioned above, or like the French government's requirement to include positive health messages in adverts of manufactured food products (*e.g.* "for your health, eat at least five portions of fruit and vegetables a day", or "for your health, practice physical activity regularly", see *http://mangerbouger.fr*), might generate a similar effect is not known.

The extent to which the types of initiatives taken within the private sector may have an impact on lifestyles and chronic diseases may partly be gauged from the findings of a micro-simulation modelling exercise presented in the following chapters. However, there is at present very limited empirical evidence that market-based solutions can contribute significantly to containing overweight and obesity. Much of the existing evidence relates to industry compliance with self-regulatory initiatives, consumer awareness and consumer perceptions. It is in the interest of all stakeholders to expand and strengthen the existing evidence-base through new and improved research on how market-based initiatives may reduce exposure to potentially harmful environmental influences and change individual behavioural and consumption patterns in ways that promote healthy lifestyles.

Key messages

- Governments can increase choice by making new healthy options available, or by making existing ones more accessible and affordable.

- Governments can use persuasion, education and information to make healthy options more attractive. These are often advocated as minimally intrusive interventions, but governments may not always deliver persuasion effectively and in the best interest of individuals, and it is difficult to monitor whether they do so.

- Regulation and fiscal measures are more transparent and contestable interventions, although they hit all consumers indiscriminately, may be difficult to organise and enforce and may have regressive effects.

- Interventions that are less intrusive on individual choices tend to have higher costs of delivery. Interventions that are more intrusive have higher political and welfare costs.

- OECD governments have been taking action in the last five to ten years in response to calls by international organisations and pressure by the media and the public health community, but without a strong body of evidence on the effectiveness, efficiency and distributional impact of interventions.

- Governments have been trying to influence diet more than physical activity. The vast majority of interventions has been based on the delivery of health education and health promotion through public health campaigns, the education system and at the workplace.

- The private sector, including employers, the food and beverage industry, the pharmaceutical industry, the sports industry and others, has made a potentially important contribution to tackling unhealthy diets and sedentary lifestyles, often in co-operation with governments and international organisations.

- Evidence of the effectiveness of private sector interventions is still insufficient, but an active collaboration between the public and the private sector will enhance the impact of any prevention strategies and spread the costs involved more widely. Key areas in which governments expect a contribution from the food and beverage industry are: food product reformulation; limitation of marketing activities, particularly to vulnerable groups; transparency and information about food contents.

Bibliography

Abadie, A. and S. Gay (2006), "The Impact of Presumed Consent Legislation on Cadaveric Organ Donation: A Cross-Country Study", *Journal of Health Economics*, Vol. 25, pp. 599-620.

Arnade, C. and M. Gopinath (2006), "The Dynamics of Individuals' Fat Consumption", *American Journal of Agricultural Economics*, Vol. 88, No. 4, pp. 836-850.

Cawley, J. and J.A. Price (2009), "Outcomes in a Programme that Offers Financial Rewards for Weight Loss", NBER Working Paper No. 14987, Cambridge, MA.

Cerin, E. and E. Leslie (2008), "How Socio-Economic Status Contributes to Participation in Leisure-Time Physical Activity", *Social Science and Medicine,* Vol. 66, pp. 2596-2609.

Fogarty, J. (2004), "The Own-Price Elasticity of Alcohol: A Meta-Analysis", Economic Programme Working Papers, University of Western Australia, Crawley.

Gallet, C.A. (2007), "The Demand for Alcohol: A Meta-Analysis of Elasticities", *Australian Journal of Agricultural and Resource Economics*, Vol. 51, pp. 121-135.

Gallet, C.A. and J.A. List (2003), "Cigarette Demand: A Meta-Analysis of Elasticities", *Health Economics*, Vol. 12, No. 10, pp. 821-835.

Ippolito, P. and A.D. Mathios (1990), "Information, Advertising and Health Choices: A Study of the Cereal Market", *RAND Journal of Economics,* Vol. 21, pp. 459-480.

Ippolito, P. and A.D. Mathios (1995), "Information and Advertising: The Case of Fat Consumption in the United States", *American Economic Review,* Vol. 85, No. 2, May.

Ippolito, P. and A.D. Mathios (1996), "Information and Advertising Policy, A Study of Fat and Cholesterol Consumption in the United States, 1977-1990", Bureau of Economics Staff Report, Federal Trade Commission, Washington DC, September.

Kenkel, D.S. (2007), "The Evolution of the Schooling-Smoking Gradient", Paper presented at the Population Association of America 2007 Annual Meeting, 29 March.

Madden, D. (2007), "Tobacco Taxes and Starting and Quitting Smoking: Does the Effect Differ by Education?", *Applied Economics*, Vol. 39, No. 4-6, pp. 613-627.

O'Donoghue, T. and M. Rabin (2006), "Optimal Sin Taxes", *Journal of Public Economics,* Vol. 90, pp. 1825-1849.

Paul-Ebhohimhen, V. and A. Avenell (2008), "Systematic Review of the Use of Financial Incentives in Treatments for Obesity and Overweight", *Obesity Reviews*, Vol. 9, pp. 355-367.

Sunstein, C.R. and R.H. Thaler (2003), "Libertarian Paternalism is Not an Oxymoron", *University of Chicago Law Review*, Vol. 70, No. 4, pp. 1159-1202.

Townsend, J., P. Roderick and J. Cooper (1994), "Cigarette Smoking by Socioeconomic Group, Sex, and Age: Effects of Price, Income, and Health Publicity", *British Medical Journal*, Vol. 309, No. 6959, pp. 923-927.

Volpp, K.G., L.K. John, A.B. Troxel, L. Norton, J. Fassbender and G. Lowenstein (2008), "Financial Incentive-Based Approaches for Weight Loss: A Randomized Trial", *JAMA*, Vol. 300, No. 22, pp. 2631-2637.

Wilcox, K., B. Vallen, L. Block and G.J. Fitzsimons (2009), "Vicarious Goal Fulfillment: When the Mere Presence of a Healthy Option Leads to an Ironically Indulgent Decision", *Journal of Consumer Research*, Vol. 36, No. 3, pp. 380-393.

Special Focus IV.
Community Interventions for the Prevention of Obesity

by

Francesco Branca, World Health Organisation

in collaboration with Vasiliki Kolovou Delonas,
University of Warwick, and Trudy Wijnhoven,
World Health Organisation, Regional Office for Europe

Community interventions: Why, who, what and where?

Community settings offer a unique set of opportunities to reach various individuals and groups at the local level (WHO, 2007) and are a necessary complement to the implementation of high-profile, macro-level policies. Members of a community share cultural or ethnic backgrounds and are exposed to the same environmental determinants. The rationale of acting at the local level is its capacity to facilitate cross-sector efforts (King and Gill, 2009). Within a community, there is a potential to mobilise human resources such that different dynamics and synergies translate into better possibilities to "partner, collaborate, expand and enrich" an intervention (Economos and Irish-Hauser, 2007). This is particularly important given that increased and effective engagement of stakeholders enhances the prospects of a successful implementation of interventions aimed at changing lifestyles (WHO, 2007; King and Gill, 2009).

Most community programmes have been designed to target children and have used schools as an entry point. Others have targeted lower income groups (see the examples from Wales and Germany below) or groups prone to become sedentary (as in the Dutch example).

Community interventions typically entail a variety of measures addressing the supply of, and demand for, food as well as physical activity.

Interventions are implemented in a combination of local settings apart from schools, including workplaces, communal sites, religious and cultural centres, health and social care facilities or neighbourhoods. They may target all the population or only selected groups, such as children, housewives, pregnant women, the disabled, high-risk groups such as diabetics, the elderly, families, and socially disadvantaged groups.

Community interventions in the OECD area

Community interventions addressing lifestyle were first designed in the 1970s to address non-communicable diseases. The "North Karelia Project" in Eastern Finland (Puska *et al.*, 1989; Vartiainen *et al.*, 2009) and the "Stanford Three Community Study" in the United States (Fortmann *et al.*, 1981) illustrated the great potential of community interventions to reduce lifestyle risk factors. Typically interventions include a combination of actions addressing both demand and supply. For example, "Heart Health Nova Scotia" (Nova Scotia Heart Health Program, 1993), implemented in 1989-95 as part of the Canadian Heart Health Initiative, included a retail point-of-purchase demonstration project; a campaign promoting the consumption of lower fat breakfasts, a continuing education programme for chefs, and consumer-friendly nutrition labelling.

A new generation of community interventions has recently been designed to address the challenge of obesity.

- *Europe*. In 2006, the European Charter on counteracting obesity was signed by the health ministers of European countries. It stressed the need for action against obesity to be taken at both macro and micro level and in different settings (WHO, 2006). In view of this commitment, international and national policies (macro level) should be complemented by activities and initiatives at the community level (micro level). Interventions should include as many components and address as many areas of daily activity simultaneously in order to facilitate healthy options and create healthy instead of so-called "obesogenic" environments (Lemmens *et al.*, 2008).

  The "Shape Up" project (*www.shapeupeurope.net*) was implemented in 21 European cities in 2006-08 to promote healthy lifestyles through school and community.

  - The healthy eating component involved increased nutritional quality and variety of food available in school canteens; parental awareness about the links between healthy eating, learning and prevention; as well as better access to healthy food in the school neighbourhood.

  - The physical activity component involved increased number, attractiveness and variety of possibilities for physical activity, information and skills in schools; parental awareness of mobility patterns and health; changed family patterns in terms of mobility/bringing children to school; and increased number, attractiveness and variety of possibilities for physical activity provided by the environment surrounding the school, creating more possibilities for active mobility.

- *United Kingdom.* The Department of Health has established a Childhood Obesity National Support Team to provide support to local partnerships in achieving the Government's key deliverables for childhood obesity. The team is meant to help local authorities, primary care trusts and other partners to improve their capacities to address the obesity agenda. They provide recommendations on data and needs assessment, on evaluation/ performance management, on how to establish and run preventive activities aimed at very young and school-age children, on weight management programmes, on working with families, the built environment, training and workforce development, and communication.

- *Wales.* "Food Coops" started in 2004 and involved 26 sustainable food co-operatives to promote consumption of fruits and vegetables among low socio-economic status groups. The programme allows the purchase of fresh fruit and vegetables at wholesale prices through direct supply by local farmers.

- *France.* Municipalities can receive the national government's "Healthy Cities" label if they conform with the *Plan National Nutrition et Santé*. This can be accomplished by implementing a range of interventions, including: activities aimed at improving the nutrition of infants and young children (information and education, monitoring); improving the situation in schools (better catering, fruit distribution, water fountains, education about nutrition, physical education); improving the possibilities for physical activity (active transport, sports events, support to sport associations); aid for socially deprived groups (support to the structures and the staff providing food aid, information and promotion of physical education); support for elderly people (cooking classes, access to physical activity, social networking); actions aimed at economic agents (bakers, fruit and vegetable distributors, retailers, workplaces, public catering, information for operators); communication to the public (nutrition information in public documents and through public channels, public events). Currently 195 cities have adhered, for a total of approximately 10 million people.

- *Iceland.* "Everything Affects Us, Especially Ourselves" was started in 2005 in 25 municipalities to promote healthy lifestyles of children and their families by emphasising increased physical activity and improved diet.

- *Netherlands.* "Communities on the Move" was established by the Netherlands Institute for Sports and Physical Activity (*www.communities*

inbeweging.nisb.nl/cat). It has developed a community approach to promoting an active lifestyle among groups that tend to become more sedentary through active participation of the target group in the organisation, the execution and the atmosphere of the activity and through the introduction of the element of enjoyment.

- *Finland.* "Fit for Life" (*www.likes.fi*) encourages people over 40 years of age to include physical activity in their daily lives. It is implemented in co-operation with municipal sports and health services, workplaces, occupational health care, sports clubs, various associations and public health organisations.

- *Spain.* In the "Exercise Looks after You" project in Extremadura, (*www.ejerciciotecuida.es*) general practitioners refer elderly people with a risk of metabolic syndrome or moderate depression to a sports centre, where professionals periodically assess participants (with fitness, psychosocial and biological tests) and deliver a structured, walk-based programme four days a week. Preliminary results showed the cost-effectiveness of the programme based on a reduction in primary care consultations and improvements in fitness and health-related quality of life.

- *Germany.* The "BIG" project (*Bewegung als Investition in Gesundheit*, "Movement as Investment for Health") targeted women of low socio-economic status or minority background in the city of Erlangen (2005-07). The sports administration was responsible for organising the local activities, promoting networking among the different settings and providing contact and information for other municipal branches.

- *Australia.* "Eat Well Be Active Community Program" (Wilson, 2009) worked in partnership with a variety of sectors such as health, education, welfare, neighbourhoods and food supply by addressing both environmental and individual barriers to healthy eating and physical activity in schools and the community.

Evaluating community interventions

A systematic review of interventions for preventing obesity in children (Summerbell *et al.*, 2005) highlighted the paradox that only a limited number of studies provide findings on what works, despite the recognition that obesity is a priority for public health. The clinical trial philosophy of randomised controlled trials is not ideal to appraise community interventions, as it would miss important aspects such as the intervention-context interaction. One possibility to capture such insights is the ecological approach, which seeks to preserve and manage resources such as people, settings and events and encompass the notion of context (Hawe and Riley, 2005; McLaren and Hawe, 2005).

Knowledge coming from unsuccessful interventions fails to make a distinction between the evaluation process and the intervention's concept itself, whereas the restricted generalisability (external validity) and transferability of the results should be stressed (Rychetnik *et al.*, 2002).

As an alternative, observational epidemiological methods such as non-randomised trials, prospective and retrospective cohort studies and case-control studies could also be used (Black, 1996).

Results of community interventions

There are however important experiences that indicate the value of community projects for the control of obesity. In Europe, the EPODE project, which has been implemented in several European countries since 2004 and which involves multiple local stakeholders, has shown a reduction of the prevalence of being overweight or obese (Westley, 2007; Katan, 2009; Romon *et al.*, 2009). Similarly, the "Programme for Nutrition, Prevention and Health of Children and Adolescents" implemented in 2004 in the Aquitaine region of France indicated decreased the prevalence of being overweight among 6-year-old children in Bordeaux (Baine, 2009).

A 2009 WHO review of 65 community interventions addressing diet and physical activity (20 focusing on disadvantaged communities and three from low- or middle-income countries) indicated that "the most successful community interventions generally comprised many different activities and usually included both diet and physical activity components", although information on cost-effectiveness is not available (WHO, 2009). An explicit obesity reduction target has not always been formulated.

Data will be soon available from the "Pacific OPIC" Project (Obesity Prevention in Communities) (Swinburn *et al.*, 2007; Schultz *et al.*, 2007), a comprehensive, community-based intervention comprising programmes, events, social marketing and environmental change involving over 14 000 youth in Fiji, Tonga, New Zealand, and Australia; and from the Stanford GEMS (Girls Health Enrichment Multi-site Studies) (Robinson *et al.*, 2008). GEMS addressed low-income, pre-adolescent African-American girls and compared a culturally tailored after-school intervention and a home/family-based intervention to reduce screen media use with an information-based community health education programme.

Designing community interventions

Existing community interventions indicate that comprehensive interventions are preferable and should include a combination of actions to address the offer and the demand of food and action to address the demand and offer of physical activity.

In 2009, the US Institute of Medicine (Parker *et al*., 2009) carried out an analysis at the community level and identified a series of potentially effective actions to promote healthy eating and to increase physical activity. The list of measures aimed to improve diet includes:

- Increase community access to healthy foods through supermarkets, grocery stores, and convenience/corner stores.
- Improve the availability and identification of healthful foods in restaurants.
- Promote efforts to provide fruits and vegetables in a variety of settings, such as farmers' markets, farm stands, mobile markets, community gardens, and youth focused gardens.
- Ensure that publicly run entities such as after-school programmes, child care facilities, recreation centres, and local government worksites implement policies and practices to promote healthy foods and beverages and reduce or eliminate the availability of calorie-dense, nutrient-poor foods.
- Increase participation in federal, state, and local government nutrition assistance programmes.
- Encourage breastfeeding and promote breastfeeding-friendly communities.
- Increase access to free, safe drinking water in public places to encourage consumption of water instead of sugar-sweetened beverages.
- Implement fiscal policies and local ordinances that discourage the consumption of calorie-dense, nutrient-poor foods and beverages.
- Promote media and social marketing campaigns on healthy eating and childhood obesity prevention.

A similar list for the promotion of physical activity includes:

- Encourage walking and bicycling for transportation and recreation through improvements in the built environment.
- Promote programmes that support walking and bicycling for transportation and recreation.
- Promote other forms of recreational physical activity.
- Promote policies that build physical activity into daily routines.
- Promote policies that reduce sedentary screen time.
- Develop a social marketing campaign that emphasizes the multiple benefits for children and families of sustained physical activity.

Apart from the limited evidence on what works in programmes for public health there is the inherent complexity of selecting among the interventions that work. The ANGELO framework (Analysis Grid for Environments Linked to Obesity) was developed in Australia to guide the process of prioritising actions for obesity prevention within communities. ANGELO distinguishes the size (micro: settings, macro: sectors) and the type (physical, economic, political and sociocultural) of environment; analyses the "obesogenic" influences within a sector or setting; and allows possible actions among a portfolio of different actions to be identified and prioritised (Swinburn *et al.*, 1999; Simmons *et al.*, 2009).

The evaluation system, apart from assessing the objectives of the project with clear process, output and outcome indicators (WHO, 2008), should also explore the specific context of the setting in which the intervention is applied.

Conclusion: Involving stakeholders

The effective involvement of the right stakeholders is crucial (WHO, 2007; Flynn *et al.*, 2006). Different sectors of national and local government, local leaders, local councils, sport associations, parent-teacher associations, and clubs, NGOs, academics, the media and the private sector need to be implicated and involved in different forms of dialogue and partnerships. The establishment of a good governance mechanism is central, as well as effective channels of communication stakeholders.

Stakeholders can commit human and financial resources to the project, as well as establish or review their practices to comply with the project objectives. Community interventions are supported by public funds (national or local), as well as by charities and other private sources, including corporate sponsorships. Whenever this happens it is important to emphasize the need for transparency, public disclosure and strict ethical rules, especially when the funding is accepted from private sources that might have a conflict of interest with the project objectives.

Bibliography

Baine, M., S. Maurice-Tison and H. Thibault (2009), "Enquête : Habitudes alimentaires, mode de vie et prévalence de l'obésité en grande section de maternelle", available at *www.nutritionenfantaquitaine.fr/PNNS/enquetes/2009/Rapport_-GS_2007-2008.pdf*, accessed 30 June 2010.

Black, N. (1996), "Why We Need Observational Studies to Evaluate the Effectiveness of Health Care", *British Medical Journal*, Vol. 312, No. 7040, pp. 1215-1218, 11 May.

Economos, C.D. and S. Irish-Hauser (2007), "Community Interventions: A Brief Overview and their Application to the Obesity Epidemic", *J. Law Med. Ethics*, Vol. 35, No. 1, pp. 131-137.

Flynn, M.A.T., D.A. Mcneil, B. Maloff, D. Mutasingwa, M. Wu, C. Ford and S.C. Tough (2006), "Reducing Obesity and Related Chronic Disease Risk in Children and Youth:

A Synthesis of Evidence with 'Best Practice' Recommendations", *Obesity Reviews*, Vol. 7, pp. 7-66, February.

Fortmann, S.P., P.T. Williams, S.B. Hulley, W.L. Haskell, J.W. Farquhar (1981), "Effect of Health Education on Dietary Behavior: The Stanford Three Community Study", *Am. J. Clin. Nutr.*, Vol. 34, No. 10, pp. 2030-2038, October.

Hawe, P. and T. Riley (2005), "Ecological Theory in Practice: Illustrations from a Community-Based Intervention to Promote the Health of Recent Mothers", *Prev. Sci.*, Vol. 6, No. 3, pp. 227-236, September.

Katan, M.B. (2009), "Weight-Loss Diets for the Prevention and Treatment of Obesity", *N. Engl. J. Med.*, Vol. 360, No. 9, pp. 923-925, 26 February.

Lemmens, V.E., A. Oenema, K.I. Klepp, H.B. Henriksen and J. Brug (2008), "A Systematic Review of the Evidence Regarding Efficacy of Obesity Prevention Interventions among Adults", *Obes. Rev.*, Vol. 9, No. 5, pp. 446-455, September.

Lynn Parker, A., C. Burns and E. Sanchez (eds.), (2009), *Local Government Actions to Prevent Childhood Obesity*, Committee on Childhood Obesity Prevention Actions for Local Governments, Institute of Medicine, National Research Council.

McLaren, L. and P. Hawe (2005), "Ecological Perspectives in Health Research", *J. Epidemiol. Community Health*, Vol. 59, No. 1, pp. 6-14, January.

Nova Scotia Heart Health Program (1993), *Report of the Nova Scotia Nutrition Survey*, Nova Scotia Department of Health, Health and Welfare Canada, Halifax, N.S., Canada.

Puska, P., J. Tuomilehto, A. Nissinen, J.T. Salonen, E. Vartiainen, P. Pietinen, K. Koskela and H.J. Korhonen (1989), "The North Karelia Project: 15 Years of Community-Based Prevention of Coronary Heart Disease", *Ann. Med.*, Vol. 21, No. 3, pp. 169-173, June.

Robinson, T.N., H.C. Kraemer, D.M. Matheson, E. Obarzanek, D.M. Wilson, W.L. Haskell, L.A. Pruitt, N.S. Thompson, K.F. Haydel, M. Fujimoto, A. Varady, S. McCarthy, C. Watanabe and J.D. Killen (2008), "Stanford GEMS Phase 2 Obesity Prevention Trial for Low-Income African-American Girls: Design and Sample Baseline Characteristics", *Contemp. Clin. Trials*, Vol. 29, No. 1, pp. 56-69, January.

Romon, M., A. Lommez, M. Tafflet, A. Basdevant, J.M. Oppert, J.L. Bresson, P. Ducimetiere, M.A. Charles, J.M. Borys (2009), "Downward Trends in the Prevalence of Childhood Overweight in the Setting of 12-year School- and Community-Based Programmes", *Public Health Nutr.*, Vol. 12, No. 10, pp. 1735-1742, October.

Rychetnik, L., M. Frommer, P. Hawe and A. Shiell (2002), "Criteria for Evaluating Evidence on Public Health Interventions", *J. Epidemiol. Community Health*, Vol. 56, No. 2, pp. 119-127, February.

Schultz, J., J. Utter, L. Mathews, T. Cama, H. Mavoa and B. Swinburn (2007), "The Pacific OPIC Project (Obesity Prevention in Communities): Action Plans and Interventions", *Pac Health Dialog*, Vol. 14, No. 2, pp. 147-153, September.

Simmons, A., H.M. Mavoa, A.C. Bell, M. de Courten, D. Schaaf, J. Schultz and B.A. Swinburn (2009), "Creating Community Action Plans for Obesity Prevention Using the ANGELO (Analysis Grid for Elements Linked to Obesity) Framework", *Health Promot. Int.*, Vol. 24, No. 4, pp. 311-324, December.

Summerbell, C.D., E. Waters, L.D. Edmunds, S. Kelly, T. Brown and K.J. Campbell (2005), "Interventions for Preventing Obesity in Children", *Cochrane Database of Systematic Reviews*, Vol. 3.

Swinburn, B., G. Egger and F. Raza (1999), "Dissecting Obesogenic Environments: The Development and Application of a Framework for Identifying and Prioritizing Environmental Interventions for Obesity", *Prev. Med.*, Vol. 29, No. 6, Pt 1, pp. 563-570, December.

Swinburn, B., J. Pryor, M. McCabe, R. Carter, M. de Courten, D. Schaaf and R. Scragg (2007), "The Pacific OPIC Project (Obesity Prevention in Communities) – Objectives and Designs", *Pac Health Dialog*, Vol. 14, No. 2, pp. 139-146, September.

Vartiainen, E., T. Laatikainen, M. Peltonen, A. Juolevi, S. Mannisto, J. Sundvall, P. Jousilahti, V. Salomaa, L. Valsta and P. Puska (2009), "Thirty-Five-Year Trends in Cardiovascular Risk Factors in Finland", *Int. J. Epidemiol.*, 3 December.

Westley, H. (2007), "Thin Living", *British Medical Journal*, Vol. 335, No. 7632, pp. 1236-1237, 15 December.

WHO (2006), *European Charter on Counteracting Obesity*, World Health Organisation, Istanbul.

WHO (2007), *The Challenge of Obesity in the WHO European Region and the Strategies for Response*, WHO Regional Office for Europe, Copenhagen.

WHO (2008), *WHO Global Strategy on Diet, Physical Activity and Health: A Framework to Monitor and Evaluate Implementation*, World Health Organisation, Geneva.

Wilson, A.M., A.M. Magarey, J. Dollman, M. Jones and N. Mastersson (2009), "The Challenges of Quantitative Evaluation of a Multi-Setting, Multi-Strategy Community-Based Childhood Obesity Prevention Programme: Lessons Learnt from the Eat Well Be Active Community Programs in South Australia", *Public Health Nutr.*, Vol. 13, pp. 1-9, October.

Chapter 6

The Impact of Interventions

Governments in OECD countries have intervened in a variety of ways to improve diets, increase physical activity and tackle obesity in recent years. The preventive interventions assessed in this analysis are drawn from the most commonly used approaches, including: health education and health promotion (mass media campaigns, school-based interventions, worksite interventions); regulation and fiscal measures (fiscal measures altering the prices of healthy and unhealthy foods, regulation of food advertising to children and mandatory nutrition labelling); and, counselling of individuals at risk in primary care. This chapter examines the characteristics, the costs and the relative success of each approach in improving health outcomes and social disparities in health, with a focus on five OECD countries: Canada, England, Italy, Japan and Mexico.

What interventions really work?

Governments in OECD countries have considered or implemented numerous interventions to improve diets, increase physical activity and tackle obesity in recent years (see Chapter 5 for a full discussion). Building on reviews[1] by WHO and OECD, it has been possible to identify a relatively small but important evidence base on the impact of nine different health interventions on individual health-related behaviours, obesity and other risk factors for chronic diseases. The nine interventions, listed below within three main groups, formed the object of an economic analysis undertaken by the OECD to assess the cost-effectiveness and the distributional impacts of different means of preventing chronic diseases, based on a mathematical model jointly developed with the WHO (Sassi et al., 2009).

Health education and health promotion interventions	Regulation and fiscal measures	Primary-care based interventions
Mass media campaigns	Fiscal measures altering the prices of fruit and vegetables and foods high in fat	Physician counselling of individuals at risk
School-based interventions	Government regulation or industry self-regulation of food advertising to children	Intensive physician and dietician counselling of individuals at risk
Worksite interventions	Compulsory food labelling	

The quality and quantity of the evidence available for different interventions vary widely,[2] but mathematical models like the OECD/WHO one can be used to combine multiple sources of evidence to make up for the limitations of individual sources.

The OECD/WHO analysis relies on the existing effectiveness evidence to identify possible key characteristics of the nine interventions. Therefore, the interventions considered here reflect the characteristics of those assessed in existing experimental and observational studies, and not necessarily those of interventions which specific countries may have adopted or which countries may be considering to adopt. Interventions may be designed and implemented in a variety of ways, and the evidence presented in this chapter should serve as a guide to policy makers as to what impact may be expected.

The preventive interventions assessed in the analysis reflect a wide variety of approaches and are based in diverse settings. The costs associated with those interventions may arise in different jurisdictions. Some of the costs are typically paid through public expenditure (*e.g.* the costs associated with regulatory measures), others typically not (*e.g.* most of the costs associated with worksite interventions). Some of the costs arise within the health sector, others arise within other sectors of government intervention (*e.g.* most of the costs associated with school-based interventions). Only public sector costs are accounted for in the analysis, while costs borne by the private sector are excluded. All costs are reported in US dollar Purchasing Power Parities (USD PPPs), with 2005 the chosen base year, a unit that is commonly used to account for differences in purchasing power across countries.

The analysis focuses on five OECD countries: Canada, England, Italy, Japan and Mexico. These reflect a wide geographical spread, as well as markedly different epidemiological characteristics in terms of risk factors and chronic diseases. This group includes countries with some of the highest rates of obesity in the OECD area, such as Mexico and England, as well as the country with the lowest rate, Japan, with Italy and Canada faring, respectively, in the lower and upper sections of the ranking (as shown in Chapter 2, Figure 2.1).

Health education and health promotion interventions

We consider three types of health education and health promotion interventions, targeting different populations. The first is a campaign run through the mass media, designed to deliver health promotion messages to the adult population. The second intervention targets children within schools, while the third targets working age adults who are employed by large firms through a series on initiatives run at the workplace.

Exploiting the power of the media

The mass media can reach vast audiences rapidly and directly. Health promotion campaigns broadcast by radio and television may raise awareness of health issues and increase health information and knowledge in a large part of the population.

The campaign is assumed to be broadcast on television and radio channels at the national and local levels, and to follow a two year pattern alternating six months of intensive broadcasting with three months of less intensive broadcasting. During the more intensive phases television and radio channels broadcast 30 second advertisements six times a day, seven days a week. In the less intensive phases they broadcast 15 second advertisements three times a day, seven days a week. Advertisements contain messages both on diet and physical activity. Broadcast messages are associated with the distribution of printed material, both of which are assumed to reach 10% of households.

Targeting children

School enrolment is nearly universal in the OECD area at younger ages; therefore, schools provide the means for reaching a large audience of children from all backgrounds. Additionally, food preferences are formed during childhood and helping children to develop a taste for healthier foods may have an effect on their diets persisting into their adult life.

The intervention targets all children attending school in the age group 8-9, but it is assumed that just above 60% of children will fully participate in the activities which form part of the intervention.

The intervention entails the integration of health education into the existing school curriculum with support from indirect education and minor environmental changes such as healthier food choices in cafeterias. The main component is represented by an additional 30 hours per school year (about one hour per week) of health education focused on the benefits of a healthy diet and an active lifestyle. This is associated with an opening lecture held by a guest speaker, and further activities during ordinary teaching hours (*e.g.* science) with the support of school nurses. Indirect education consists of the distribution of brochures or posters, while environmental changes are pursued by re-negotiating food service contracts and re-training of staff.

Healthy workplaces

Working adults spend a large part of their time at the workplace, where they are exposed to a number of factors that may influence their lifestyles and health habits. Existing evidence suggests that health education, peer pressure, and changes in the work environment contribute to changing lifestyles and preventing certain chronic diseases.

The intervention targets individuals between the ages of 18 and 65 working for companies with at least 50 employees. It is assumed that 50% of employers, and 45% of their employees, will participate in the programme.

The intervention involves an introductory lecture by a guest speaker and a series of 20 minute group sessions with a nutritionist every two weeks for 20 months. Messages are reinforced by the distribution of information materials and posters in common areas and cafeterias. Other activities are co-ordinated by volunteers who also act as peer educators and organise "walk-clubs" or similar initiatives. As part of the intervention, catering staff are re-trained to prepare healthy dishes and food service contracts are re-negotiated.

Box 6.1. **Health education and health promotion**

Mass media campaigns

Main sources of evidence. Intervention characteristics and effectiveness are modelled on the basis of a selection of studies selected from a broader literature (Dixon *et al.*, 1998; Foerster *et al.*, 1995; Craig *et al.*, 2007).

Effects of the intervention. The intervention will increase consumption of fruit and vegetables by an average of slightly more than 18 grams per day, and it will increase the proportion of the population undertaking adequate levels of physical activity by approximately 2.35%.

Intervention costs. The estimated cost of per capita of a mass media campaign ranges between USD PPPs 0.5 and 2 in the five countries examined. Almost two-thirds of this cost is spent in broadcasting advertisements on national and local radio and television channels and on producing and distributing flyers and leaflets. The remaining resources are mainly devoted to hiring personnel to design, run and supervise the programme. We assume that public health specialists are involved in designing the prevention programme. Planning and administration costs are spread over a large target population.

School-based interventions

Main sources of evidence. Intervention characteristics and effectiveness are modelled on the basis of a selection of studies selected from a broader literature (Gortmaker *et al.*, 1999; Luepker *et al.*, 1998; Perry *et al.*, 1998; Reynolds *et al.*, 2000).

Effects of the intervention. The intervention will modify distal risk factors, particularly by increasing the intake of fruit and vegetables by almost 38 grams per day during the course of the intervention and by decreasing the proportion of energy intake from fats of nearly 2%. The BMI of children exposed to the intervention will be reduced by 0.2 points. The analysis is based on the assumption that children will enjoy the benefits of the intervention throughout the course of their lives, although dietary changes will be reduced after exposure to the programme ceases.

Intervention costs. The estimated cost per capita of a school-based intervention ranges between one and two USD PPPs in the five countries examined. About half of this is spent in programme organisation costs, while the remaining half is split between training of teachers and food service staff, extra teaching and additional curricular activities, *e.g.* guest speakers, brochures, books, posters and equipment. The single most expensive item is extra teaching hours. Costs do not include changes in food service contracts, vouchers/coupons from sponsors and school nurse time.

> ### Box 6.1. **Health education and health promotion** (*cont.*)
>
> **Worksite interventions**
>
> *Main sources of evidence.* Intervention characteristics and effectiveness are based on evidence provided in Sorensen *et al.* (1996; 1998; 1999), Emmons *et al.* (1999) and Buller *et al.* (1999).
>
> *Effects of the intervention.* The intervention will increase the consumption of fruit and vegetables by an average of almost 46 grams per day and the proportion of physically active employees by 12%. It will also decrease the proportion of total energy intake from fats by over 2%. Employees exposed to the intervention will have their BMI reduced by, on average, half a point.
>
> *Intervention costs.* The estimated cost of per capita of a national worksite intervention ranges between USD PPPs 2.5 and 5.5 in the five countries examined. Organisation and training of peer-educators and food service staff account for less than one-tenth of these costs, while the largest component is represented by seminar organisation and nutritionist fees. Other costs include information materials and a guest speaker. Although the intervention is delivered by employers, its costs are assumed to be fully subsidised by the public sector. The costs involved in re-negotiating food service contracts or accessory measures (*e.g.* installation of bicycle racks) were not included in the analysis.

Regulation and fiscal measures

Governments may pull different regulatory and fiscal levers in their fight against obesity. We consider three types of interventions in this category. The first is a broadly defined set of fiscal measures combining initiatives to alter the relative prices of different types of foods. The second intervention involves the regulation of food advertising to children, which may also be designed as a self-regulation intervention driven by the food and beverage industry. Finally, we consider the introduction of compulsory nutritional labelling of foods.

Using fiscal levers to change people's diets

Fiscal incentives can directly affect consumption behaviours, and therefore influence lifestyle choices. Taxes, tax exemptions and subsidies are widely used in agriculture and food markets in the OECD area. Differential taxation of food products is relatively common. Sales taxes, or value added taxes, are often applied at different rates to different types of food. In many countries most foods are exempt, or subject to a reduced rate taxation, but certain foods are often subject to higher rates, particularly manufactured foods, or foods containing larger amounts of certain ingredients, such as sugar. Food taxes are often viewed as not particularly effective in changing patterns of food consumption, but several studies suggest that they can have an impact on both consumption of unhealthy foods and people's weight, although evidence of the latter is weaker (Powell and Chaloupka, 2009). Fiscal measures may be complex to design and enforce, and their impacts may be somewhat unpredictable as the price elasticity of lifestyle commodities varies across individuals and population groups, and substitution effects are not always obvious. However, the demand for foods which might be subjected to taxation in the pursuit of health objectives is generally inelastic. As discussed in Sassi and Hurst (2008), this is associated with more limited substitution. Rather, individuals end up consuming less of the taxed commodity while at the same time spending more of their income on that same commodity, which may also displace other forms of consumption to a certain degree. The combined use of taxes and subsidies on different types of foods whose demand is similarly inelastic may neutralise such displacement effect, although empirical evidence of the effects of similar combined measures is lacking at present. Fiscal measures also have potentially large re-distributive effects, which are mostly dependent upon existing differences in price elasticities between socio-economic groups, overall consumption of the foods targeted by fiscal measures, and cross-elasticities between the demand for these and for other foods. Income distribution effects are not explicitly addressed in the analyses reported in this chapter.

Taxes and subsidies typically affect all consumers. The intervention assessed in the analysis involves fiscal measures that will both increase the price of foods with a high fat content (e.g. many dairy products) by 10% and will decrease the price of fruit and vegetables in the same proportion. No assumptions are made as to what specific measures should be taken to achieve those price changes.

In modelling our "fiscal measures" intervention, we deliberately avoided to specify the detailed nature of the measures that governments may wish to use to cause a rise in the prices of foods high in fat and a fall in the prices of fruit and vegetables. Therefore, we only expect our estimates of the costs associated with the intervention to reflect a realistic average across a range of possible options.

Interventions to influence food prices might rely on the infrastructure of existing agricultural policies. The overall cost of agricultural policies may be high, but the additional administrative cost of incremental measures to influence the prices of selected foods is likely to be substantially lower. Alternatively, the prices of foods high in fat may be raised by imposing indirect taxes. If our modelling assumptions were applied to household expenditure data from the United Kingdom (Expenditure and Food Survey, 2007) it could be roughly estimated that a tax on foods high in fat leading to a 10% price increase and eliciting a 2% reduction in consumption would yield revenues in the region of USD PPPs 1 billion in the United Kingdom, while the estimated administrative cost of the tax, based on our modelling assumptions, would be up to USD PPPs 16.8 million, or 1.6% of the total revenue yield of the tax.

Protecting children from food advertising

Heavy marketing of fast food and energy-dense food is regarded as a potential causal factor in weight gain and obesity, particularly because of its impact on dietary habits in children and teenagers. Most advertising explicitly directed to children is broadcast on television. Some countries have already taken formal regulatory steps to limit food advertising to children. Furthermore, major international players in the food industry are adopting forms of self-regulation, which may be viewed as an alternative, or a complement, to government regulation.

The intervention is targeted to children between the ages of 2 and 18. The intervention is intended to limit children's exposure to food advertising on television, particularly in programmes primarily aimed at children and during times of the day when a large proportion of the audience is made up by children in the above age group. Two versions of the intervention were assessed in the analysis: the first involving formal government regulation introduced by law and enforced by communication authorities; the second involving self-regulation by the food industry and broadcasters, with the government acting only in a monitoring and supervisory role.

Informing consumers on food nutritional contents

Disclosure of the nutritional characteristics of food sold in stores through labels reporting easy-to-read "nutrition facts" helps consumers choose healthier diets and may provide strong incentives for food manufacturers to decrease serving size and reformulate packaged food with healthier nutrients.

Although the intervention is intended to affect all consumers, empirical evidence suggests that only about two-thirds of store customers actively read labels. The intervention entails the adoption of a mandatory food labelling scheme for food sold in stores. Labels will deliver information about nutrient contents and serving size. Retailers will post information about how to read labels and about the benefits of a healthy diet. The intervention does not involve other forms of communication. The accuracy of the information reported on labels is verified through an extensive programme of food inspection.

Counselling individuals at-risk in primary care

In many OECD countries most citizens have a primary care physician who acts as their first point of contact with the health service and as a usual source of primary health care. Primary care physicians are also an important source

---

Box 6.2. **Regulation and fiscal measures**

Fiscal measures

Main sources of evidence. We modelled the effects of fiscal interventions only through changes in consumption of fat and fruit and vegetables, based on some of the most conservative estimates of the price elasticity of demand for foods high in fat and for fruit and vegetables, among the nine studies reviewed in a recent French Government report (Hespel and Berthod-Wurmser, 2008).

Effects of the intervention. A 10% change in price will produce, on average, a 2% change in consumption in the opposite direction. Depending on the baseline levels of consumption in the countries concerned, the above price change will generate increases of between 4 and 11 grams of fruit and vegetable consumption per day, on average, and reductions in the proportion of total energy intake from fats between 0.58% and 0.76%. Price elasticity is assumed equal across population groups, which may slightly overestimate the responsiveness of low income groups to changes in the prices of fruit and vegetables, and correspondingly underestimate the responsiveness of high-income groups.

Intervention costs. The estimated cost of per capita of fiscal measures ranges between USD PPPs 0.03 and 0.13 in the five countries examined. We modelled the costs of fiscal measures to include basic administration, planning, monitoring and enforcement at the national level. The latter, in particular, accounts for most of the cost. Potential revenues from the tax, as well as expenditures originating from the subsidy, are not accounted for in the analysis, as they represent transfers rather than costs. Tax operating costs, also not included in the analysis, may be driven by a broad range of factors (associated with the nature of the tax base or with characteristics of the tax) which makes it difficult to generalise existing estimates to new taxes or settings. A review of studies up to 2003 concluded that "studies that do address administrative costs suggest that they rarely exceed 1% of the revenue yield, and more usually come in well below 1%" (Evans, 2003).

Regulation of food advertising to children

Main sources of evidence. The effects of children's exposure to (fast) food advertising on BMI was estimated on the basis of the findings reported by Chou *et al.* (2008). The impact of government regulation on children's exposure to food advertising was based on an evaluation of the impact of Ofcom's regulatory measures in the United Kingdom (Ofcom, 2008).

Effects of the intervention. As a result of restrictions in advertising, children aged 4-9 will see 39% less advertising of foods high in fat, salt, or sugar, while children aged 10-15 will see 28% less. Depending on the overall amount of

---

Box 6.2. **Regulation and fiscal measures** (cont.)

television viewing by children in different countries, and on the amount of food advertising broadcast, children's BMI in the above age groups will be reduced by 0.13 to 0.34 points. This effect takes into account children's residual exposure to a certain amount of advertising, either because they watch television programmes outside the hours in which restrictions are enforced, or because advertisers may switch from television to other forms of advertising to which children remain exposed. The effects of the intervention were assumed to persist into adult life in a reduced form. In the case of self-regulation, the effects of the intervention were assumed to be half of those produced by formal regulatory measures, because of possibly looser limitations self-imposed on advertising and a less than universal compliance to the voluntary arrangements.

Intervention costs. The estimated cost of per capita of government regulation of food advertising to children ranges between USD PPPs 0.14 and 0.55 in the five countries examined, while the industry self-regulation option would cost between USD PPPs 0.01 and 0.04 per capita. The intervention involves basic administration and planning costs at the national and local levels, as well as monitoring and enforcement costs. In addition, minor training may be required for communication authority staff charged with the task of overseeing the implementation of the scheme. In the case of self-regulation, basic administration, facilitation and supervision costs will arise at the national level. Enforcement costs will be largely reduced, but there will remain a need for monitoring of compliance and effects.

Compulsory food labelling

Main sources of evidence. Intervention characteristics and effectiveness are based on evidence provided in Variyam and Cawley (2006) and Variyam (2008).

Effects of the intervention. Food labelling helps conscious consumers follow a healthy diet. Evidence suggests that this will increase the consumption of fruit and vegetables by an average of 10 grams per day, and reduce the proportion of total energy intake from fats by 0.42%. The average BMI reduction that will be achieved in the population exposed to the intervention is 0.02 points.

Intervention costs. The estimated cost of per capita of introducing compulsory food labeling regulation ranges between USD PPPs 0.33 and 1.1 in the five countries examined. The costs of the intervention include basic administration, planning, enforcement, preparation and distribution of posters and, finally, resources needed to manage the programme of food inspection. The programme does not account for the additional packaging costs associated with designing and printing nutrition labels and for the potential cost associated with the reformulation of certain foods, likely to be borne by the private sector.

of information and advice on lifestyles and the prevention of chronic diseases. However, such advice is not offered systematically, and is generally provided in response to specific individual demands.

The intervention targets individuals between the ages of 25 and 65 who present at least one of the following risk factors: a BMI of 25 kg/m^2 or above, high cholesterol (75th percentile or above), high systolic blood pressure (> 140 mmHg), and type 2 diabetes. It is assumed that 80% of primary care physicians will join the programme and that 90% of eligible individuals will choose to participate in the programme. Of the latter, 75% will complete the programme successfully.

Candidates are either recruited opportunistically, by screening patients waiting for a consultation, or identified using the information contained in practice records and invited for a consultation through a telephone call. Individuals are asked to complete a health and lifestyle questionnaire while they wait for their consultation, which will be used to tailor physician advice.

Box 6.3. **Counselling of individuals at risk in primary care**

Main sources of evidence. Intervention characteristics and effectiveness are modelled on the basis of a selection of studies which provide accounts of controlled experiments of counselling interventions in primary case (Ockene *et al.*, 1996; Herbert *et al.*, 1999; Pritchard *et al.*, 1999).

Effects of the intervention. The intervention will modify risk factors at all the three levels modelled in the analysis. In its more intensive form (physician and dietician counseling), the intervention will decrease the proportion of total energy intake from fats by almost 10%, on average (1.6% in the less intensive version, in which counseling is only provided by physicians), it will reduce BMI by 2.32 points (0.83 in the less intensive version), it will reduce blood cholesterol by 0.55 mmol/l (0.12), and systolic blood pressure and by 12 mmHg (2.30).

Intervention costs. The estimated cost of per capita of a counseling intervention run by physicians and dieticians in primary care ranges between USD PPPs 9 and 20 in the five countries examined, while the cost of the less intensive version of the programme ranges between USD PPPs 4.5 and 9.5. A large part of these costs (up to three-quarters in the intensive intervention) covers the cost of extra working hours of physicians and other health professionals, including dieticians and office support staff. In particular, we assume that target individuals spend on average 25 minutes over 2.6 sessions with their physician. The intervention also includes laboratory costs, training of health professionals and basic organisation costs.

Physicians spend roughly 8-10 minutes providing information and advice on lifestyle, and particularly on diet. The same information is repeated in following consultations.

A second, more intensive, version of the intervention involves additional counselling provided by a dietician upon referral. This consists of a first 45 minute individual session, followed by five group sessions of 15 minutes and by a final 45 minute individual session.

Cost-effectiveness analysis: A generalised approach

Cost-effectiveness analysis (CEA) is concerned with how to make the best use of scarce health resources. The large and growing literature on the topic is dominated by comparisons of interventions aimed at a particular disease, risk factor or health problem, which provides relevant information to programme managers or practitioners with this specific disease mandate. In practice, however, different types of policy makers and practitioners have different demands. Managers of hospital drug formularies must decide which of a vast array of pharmaceuticals they should stock, taking into account the available budget. Countries where health is funded predominantly from the public purse make decisions on what type of pharmaceuticals or technologies can be publicly funded or subsidised, while all types of health insurance – social, community or private – must select a package of services that will be provided. These types of decisions require a broader set of information, involving comparisons of different types of interventions across the entire health sector – whether they are aimed at treating diabetes, reducing the risk of stroke, or providing kidney transplants. This type of analysis can be referred to as "sectoral cost-effectiveness analysis".

Although the number of published cost-effectiveness studies is now very large, there are a series of practical problems in using them for sectoral decision making (Hutubessy et al., 2003). The first is that most published studies take an incremental approach, addressing questions such as how best should small changes (almost always increases) in resources be allocated, or whether a new technology is cost-effective relative to the existing one it would replace. Traditional analysis has not been used to address whether existing health resources are allocated efficiently, despite evidence that in many settings current resources do not in fact achieve as much as they could (Tengs et al., 1995). A second problem is that most studies are very context specific. The efficiency of additional investment in an intervention aimed at a given disease depends partially on the level and quality of the existing health infrastructure (including human resources). This varies substantially across settings and is related to a third problem – individual interventions are almost always evaluated in isolation despite the fact that the effectiveness and costs of most will vary according to whether other related interventions are currently undertaken or are likely to be introduced in the future.

In response to these concerns, a more generalised approach to CEA has been developed by WHO in order to allow policy makers to evaluate the efficiency of the mix of health interventions currently available and to maximise the generalisability of results across settings. Generalised cost-effectiveness analysis (GCEA) and its implementation *via* the CHOICE (CHOosing Interventions that are Cost Effective) project allows for an assessment of the efficiency of the current mix of interventions by analysing all interventions and combinations incremental on doing nothing (Murray *et al.*, 2000; Tan Torres *et al.*, 2003; *www.who.int/choice*). The approach adopted by the OECD and the WHO in their joint analysis of the impact of strategies to improve diets and increase physical activity is a modified version of the generalised CEA approach used in previous CHOICE analyses. The main difference between the two is that while the counterfactual adopted in applied CHOICE studies is defined in terms of what would happen to population health if all interventions being provided now were stopped, in the OECD/WHO analysis the counterfactual is a situation in which no prevention were systematically delivered but chronic diseases were treated as they emerged with the conventional medical means available in the health services of OECD countries. A further difference relative to the traditional CHOICE approach is that the OECD/WHO model was specifically designed to assess the impacts of interventions on health inequalities, in addition to their health impacts and cost-effectiveness.

Many interventions interact in terms of either costs or effects at the population level and interacting interventions are undertaken in different combinations in different settings. Neither the health impact of undertaking two interventions together nor the costs of their joint production are necessarily additive. To understand whether they are efficient uses of resources independently or in combination requires assessing their costs and health effects independently and in combination.

GCEA has now been applied to a wide range of specific diseases (including malaria, tuberculosis, cancers and mental disorders) as well as risk factors (for example, child under-nutrition, unsafe sex, unsafe water, hygiene and sanitation, hypertension and smoking) (see, for example, Chisholm *et al.*, 2004a; Chisholm *et al.*, 2004b; Groot *et al.*, 2006; Murray *et al.*, 2003; Shibuya *et al.*, 2003; WHO, 2002).

Effects of the interventions on obesity, health and life expectancy

Interventions to improve diets and increase physical activity have the potential to reduce obesity rates, decrease the incidence of ischaemic heart

Box 6.4. **The Chronic Disease Prevention model**

The OECD and the WHO jointly developed a micro-simulation model called Chronic Disease Prevention (CDP) which implements a "causal web" of lifestyle risk factors for selected chronic diseases. This model was initially used to estimate the impact of interventions (the same examined here) in the EUR-A WHO region (Sassi *et al.*, 2009). Risk factors range from more distant exposures ("distal risk factors"), which are several steps away from disease events in the chain of causation, to more proximate exposures ("proximal risk factors"), more immediately connected to disease events. The causal web concept involves mutual influences among risk factors, which therefore have both direct and indirect impacts on chronic diseases. The model explicitly accounts for three groups of chronic diseases: stroke, ischemic heart disease and cancer (including lung, colorectal and female breast cancer). Proximal risk factors, such as high blood pressure, high cholesterol and high blood glucose, have a direct influence on the probability of developing the above chronic diseases, based on established pathophysiological mechanisms. Conversely, distal risk factors such as low intake of fruit and vegetables, high fat intake and insufficient physical activity have an indirect influence on chronic diseases. The indirect effect is mediated in part by the body mass index (BMI), which acts on proximal risk factors as well as directly on disease events. The model accounts for mortality from all causes of death and assumes that mortality associated with diseases that are not explicitly modelled remains stable at the rates currently observed in the relevant populations. The model simulates the dynamics of a given country or regional population over a lifetime period (set at 100 years in order to capture the full effectiveness of all interventions, including those targeting young children), although impacts can be assessed at any point in time. Births, deaths and the incidence and prevalence of risk factors and chronic diseases are modelled accordingly, based on the best existing epidemiological evidence for the relevant countries from a range of sources, including WHO, FAO and IARC datasets, national health surveys and published studies. A diagrammatic representation of the model is shown in the figure below. Future costs, as well as future health effects, were discounted at a 3% rate. The model was programmed using a software called ModGen (*www.statcan.gc.ca/spsd/Modgen.htm*), which is a generic "Model Generator" language created by Statistics Canada for developing and working with micro-simulation models.

The CDP model requires a series of epidemiological input data by gender, class of age (0 to 100) and socio-economic status. A first group of parameters allows the software to model population changes over time. This includes global mortality, fertility and the demographic structure of the population. A second group of parameters relates to the three levels of risk factors (*i.e.* distal, intermediate and proximal). This group includes the following epidemiological parameters: prevalence, incidence of new cases, remission rates, and relative risks (RRs) for higher level risk factors. A third and last group of parameters is used to model

Box 6.4. **The Chronic Disease Prevention model** (*cont.*)

diseases. This includes prevalence, incidence rates, remission rates, relative rates (RRas) of disease for different risk factors, and case-fatality hazards (risk of dying of a disease for individuals who have that chronic disease).

We used the best available sources of information on the epidemiology of risk factors and chronic diseases to populate the micro-simulation model. When it was not possible to find input parameters from existing sources, these were calculated based on other parameters using the WHO software DisMod II, or through the analysis of data from national health surveys.

Figure Box 6.4. **The Chronic Disease Prevention model**

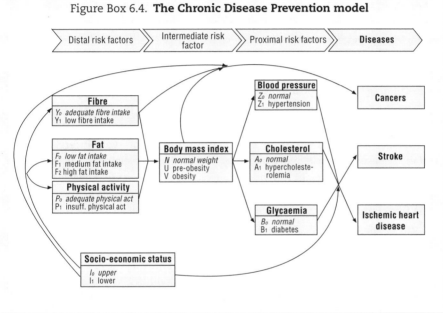

disease, stroke and, to a lesser extent, the incidence of at least three forms of cancer. The impact of interventions on the morbidity associated with these chronic diseases is generally larger than their impact on mortality. Prevention in many cases delays the onset of chronic diseases, rather than preventing them altogether.

If they were to be implemented in isolation, interventions would generate a reduction in the number of people who are obese in the order of four to five percent, at best, in most OECD countries, although the majority of interventions would have substantially smaller impacts. This may seem a modest achievement, but in fact measuring changes in obesity rates is a rather inadequate way of assessing the value of such interventions. Many more people benefit from prevention than those who actually make it across the line that formally separates obesity from non-obesity thanks to those interventions. Improving one's own lifestyle and loosing weight will generate beneficial effects on health regardless of the BMI category in which someone is classified.

The outcomes that matter the most when assessing the impacts of prevention are mortality and the occurrence of chronic diseases, or morbidity. Accordingly, health outcomes are measured in this analysis in terms of life years (LYs) gained through prevention (reflecting improvements in mortality) and disability-adjusted life years (DALYs) averted (reflecting the combined effect of prevention on mortality and morbidity). These outcomes capture comprehensively the ultimate impacts of prevention on health and longevity, although they fall short of reflecting some of the more subtle effects of improved lifestyles on quality of life, particularly in terms of psychological well-being and social functioning. Life years and DALYs are also widely used as outcome measures in economic evaluations of health interventions in areas other than prevention, which facilitates comparisons across a broad spectrum of options in setting priorities for health expenditures.

All but one of the interventions examined by the OECD have the potential to save, every year, a total of between 25 and 75 000 life years in the five countries, relative to a situation in which no prevention were offered and chronic diseases were treated when they emerged. An intervention based on the intensive counselling of individuals at risk in primary care, however, was found to have a substantially larger impact, with over 240 000 life years gained in the five countries. This is shown in the right-hand panel of Figure 6.1.

When the reduction in morbidity from chronic diseases is taken into account (left-hand panel of Figure 6.1) the annual benefits of prevention increase to 40-140 000 disability-adjusted life years (DALYs) saved, and those obtainable though an intensive counselling of individuals at risk in primary care rise to almost half a million DALYs saved.

As indicated, Figure 6.1 shows the average annual gain in life years and DALYs generated by each intervention over the entire simulation (100 years). However, the distribution of gains over time is particularly uneven for interventions targeting children, with most gains concentrated in the final part of the period and little or no gains during the first several decades. When the value of health gains is appropriately discounted, based on the time at which gains occur, it is precisely interventions aimed at children, whose benefits are farthest away, which are penalised the most. So, even regulation of food advertising to children, which ranks fourth in terms of average annual gains in Figure 6.1, in fact has a lower overall effectiveness than most interventions, similar to mass media campaigns at the end of the simulation, but lower than the latter throughout the first 85 years. This is illustrated in

Figure 6.1. **Health outcomes at the population level (average effects per year)**

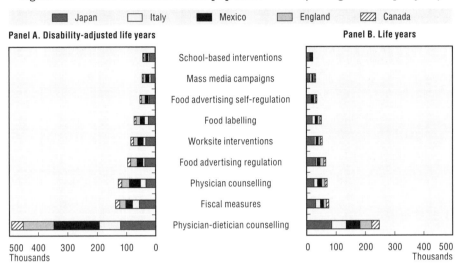

Panel A. Disability-adjusted life years   Panel B. Life years

Source: CDP model-based analysis relying on input data from multiple sources, listed in Table A.2 in Annex A.
StatLink ᵃⁱˢᵖ *http://dx.doi.org/10.1787/888932316077*

Figure 6.2, which shows the value of cumulative gains in DALYs associated with each intervention, after those gains have been discounted at an annual rate of three percent. Consistently with 6.1, Figure 6.2 shows that counselling individuals at risk in primary care is the intervention associated with the largest numbers of DALYs saved, with the intensive counselling option outperforming all other interventions by a large margin, followed by fiscal measures and worksite interventions. At the other end of the spectrum we find interventions aimed at children, whose benefits are more heavily penalised by discounting, due to their later occurrence. Interventions targeting adults have health impacts which are more evenly distributed over time, because they start to generate benefits shortly after their implementation, and impacts are even faster when interventions narrowly target higher-risk individuals and age groups, as in the case of primary-care based counselling.

The health impacts of interventions vary in different age groups. Health gains below age 40 are barely noticeable, while the largest benefits tend to be realised from the age of 40 up to the eighth or ninth decade of life. In the latter group, interventions tend to delay the onset of chronic diseases more than they reduce mortality from those diseases. This pattern is reflected in larger numbers of DALYs averted than LYs gained in the same age group. For instance, physician counselling in primary care can generate twice as large gains in DALYs than in LYs in Canada, and proportionally even larger are the DALYs averted by school-based interventions in Italy, relative to LYs gained

Figure 6.2. **Cumulative DALYs saved over time**

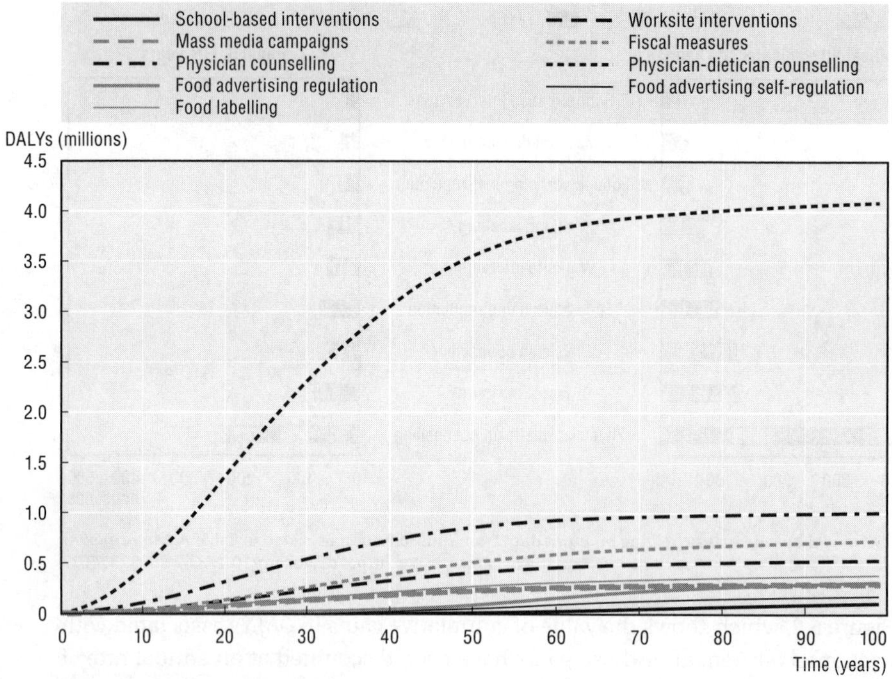

Source: CDP model-based analysis relying on input data from multiple sources, listed in Table A.2 in Annex A.
StatLink 🔗 *http://dx.doi.org/10.1787/888932316096*

(see Panels A and C in Figure 6.3). Among the longest survivors, many will be enjoying the benefits of prevention in terms of a delayed onset of chronic diseases or will be spared altogether. In this age group, the balance between DALYs averted and LYs gained is reversed, with twice as many LYs gained as DALYs saved through intensive counselling in primary care in Canada, and 50% more LYs than DALYs through school-based interventions in Italy.

The impacts of interventions on health care expenditure reflect a mirror image of the patterns of effectiveness described above, as shown in the right-hand panels in Figure 6.3. Interventions have virtually no effects on expenditure up to age 40; they reduce health expenditure for several decades thereafter, consistently with a greater reduction in morbidity than in mortality; and, they increase expenditure in later years of life because of increased survival and need for medical care. The increase in health expenditure in the oldest age groups tends to be directly proportional to the decrease in expenditure realised at earlier ages, *i.e.* the largest the benefits of prevention in terms of reduced morbidity from chronic diseases, the more substantial the upturn in health expenditure among those surviving the

Figure 6.3. **Effects of selected interventions in different age groups**

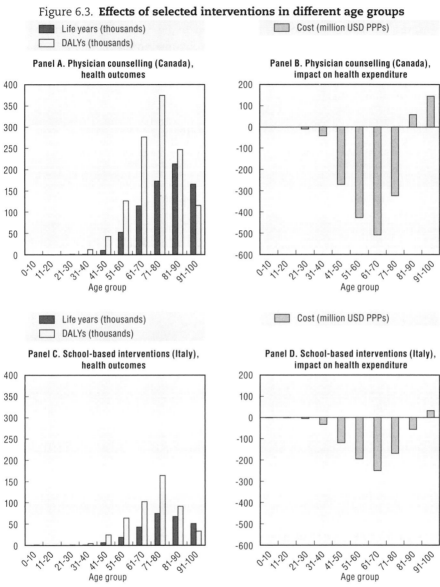

■ Life years (thousands)
☐ DALYs (thousands)
☐ Cost (million USD PPPs)

Source: CDP model-based analysis relying on input data from multiple sources, listed in Table A.2 in Annex A.
StatLink ⟨⟨≫⟩ http://dx.doi.org/10.1787/888932316115

longest. Over the entire period covered by the simulation, all interventions except the two forms of regulation of food advertising to children (government regulation and industry self-regulation) generate net savings in health expenditure, as shown in Figure 6.4. The largest savings are associated with the most effective intervention, intensive counselling of individuals at risk in primary care, which generates savings three times as large as those of fiscal measures, the next most effective intervention. In the case of food advertising regulation, the savings in health expenditure obtained in the middle decades of life are more than offset (although by a thin margin) by increases in health expenditure in older age groups, with a slight increase in health expenditure as the overall net effect.

Figure 6.4. **Cumulative impact on health expenditure over time**

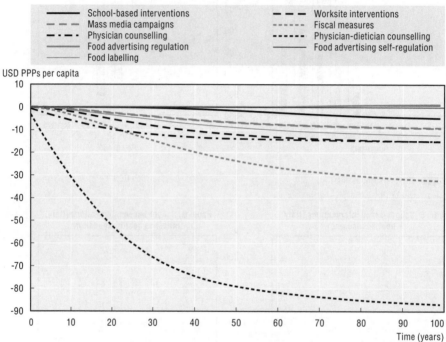

Source: CDP model-based analysis relying on input data from multiple sources, listed in Table A.2 in Annex A.
StatLink ᴍ𝔰⬛ http://dx.doi.org/10.1787/888932316134

The costs and cost-effectiveness of interventions

The costs of delivering the interventions in the countries examined are often several times larger than the interventions' impacts on health expenditure. Therefore, even accounting for the reduced health expenditure, governments wishing to implement the interventions assessed here will bear extra costs, which will be higher at the start and will be progressively attenuated once interventions start to generate their health benefits. While investments in prevention need to be made available upfront, potential savings are usually deferred.

Figure 6.5. **Economic impact at the population level (average effects per year)**

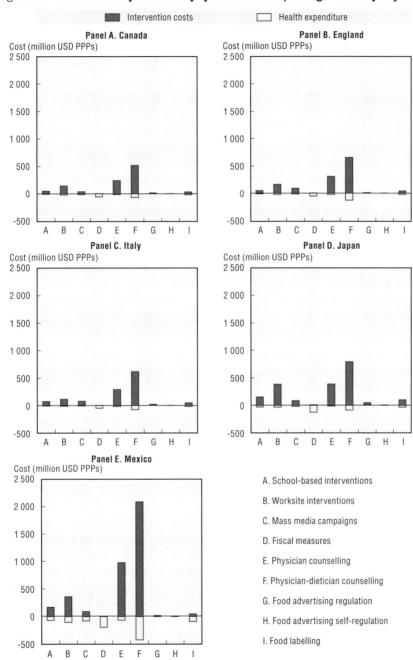

Source: CDP model-based analysis relying on input data from multiple sources, listed in Table A.2 in Annex A.
StatLink ᵐᵖ http://dx.doi.org/10.1787/888932316153

The average annual costs of delivering individual interventions, as well as the average annual savings in health expenditure associated with each intervention, are illustrated in Figure 6.5. Once differences in purchasing power among countries are accounted for, the results are remarkably consistent, with primary care counselling interventions displaying not only the largest savings in health expenditure but also the largest costs of delivery. Health promotion interventions are the next most expensive to deliver. The most expensive in this group are worksite interventions, generally followed by school-based interventions and mass media campaigns. Regulatory and fiscal interventions, on the other hand, are the least expensive interventions among those examined by the OECD. In particular, the relatively small cost of implementation and the relatively large effectiveness of fiscal measures make these the only intervention likely to pay for itself, *i.e.* the only one which generates larger savings in health expenditure than costs of delivery.

Combining the health and economic outcomes of interventions into incremental cost-effectiveness ratios shows patterns of cost-effectiveness declining over time, reflecting an increasing efficiency of the interventions in question as their health benefits build up over time. The one exception is fiscal measures, which are consistently cost saving throughout the period covered by the simulation in all of the five countries examined.

In the first 20-30 years from the initial implementation of interventions, cost-effectiveness ratios tend to be very high. In general, the scale of the impact of individual interventions is limited by the difficulties involved in reaching a large proportion of the population, either because only certain age groups are targeted by the intervention, in which case it may take many years before a large share of the population receives some exposure to the intervention, or because response rates are relatively low, as is typically the case for some of the interventions examined (*e.g.* worksite interventions), based on existing evidence. While cost-effectiveness ratios tend to be favourable for all interventions by the end of the simulation, the patterns of decline over time vary across interventions. Interventions that target children tend to have incommensurable cost-effectiveness ratios during the first several decades, while the measurable health benefits of those interventions are close to zero. However, when health benefits do begin to materialise, the cost-effectiveness of interventions such as school-based health education and health promotion or regulation of food advertising to children has a very steep drop, gradually approaching levels that are commonly regarded as favourable. This is shown clearly in Figure 6.6, in which we may consider the USD PPPs 50 000 per DALY line to broadly reflect an acceptable level of cost-effectiveness in OECD countries.

Figure 6.6. **Cost-effectiveness of interventions over time**

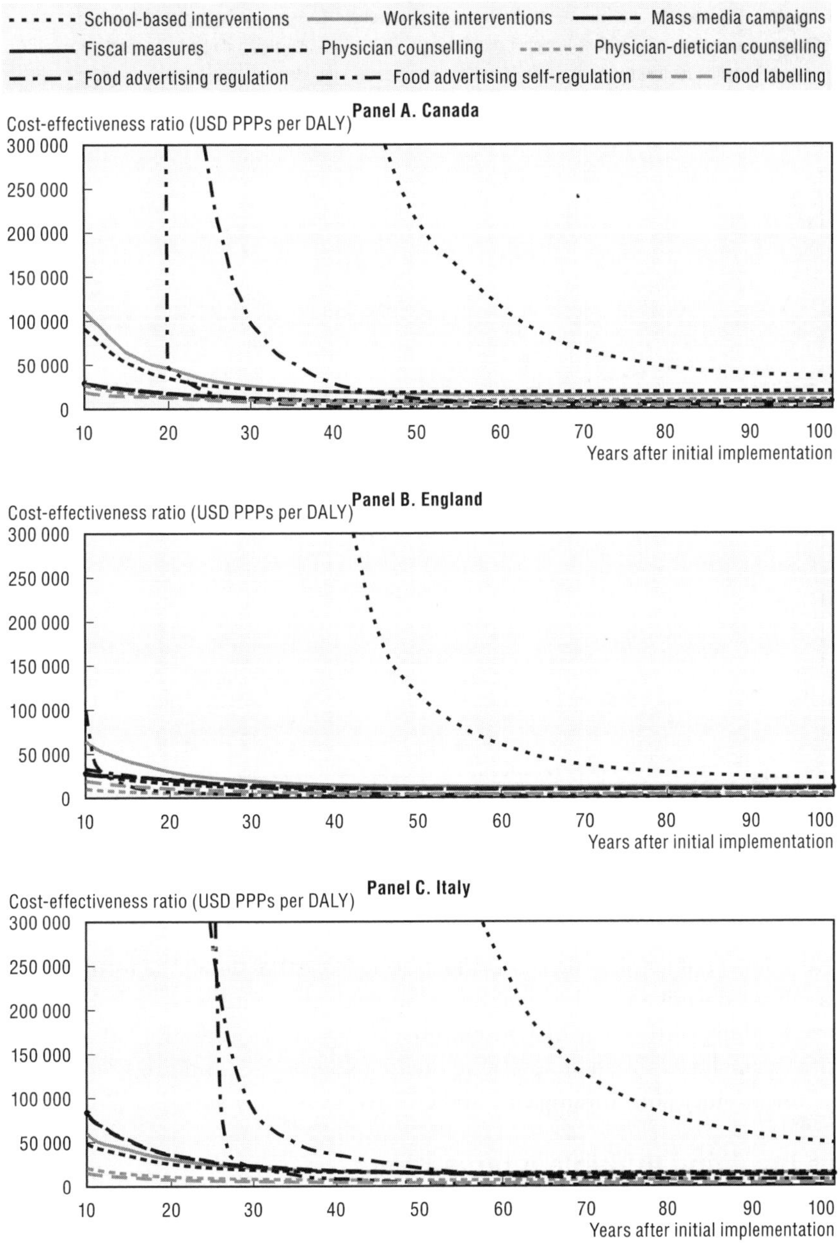
School-based interventions
Worksite interventions
Mass media campaigns
Fiscal measures
Physician counselling
Physician-dietician counselling
Food advertising regulation
Food advertising self-regulation
Food labelling
Panel A. Canada
Cost-effectiveness ratio (USD PPPs per DALY)
300 000
250 000
200 000
150 000
100 000
50 000
0
10
20
30
40
50
60
70
80
90
100
Years after initial implementation
Panel B. England
Cost-effectiveness ratio (USD PPPs per DALY)
Years after initial implementation
Panel C. Italy
Cost-effectiveness ratio (USD PPPs per DALY)
Years after initial implementation

Source: CDP model-based analysis relying on input data from multiple sources, listed in Table A.2 in Annex A.

StatLink http://dx.doi.org/10.1787/888932316172

Figure 6.6. **Cost-effectiveness of interventions over time** (*cont.*)

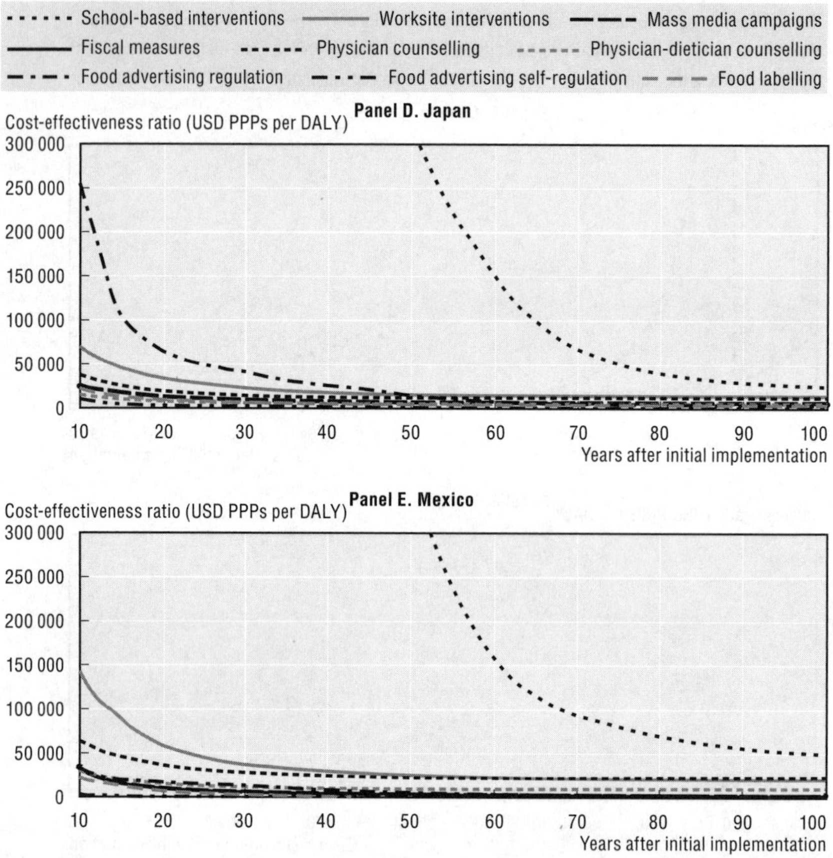

Source: CDP model-based analysis relying on input data from multiple sources, listed in Table A.2 in Annex A.
StatLink ⬛⬛⬛ http://dx.doi.org/10.1787/888932316172

A fuller set of graphs and tables illustrating in further detail the results of the analyses described in this chapter for individual countries is available in Annex A, along with a set of figures illustrating the results of a range of sensitivity analyses aimed at assessing the robustness of the findings relative to the uncertainty surrounding cost and effectiveness estimates.

Strategies involving multiple interventions

If evidence of the effectiveness of individual interventions is not abundant, evidence of the combined effectiveness of multiple interventions implemented simultaneously is virtually nonexistent. It is difficult to predict whether combinations of interventions would create synergies which would translate into an overall effect larger than the sum of individual intervention effects, or whether the opposite would be true and adding interventions to a prevention strategy would have decreasing incremental returns. However, a micro-simulation model like CDP can be used to assess at least some of the effects to be expected from combining multiple interventions into a prevention strategy which targets different population groups. Only for the groups exposed to more than one intervention at the same time, an assumption is required as to what the combined effect of the interventions will be. The assumption made in this analysis is a conservative one, estimating that the overall effect of interventions is less than additive, relative to the effects of individual interventions.

The potential impact of a combination of five interventions was explored, including regulatory interventions such as compulsory food labelling and industry self-regulation of food advertising to children, worksite and school-based health promotion programmes, and intensive counselling of individuals at risk in primary care. This combination of interventions provides a balanced coverage of different age groups (children and adults) using both regulation and health promotion approaches. In addition, it targets high-risk individuals with a more focused intervention which has been shown to be particularly effective in previous analyses.

The estimated impacts of the combined intervention on population health and health expenditure are illustrated in Figure 6.7 for the five countries concerned. Health impacts are up to twice as large as those attributable to the single most effective intervention (intensive counselling in primary care), while the cost-effectiveness profile of the multiple-intervention strategy is very similar to that of the former. Once differences in population size among the five countries are accounted for, England would appear to have the largest health returns from a combination of the five strategies listed above, while Mexico would enjoy the largest reduction in health expenditure.

The reason why some countries benefit more from the prevention package in terms of health gains while others benefit more in terms of reduction in health expenditure is that these two outcomes are driven by partly different effects. In particular, the incidence and prevalence of the risk factors considered in the CDP model have a much greater influence on health expenditure than on health gains measured in terms of life years and DALYs, because risk factors may be expensive to treat but have a less direct impact on health outcomes. Accordingly, the health gains generated by the interventions discussed in this chapter are less affected by changes in risk factors produced by the same interventions than are health expenditure. The result is that reductions in health expenditure in the five countries, as illustrated in the Panel B of Figure 6.7, reflect more closely than health gains the prevalence of risk factors in the same countries. Mexico would enjoy the largest reduction in health expenditure from a multiple-intervention strategy, in line with a very

Figure 6.7. **Estimated impacts of a multiple-intervention strategy (average effects per year)**

Panel A. Health outcomes

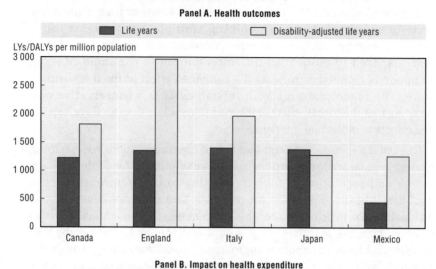

Panel B. Impact on health expenditure

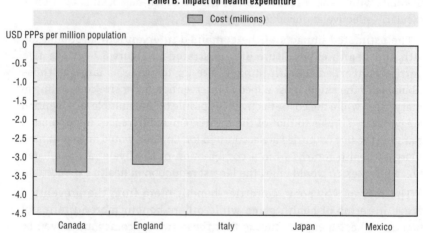

Source: CDP model-based analysis relying on input data from multiple sources, listed in Table A.2 in Annex A.
StatLink 🔗 http://dx.doi.org/10.1787/888932316191

high prevalence of obesity and proximal risk factors such as diabetes, and therefore with a greater scope for improvement through the interventions in question. On the other hand, Japan and Italy, with a more favourable risk profile, would enjoy lesser, but still significant, reductions in health expenditure. Differences in health gains among the five countries, as illustrated in the Panel A of Figure 6.7, are mostly driven by different factors, including the incidence and prevalence of chronic diseases and the proportion of the population covered by the interventions in question.

The cost of delivering the package of interventions varies between USD PPPs 12 per capita in Japan to USD PPPs 24 in Canada, a tiny fraction of health expenditure in those countries, and also a small proportion of what is currently spent on prevention in the same countries. Moreover, part of the above costs would be offset by the savings in health expenditure generated by the interventions, as shown in the Panel B of Figure 6.7.

Distributional impacts of preventive interventions

The issue of the impact of prevention on equity and health inequalities is widely debated in academic and policy circles, although arguments often rest on speculation and anecdotal evidence, rather than sound empirical data. The CDP model was explicitly designed to assess, among other things, the distributional impact of prevention strategies. The model accounts for one dimension of socio-economic status along which two main groups are identified with different risk factor profiles and consequent chronic disease morbidity and mortality rates. In the analysis reported here, the two groups correspond to occupation-based social classes and broadly reflect the distribution of the five countries' populations into blue and white collar workers, or manual and non-manual occupations.

There are two main ways in which the impacts of prevention may vary across different socio-economic groups. First, different groups are characterised by different levels of morbidity and mortality from the risk factors and chronic diseases to be prevented. Which group will benefit the most from preventive interventions is mainly determined by the relative sizes of incidence, prevalence and mortality rates in the different groups. As a general rule of thumb, socio-economic groups that have a less favourable risk profile and bear a higher burden of chronic diseases are likely to benefit more from prevention. But in practice the distributional effect of prevention depends on a very large number of factors, including, for instance, the age-distribution of risk factors and intervention effects.

On the other hand, a second mechanism may be at play in chronic disease prevention. Different socio-economic groups may be more or less likely to respond favourably to prevention programmes, *e.g.* to comply with health promotion messages, use the information delivered through programmes, or change their consumption in response to price changes. There is at least some evidence that individuals in higher socio-economic groups, who tend to have higher levels of education, are more likely than others to respond favourably to prevention programmes that involve the delivery of health promotion or health education messages. But there is also some evidence that more cogent interventions, such as fiscal measures altering the prices of lifestyle commodities, elicit a greater response from individuals in lower socio-economic groups. Therefore, whether differences in response and intervention effectiveness across socio-economic groups are likely to reduce or increase health disparities depends largely on the nature of the interventions in question.

In the analysis presented here, we were able to account for the different incidence and prevalence rates of risk factors and chronic diseases in the two socio-economic groups (the first effect), but we could account only to a very limited extent for differences in response to interventions by different groups, because of the paucity, or even absence, of reliable quantitative evidence that could be used as an input into the CDP model-based analysis. In practice, we could only account for different responses to fiscal measures, which generate price incentives, based on existing estimates of price elasticity of the demand for different foods in different socio-economic groups, ranging from a greater response in the less well-off (the vast majority of estimates) to a greater response in the better-off.

When only the effect of differences in morbidity and mortality between socio-economic groups are accounted for, the analysis shows mixed results. England is the only country in which interventions generate consistently larger health gains in the lower socio-economic group (up to 50% larger, in proportion, than in the higher socio-economic group for school-based interventions and fiscal measures). In the other four countries, fiscal measures have consistently more favourable effects in the lower socio-economic group but other interventions have different distributional effects in different countries, depending on the epidemiological characteristics of those countries. Canada has the largest variability in distributional effects across interventions, with counselling in primary care, worksite interventions and food labelling displaying more favourable effects in the better-off, while interventions aimed at children (school-based and food advertising regulation) and fiscal measures display more favourable effects in the less well-off.

Given that fiscal measures generate consistently larger health gains in the lower socio-economic group, accounting for a different response to food price incentives in different groups further increases the advantage for the lower socio-economic group, however, the size of the change is minor. Starting from price elasticities of 2% for both socio-economic groups in the main analysis, elasticities were changed to 1.56% and 2.38%, respectively, for the higher and lower groups, in line with Mytton et al. (2007). Despite the relatively large change in elasticities, health gains were only slightly more favourable in the less well-off, relative to the better-off, than in the initial analysis, suggesting that differences in morbidity and mortality between the two groups are more important than differences in the response elicited by the intervention in explaining the health gains generated by the same intervention. Similarly, when alternative elasticities were used in the model to test for the effects of a possibly larger response in the higher socio-economic group (not widely supported by the existing evidence), in line with Allais *et al.* (2008), the advantage in health gains for the lower socio-economic group was only marginally decreased.

From modelling to policy: Key drivers of success

The findings presented in this chapter are the result of a major analytical effort, aimed at bringing together the best existing evidence on the epidemiology of risk factors and chronic diseases in the five countries concerned and the best evidence of the effectiveness of preventive interventions. However, the analysis remains a simulation and the results obtained may or may not reflect accurately the outcomes to be expected from the implementation of the interventions discussed here in real world settings. In general, the model was designed, and the input parameters were selected, with a view to minimising the risk of overestimating the impacts of interventions. So, the findings reported in this chapter may be regarded as conservative estimates of those impacts in real world settings.

The most conservative of all the assumptions made is that the only effects to be accounted for in the analysis, among those potentially generated by prevention, are the ones for which there is clear and direct evidence from existing studies. Effects for which only indirect or anecdotal evidence is available were ignored in the analysis. One example is social multiplier effects, discussed in Chapter 4, which are very likely to be triggered by at least some of the interventions discussed here. The benefits of school-based or worksite health promotion interventions, for instance, are likely to spread into the families of those who are exposed to the interventions, although the lack of quantifiable evidence of how social multiplier effects may develop prevented their formal inclusion into the analysis.

Following a similar logic, the CDP model only accounts for a set of relationships among factors, and between these and chronic diseases, which are supported by existing epidemiological evidence. In the real world, further and more complex relationships may exist that could not be reflected in the structure of the model.

Another instance in which a conservative attitude was adopted in modelling interventions is the assumption made about the long-term sustainability of the effects of interventions. With the exception of interventions such as food labelling, or fiscal measures, which essentially target the entire population, most interventions target specific age groups (*e.g.* children, working-age adults, adults at risk, etc.). As individuals targeted by interventions grow older and cease to be part of the relevant target groups, they may or may not retain some of the behaviour changes generated by the interventions while they were exposed to them. The conservative assumption made in this analysis is that they would not retain any of the effectiveness of the interventions to which they were previously exposed, and their behaviours would essentially become the same as those of individuals of the same age who had never been exposed to the interventions in question. The only exception to this rule was made for interventions aimed at children (school-based interventions and food advertising regulation) which would be of very little value if they were assumed to have no long-term effects on behaviours. Children exposed to the latter interventions were assumed to retain some of the behaviour changes associated with those interventions (half of the original effects).

Limitations in the existing epidemiological evidence-base is a further possible cause of divergence between model estimates and real world impacts. Despite major efforts made by OECD countries to collect detailed and representative information about health and lifestyles at the population level, the availability and quality of some of that information remain unsatisfactory. The greatest limitations affect behavioural risk factor data. In particular, information on aspects of diet and physical activity is derived either from surveys, which tend to be affected by various forms of bias associated with the framing of questions and with poor recollection and self-reporting, or from national sources such as food balance sheets for food consumption, which are affected by similarly important limitations (*e.g.* they do not account for waste) and only provide average consumption estimates. A further critical input parameter in the CDP model is incidence rates for chronic diseases. While reliable incidence data tend to be available for cancer, thanks to existing disease registries, information on IHD and stroke incidence is much more difficult to compile, and it is not unconceivable that some of the parameter estimates used in the analysis do not reflect the true incidence of chronic diseases in the countries concerned, leading to an underestimation of the overall effect of preventive interventions, despite adjustments made in the analysis to account for the variable quality of different input parameters.

Aside from assumptions and potential data limitations, the analysis provides some clear indications as to what the key success factors are in the prevention of chronic diseases linked to obesity.

One clear driver of success for prevention programmes is high participation rates. The numbers of people who actually benefit from some of the interventions assessed in the analysis is dramatically low. For instance, less than 10% of the population in the countries concerned is expected to benefit from worksite interventions and from counselling in primary care. This is partly the result of supply-side constraints, including the choice of target group and decisions made by employers and primary care practices as to whether they should offer the interventions, but it is also the result of individual choices to participate in the programmes by those who are offered to do so. The overall impacts of the interventions in question would be greatly enhanced if participation rates were increased. One possible strategy for increasing participation rates is generally to make adherence to interventions less dependent on an active choice to participate (both in terms of supply of interventions and uptake by individuals). As discussed in Chapter 5 in relation to the principles of libertarian paternalism, making participation in a prevention programme the default option might significantly increase uptake. For instance, employees could be automatically enrolled in health education classes, and attendance at those classes could be monitored. Employees would have to explicitly opt out if they did not wish to participate. Concerning the supply-side of preventive interventions, appropriate financial and non financial incentives may be used, particularly at the primary care level, to increase the number of professionals and practices willing to engage in counselling programmes.

Interventions will also be more effective if they produce long-lasting changes in people's behaviours. This should be an important consideration in the design of any prevention programmes. Booster interventions may have to be associated with the main interventions described in this chapter. In principle, social multiplier effects may also make behaviour changes last longer, through a mutual reinforcement of healthy habits within families and peer groups. However, at present there is no clear evidence of any effective ways of enhancing the sustainability of behaviour changes in the long term.

Finally, the time-frame within which interventions produce their effects has an important bearing on the interventions' overall impacts. As discussed above, interventions targeting adults produce their effects earlier than those targeting children, and interventions on high-risk individuals produce their effects earlier than those targeting the general population. This should not lead to the conclusion that forward looking interventions which aim at giving a healthier adult life to the youngest generations should be assigned a lower priority than interventions targeting adults at high risk. There are good reasons for attaching a high priority to the former regardless of their overall effectiveness and cost-effectiveness, but policy makers may want to consider combining interventions that produce their effects over different time horizons in order to minimise delays in returns from prevention strategies and increase their overall impacts.

Key messages

- Interventions aimed at tackling obesity by improving diets and increasing physical activity in at least three areas, including health education and promotion, regulation and fiscal measures, and counselling in primary care, have favourable cost-effectiveness ratios.

- The health impacts of individual interventions are small, when interventions are assessed in isolation, but the use of multiple-intervention strategies may significantly enhance overall impacts while retaining a favourable cost-effectiveness profile.

- Interventions, especially those aimed at children, may take a long time to make an impact and reach favourable cost-effectiveness ratios.

- Impacts on health expenditure are relatively small (in the order of 1% of original expenditures for the relevant diseases), intervention costs exceed health care cost savings for most interventions.

- Interventions with the most favourable cost-effectiveness profiles are outside the health care sector. Counselling of individuals at risk in primary care has the largest health impact, but is also the most expensive intervention of those assessed in the analysis.

- The distributional impacts of interventions are mostly determined by differences in morbidity and mortality among socio-economic groups. Fiscal measures are the only intervention producing consistently larger health gains in the less well-off. The distributional impacts of other interventions vary in different countries.

- The impacts of interventions reported in this chapter are likely to be conservative estimates of the impacts to be expected in real world settings.

- Key drivers of success for preventive interventions include high participation (on both supply and demand sides), long-term sustainability of effects, ability to generate social multiplier effects, and combination of multiple interventions producing their effects over different time horizons.

Notes

1. A WHO review of the effectiveness of interventions to improve diets and increase physical activity found that school-based interventions are those most often assessed, while fewer studies focused on other public health interventions (WHO, 2009). The OECD collated the existing evidence concerning the impacts of interventions on diet and physical activity, of which the above WHO review includes a large part. The OECD retrieved a number of studies which were not covered in the WHO review because published after June 2006, not indexed in the literature databases used in the review, or because the relevant interventions were out of the scope of the review.

2. Rigorous prospective controlled studies have only been used in a few instances to assess the effectiveness of interventions (*e.g.* primary-care based interventions). In some cases (*e.g.* fiscal measures), the only evidence available is from regression modelling studies based on retrospective data. The impacts of interventions are generally measured in terms of behaviour change, while longer-term outcomes are seldom assessed.

Bibliography

Allais, O., P. Bertail, and V. Nichéle (2008), "The Effects of a Fat Tax on French Households' Purchases: A Nutritional Approach", *American Journal of Agricultural Economics*, Vol. 92, No. 1, pp. 228-245.

Buller, D.B. *et al.* (1999), "Randomized Trial Testing the Effect of Peer Education at Increasing Fruit and Vegetable Intake", *Journal of the National Cancer Institute*, Vol. 91, No. 17, pp. 1491-1500.

Chisholm, D., J. Rehm, M. van Ommeren and M. Monteiro (2004b), "Reducing the Global Burden of Hazardous Alcohol Use: A Comparative Cost-Effectiveness Analysis", *Journal of Studies on Alcohol*, Vol. 65, pp. 782-793.

Chisholm, D., K. Sanderson, J.L. Ayuso-Mateos and S. Saxena (2004a), "Reducing the Global Burden of Depression: Population-Level Analysis of Intervention Cost Effectiveness in 14 World Regions", *British Journal of Psychiatry*, Vol. 184, pp. 393-403.

Chou, S., I. Rasha and M. Grossman (2008), "Fast-Food Restaurant Advertising on Television and its Influence on Childhood Obesity", *Journal of Law and Economics*, Vol. 51, pp. 599-618.

Craig, C.L., C. Tudor-Locke and A. Bauman (2007), "Twelve-Month Effects of Canada on the Move: A Population-Wide Campaign to Promote Pedometer Use and Walking", *Health Education Research*, Vol. 22, No. 3, pp. 406-413.

Dixon, H., R. Borland, S. Segan, H. Stafford and S. Sindall (1998), "Public Reaction to Victoria's '2 Fruit and 5 Veg. Every Day' Campaign and Reported Consumption of Fruit and Vegetables", *Preventive Medicine*, Vol. 27, No. 4, pp. 572-582.

Emmons, K.M., L.A. Linnan, W.G. Shadel, B. and D.B. Abrams (1999), "The Working Healthy Project: A Worksite Health Promotion Trial Targeting Physical Activity, Diet and Smoking", *Journal of Occupational and Environmental Medicine*, Vol. 41, No. 7, pp. 545-555.

Evans, C. (2003), "Studying the Studies: An Overview of Recent Research into Taxation Operating Costs", *eJournal of Tax Research*, Vol. 1, No. 1, pp. 64-92.

Expenditure and Food Survey (2007), UK National Statistics Office, available at *www.statistics.gov.uk/ssd/surveys/expenditure_food_survey.asp*.

Foerster, S.B., K.W. Kizer, L.K. Disogra, D.G. Bal, B.F. Krieg and K.L. Bunch (1995), "California's '5-a-Day-for Better Health' Campaign: An Innovative Population-Based Effort to Effect Large Scale Dietary Change", *American Journal of Preventive Medicine*, Vol. 11, pp. 124-131.

Gortmaker, S.L. *et al.* (1999), "Impact of a School-Based Interdisciplinary Intervention on Diet and Physical Activity Among Urban Primary School Children: Eat Well and Keep Moving", *Archives of Pediatrics and Adolescent Medicine*, Vol. 153, No. 9, pp. 975-983.

Groot, M.T., R. Baltussen, C.A. Uyl-de Groot, B.O. Anderson and G.N. Hortobágyi (2006), "Costs and Health Effects of Breast Cancer Interventions in Epidemiologically Different Regions of Africa, North America, and Asia", *Breast Journal*, Vol. 12, Suppl. 1, pp. S81-90.

Herbert, J.R. *et al.* (1999), "A Dietician-Delivered Group Nutrition Program Leads to Reductions in Dietary Fat, Serum Cholesterol and Body Weight: the Worcester-Area Trial for Counselling in Hyperlipidaemia (WATCH)", *Journal of the American Dietetic Association*, Vol. 99, No. 5, pp. 544-552.

Hespel, V. and M. Berthod-Wurmser (2008), "La pertinence et la faisabilité d'une taxation nutritionnelle", Inspection Générale des Finances et Inspection Générale des Affaires Sociales, République Française.

Hutubessy, R., D. Chisholm and T. Tan Torres (2003), "Generalized Cost-Effectiveness Analysis for National-Level Priority-Setting in the Health Sector", *Cost Effectiveness and Resource Allocation*, Vol. 1, No. 8, available at *www.resource-allocation.com/content/1/1/8*.

Luepker, R.V. *et al.* (1998), "The Child and Adolescent Trial for Cardiovascular Health (CATCH)", *Journal of Nutritional Biochemistry*, Vol. 9, pp. 525-534.

Murray, C.J.L., D.B. Evans, A. Acharya and R.M. Baltussen (2000), "Development of WHO Guidelines on Generalized Cost-Effectiveness Analysis", *Health Economics*, Vol. 9, pp. 235-251.

Murray, C.J.L. *et al.* (2003), "Effectiveness and Costs of Interventions to Lower Systolic Blood Pressure and Cholesterol: A Global and Regional Analysis on Reduction of Cardiovascular Disease", *The Lancet*, Vol. 361, pp. 717-725.

Mytton, O. *et al.* (2007), "Could Targeted Food Taxes Improve Health?", *Journal of Epidemiology Community Health*, Vol. 61, No. 8, pp. 689-694.

Ockene, I.S. *et al.* (1996), "Effect of Training and a Structured Office Practice on Physician-Delivered Nutrition Counseling: The Worcester-Area Trial for Counseling in Hyperlipidemia (WATCH)", *American Journal of Preventive Medicine*, Vol. 12, No. 4, pp. 252-258.

Ofcom (2008), "Changes in the Nature and Balance of Television Food Advertising to Children: A Review of HFSS Advertising Restrictions", available at *www.ofcom.org.uk/research/tv/reports/hfssdec08*.

Perry, C.L. *et al.* (1998), "Changing Fruit and Vegetable Consumption Among children: the 5-a-Day Power Plus Program in St. Paul, Minnesota", *American Journal of Public Health*, Vol. 88, No. 4, pp. 603-609.

Powell, L.M. and F.J. Chaloupka (2009), "Food Prices and Obesity: Evidence and Policy Implications for Taxes and Subsudues", *Milbank Quarterly*, Vol. 87, No. 1, pp. 229-257.

Pritchard, D.A., J. Hyndman and F. Taba (1999), "Nutritional Counselling in General Practice: A Cost-Effective Analysis", *Journal of Epidemiology and Community Health*, Vol. 53, pp. 311-316.

Reynolds, K.D. *et al.* (2000), "Increasing the Fruit and Vegetable Consumption of Fourth-Graders: Results from the High 5 Project", *Preventive Medicine*, Vol. 30, No. 4, pp. 309-319.

Sassi, F. and J. Hurst (2008), "The Prevention of Lifestyle-Related Chronic Diseases: An Economic Framework", OECD Health Working Paper, No. 32, OECD Publishing, Paris.

Sassi, F., M. Cecchini, J. Lauer and D. Chisholm (2009), "Improving Lifestyles, Tackling Obesity: The Health and Economic Impact of Prevention Strategies", OECD Health Working Paper No. 48, OECD Publishing, Paris.

Shibuya, K. *et al.* (2003), "WHO Framework Convention on Tobacco Control: Development of an Evidence-Based Global Public Health Treaty", *British Medical Journal*, Vol. 327, pp. 154-157.

Sorensen, G. *et al.* (1996), "Worksite-Based Cancer Prevention: Primary Results from Working Well Trial", *American Journal of Public Health*, Vol. 86, No. 7, pp. 939-947.

Sorensen, G. *et al.* (1998), "The Effects of a Health Promotion-Health Protection Intervention on Behavior Change: The WellWorks Study", *American Journal of Public Health*, Vol. 88, No. 11, pp. 1685-1690.

Sorensen, G. *et al.* (1999), "Increasing Fruit and Vegetable Consumption through Worksites and Families in the Treatwell 5-a-Day Study", *American Journal of Public Health*, Vol. 89, No. 1, pp. 54-60.

Tan Torres, T. *et al.* (2003), "Making Choices in Health: WHO Guide to Cost-Effectiveness Analysis", World Health Organisation, Geneva.

Tengs, T.O. *et al.* (1995), "Five Hundred Life-Saving Interventions and their Cost Effectiveness", *Risk Analysis*, Vol. 15, pp. 369-390.

Variyam, J.N. (2008), "Do Nutrition Labels Improve Dietary Outcomes?", *Health Economics*, Vol. 17, pp. 695-708.

Variyam, J.N. and J. Cawley (2006), "Nutrition Labels and Obesity", NBER Working Paper No. 11956, Cambridge, MA.

WHO (2002), "Some Strategies to Reduce Risk", *World Health Report 2002: Reducing Risks, Promoting Health Life*, Chapter 5, pp. 101-144, World Health Organisation, Geneva.

WHO (2009), *Intervention on Diet and Physical Activity: What Works*, 2009, World Health Organisation, Geneva.

Special Focus V.
Regulation of Food Advertising to Children: The UK Experience

by

Jonathan Porter, on behalf of Ofcom,
the independent regulator for television, radio, telecommunications
and wireless communication services in the United Kingdom

Introduction

In December 2003, the Secretary of State for Culture, Media and Sport asked Ofcom to consider proposals to strengthen rules on food and drink advertising to children on television.

As the independent regulator for television, radio, telecommunications and wireless communication services in the United Kingdom, Ofcom has a range of duties and responsibilities set down in legislation: its broadcasting duties include responsibility for setting standards in television advertising and its statutory objectives include the protection of children. At the same time, Ofcom has other statutory obligations to secure a wide range of television services of high quality and wide appeal offered to audiences by a range of different broadcasters. Furthermore Ofcom had committed itself to carry out its duties in a proportionate, evidence-based manner. Ofcom's approach to this issue therefore needs to be set in the context of managing these different duties and regulatory objectives.

In addition, because childhood obesity is a multi-faceted issue, the consideration of restrictions on the advertising/promotion of food products to children ended up requiring a multi-disciplinary/multi-agency approach and Ofcom made use of the expertise of colleagues in the Food Standards Agency (FSA) and the Department of Health on issues such as nutritional profiling, the impact of diet on the incidence of morbidity and measures of the valuation of life.

As a result of a comprehensive review of the existing evidence of the impact of advertising on children's food preferences, and a series of public consultations, a package of measures for the regulation of food advertising to children was adopted in February 2007.

The package included the following measures:

- advertisements for HFSS* products could not be shown in or around programmes specifically made for children (including pre-school children). This measure removed all HFSS advertising from dedicated children's channels;

- advertisements for HFSS products could not be shown in or around programmes of particular appeal to children under 16; and

- these restrictions applied equally to programme sponsorship by HFSS food and drink products.

In addition to these scheduling restrictions, Ofcom also proposed that revised content rules would apply to all food and drink advertising to children irrespective of when it is scheduled. The key elements of the content rules included a prohibition on the use of licensed characters, celebrities, promotional offers and health claims in advertisements for HFSS products targeted at pre-school or primary school children.

The scope for self-regulation

In the course of Ofcom's consultation process, Ofcom did consider the option of self-regulation on the part of the food and drink industry. In terms of existing self-regulatory initiatives, a number of manufacturers argued that they already had in place policies about advertising to children and were also in the process of reformulating their products to reduce the amount of fat, salt and sugar over time. For instance, Kellogg's and Coca-Cola had a policy of not advertising their products to children under the age of 12.

Although Ofcom recognised the relevance of these self-regulatory initiatives, it did not consider that they satisfied the regulatory objectives it had set out. For instance, given the objective of reducing HFSS food advertising to children under 16 years old, the manufacturers' voluntary restrictions on advertising to under-12s did not go far enough.

Ofcom also felt that restrictions on the advertising of HFSS products combined with the FSA's NP scheme would provide at least some manufacturers with an added incentive to continue to work on the re-formulation of their products so that they might be able to advertise on TV. However, Ofcom did recognise that this would simply not be possible for some categories of products *e.g.* sweets and certain types of savoury snacks.

---

* Scheduling restrictions will be confined to food and drink products that are assessed as "high in fat, salt and sugar" (HFSS) as defined by the FSA's nutrient profiling (NP) scheme.

Key issues in the development of the policy

Definition of children

Ofcom's initial set of proposals focused on children under 10 years old. However, there was a significant amount of criticism of this approach in consultation responses. Although most manufacturers supported Ofcom's proposals, most consumer groups, health and public sector organisations and academics argued that restrictions should extend to children aged 10 and over. They argued that although older children might understand the intent of advertising, they were still susceptible to its influence. In addition, unlike younger children, they had the means to buy HFSS products. The evidence indicated that dietary quality declined from childhood to adolescence; that obesity in children was most common in the 12-15 age group; and that older children's preferences can influence those of their younger siblings.

Having reviewed the evidence and the arguments, Ofcom amended its approach to address more clearly the potential vulnerability of older children up to the age of 15, alongside that of younger children. Ofcom noted that major advertising and marketing database companies also classified children as aged 4-15 inclusive. This increased the number of channels and broadcasters that would be affected. For instance, music channels were now within the scope of the restrictions.

Programmes of appeal to children

Another issue that Ofcom had to address was the definition of programmes of appeal to children (even if not aimed specifically at them). Ofcom proposed using an audience index measure to assess programmes of appeal to children – the "120 index", which identifies programmes where the proportion of children (4-15 years old) in the audience was at least 20% higher than their proportion in the general population. The 120 index approach was also already used in the application of restrictions on alcohol advertising.

Some broadcasters argued that it would be difficult to predict in advance which programmes would have an audience index over 120. However, Ofcom rejected this argument. Ofcom was aware that when broadcasters plan where to schedule advertising airtime, they analysed the audience mix that their schedule was predicted to deliver. Where a programme series was expected to be watched by an audience with a high proportion of children, the broadcaster would "block out" that programme series, preventing unsuitable advertising (e.g. alcohol advertising) from being scheduled in or around it. The index approach was therefore already used on a predictive and judgemental basis. Ofcom made it clear that broadcasters should not necessarily be expected to identify every single programme that would index at over 120 in advance but where a programme series or time slot consistently delivered an audience rich in children then Ofcom would expect a broadcaster to apply the 120 index approach to it.

Proportionality

In assessing the impact of different scheduling restrictions, an important issue was how "efficient" particular types of restrictions were. A number of health and consumer groups pressed for restrictions on advertising in programmes when large numbers of children were likely to be watching. Effectively this would mean restrictions on HFSS advertising stretching later into the evening.

For mass audience programmes, particularly soaps or reality shows, it is true that there will be large number of children in the audience. However, that is not to say that children would make up a significant proportion of the audience and it was not necessarily the case that HFSS advertising in and around those programmes would be aimed at those children. For example, an advert for ready to eat breakfast cereal shown in the evening was likely to be aimed at adults rather than children. Given that the objective of Ofcom's advertising restrictions was to have an impact on children's food preferences and that there was no prohibition on the purchasing of HFSS food products *per se*, Ofcom was wary about extending scheduling restrictions into times of the day when the audience was likely to be mainly adults.

To assess the efficiency of different packages of restrictions Ofcom analysed the number of adult HFSS impacts that would be restricted in addition to the children's HFSS impacts, where an impact is equivalent to one viewer watching one advertisement. For instance, a hypothetical complete ban on HFSS advertising before 9 pm would remove around six adult HFSS impacts for every child impact that was removed. In comparison, restrictions in children's airtime would remove around one adult impact for every child impact that was removed.

Impact of restrictions to date

So far, the policy has:

- *Significantly reduced the exposure of children under 16 to HFSS advertising.* The latest data available indicate that children's exposure to HFSS advertising has fallen by 37% between 2005 and 2009 (compared to the 41% reduction estimated in Ofcom's Impact Assessment).

- *Enhanced protection for children as well as parents by appropriate revisions to advertising content standards.* For instance, the number of food and drink advertising spots featuring licensed characters during children's airtime fell by 84%. The same trend was apparent across the majority of advertising techniques targeted by the rule changes.

● *Avoided disproportionate impacts on the revenue of broadcasters.* Children's channels did experience a significant decline in food and drink advertising revenue. However, data provided by broadcasters indicated that overall advertising revenue on children's channels had nevertheless increased. And while the main commercial channels (ITV1, GMTV, Channel 4 and Five) saw a 6% decline in food and drink advertising revenue between 2005 and 2007/08, most other digital commercial channels had been able to increase their revenue from food and drink advertising, so mitigating the effects of restrictions to a greater degree than Ofcom had anticipated.

● *Avoided intrusive regulation of advertising during adult airtime.* As set out above, Ofcom limited the impact on adult airtime by ensuring restrictions are only applied where a disproportionate number of 4-15-year-olds are watching (120 indexing), and therefore the programme are considered to be of particular appeal to children.

Special Focus VI.
The Case for Self-Regulation in Food Advertising

by

Stephan Loerke, on behalf of the World Federation of Advertisers (WFA),
an international professional organisation representing
the common interests of marketers, Brussels, Belgium

With the global increase of overweight and obesity, food marketing communications, particularly to children, have been in the public and political spotlight. Advertisers have been duty bound to review their marketing communications strategies to ensure that they are aligned with and promote – rather than undermine – healthy diets and balanced lifestyles.

A blueprint for food and non-alcoholic beverage marketing communications

On the basis of these principles, the World Federation of Advertisers (WFA) has developed a vision for an effective policy response to public health concerns relating to food advertising to children. This vision is based on the recognition that there is no one single instrument that can effectively address the various facets of the issue and that an integrated, multi-tiered approach is necessary. This approach seeks to maximise synergies between different regulatory and self-regulatory structures and layers of rules. Each layer requires an independent monitoring component in order to create accountability and engender trust among stakeholders. A five-tiered blueprint for such a model is presented graphically below, followed by an explanation of each tier and how they interact.

At one end of the policy spectrum (the broad base of the pyramid), national regulatory frameworks set the broad parameters within which marketers are required to operate. An example of good regulatory practice along these lines is the recently adopted European Directive on Audiovisual Media Services. This directive establishes common quantitative and qualitative rules for all advertising, including strong provisions on the protection of children, while actively encouraging the establishment of codes of conduct on food advertising to children in the member States of the European Union.

At the opposite end of the policy spectrum, specific industry-led initiatives are found, such as "pledge programmes". These are framework commitments driven locally by International Food and Beverage Alliance (IFBA) members – a group of leading multinational companies, which account for the vast majority of food marketing spend globally – with a view to encouraging local operators to adopt the same basic standards. Pledge programmes thereby increase the market coverage of the framework commitments and create a level playing field among all companies. To date Pledge programmes are in place in the United States, Canada, the European Union, Switzerland, Thailand, Australia, South Africa, Brazil, Peru, Mexico, India and the GCC countries. The involvement of the leading global food advertisers in these programmes ensures that the commitments cover a significant share of the market. The effectiveness of this approach in changing the balance of food and beverage advertising to children is best demonstrated by the monitoring programme of the EU Pledge initiative in its first year of operation (2009). As well as finding virtually 100% compliance with the EU Pledge commitments, the external auditors that carried out the monitoring (Accenture Marketing Sciences) measured the change in food advertising to children under 12 in Europe since 2005, on the basis of six markets, reporting a 93% drop in advertising for products that do not meet companies' nutritional criteria in programmes with an audience composed of a majority of children, and a 56% decline in advertising for these products overall, *i.e.* in all programmes on all channels at all times. For all EU Pledge member companies'

Figure SF VI.1. **A blueprint for marketing policies on food advertising**

5. Best practice promotion (through "pledge programmes", etc.)

4. Individual corporate food marketing communications policies

3. Industry-wide self-regulatory codes for food marketing

2. National self-regulatory frameworks

1. National/regional regulatory frameworks

This diagram represents a deliberate over-simplification of the industry blueprint for the sake of understanding. Not all five layers are required in all markets; many markets can provide for robust self-regulatory frameworks for food and non-alcoholic beverage marketing communications by ensuring the existence of just one or three layers. Nor should this diagram imply any need to adopt layers chronologically. Indeed, in most markets where this model is being adopted, different layers are being reinforced simultaneously and at different speeds.

advertising across all products (*i.e.* no distinction on a nutritional basis) this represents a 61% drop in programmes with an audience composed of a majority of children, and a 30% decline overall.

The WFA's blueprint for framing food and beverage advertising in the interest of promoting balanced diets and healthy lifestyles is based on a collaborative, multi-stakeholder approach between the private and public sectors. A complete and effective strategy for regulating food advertising should include a number of elements related to restrictions, incentives, and good communication between consumers, industry and government. For one, policies should directly address the specific goal of limiting the exposure of children to advertising for food products that do not meet nutritional criteria and ensure that advertising does not condone or encourage unhealthy behaviours.

There are additional significant benefits to be gained from effective advertising self-regulation. These benefits can be reached more efficiently when government and industry propose good incentives for companies to develop responsible practices and promote healthier products. Making the changes that contribute to improving people's health has clear benefits for manufacturers in that they can realise the economic gains of these innovations as well as add positive associations to their brands by communicating them to consumers. A key part of the self-regulatory process is to empower consumers to make complaints and suggestions, and to provide for efficient and free redress.

Chapter 7

Information, Incentives and Choice:
A Viable Approach to Preventing Obesity

The basic biological causes and health effects of obesity have been common knowledge and a focus of public health concern since the mid-20th century. Still, little has been effective in slowing the upward trends of obesity in OECD populations. Adapting efficient solutions to this problem requires an understanding of the complex, interrelated factors that contribute to overweight and obesity, and the equally complex mix of tools that can remove or mitigate these causes. This chapter presents a discussion of critical factors in the design and implementation of effective prevention strategies, including considerations on how social norms form and evolve, as well as how individual approach and population approaches to chronic disease prevention can work together in the case of obesity. The chapter also discusses in further depth the meaning of a multi-stakeholder approach to prevention and the potential effects of government action on individual choice.

Tackling the obesity problem

In the face of a rising burden of chronic diseases and escalating costs to health services, individuals and the economy at large, obesity has become a priority for government efforts to build healthy societies. All OECD countries have spent large sums of money over the last decades trying to foster health in their populations, but only in the last few years they turned their attention to obesity. This book has looked at the issue by asking, among other questions, what caused the obesity epidemic, how governments have responded, and ultimately, what works. In one sense, the answer to the first question is simple: obesity is caused by an imbalance between calories taken in by the body and calories burned. Likewise, the main reasons for this imbalance are reasonably well known – a change in diets towards more energy-dense foods high in fat and sugars but low in vitamins, minerals and other micronutrients; and at the same time less physical activity due to changes in work, transportation, and lifestyles.

The risks associated with obesity have been known since the 1950s, so why have efforts to tackle the obesity epidemic been so ineffective? Is it a problem of convincing individuals to change behaviour or influencing populations? How do the elements of choice, opportunity cost, education and information contribute to shaping behaviours? What actions will achieve better results in combating obesity? There are no easy answers to these questions. We have seen that the causes of obesity are multiple and interdependent. We have looked at a range of interventions to prevent obesity in different countries and have analysed their effectiveness and efficiency. What have we learned? For one, that given the complexity of the problem, there is no magic bullet for stopping the obesity epidemic.

Finding the right solution lies in understanding how the various actors – individuals, industry decision makers, the civil society and governments – may interact. It involves understanding the psychology of personal choice and how this affects and is affected by the range of choice options that an individual has. It also requires understanding how shifts in habit and culture across societies occur. What can be done to accelerate a change to healthier habits on a large scale?

One of the most significant findings of the analyses reported in this book concerns the need for comprehensive strategies to prevent and combat obesity. Individual interventions have shown to have a relatively limited impact, therefore comprehensive strategies involving multiple interventions to address a range of determinants are required to reach a "critical mass" and have a meaningful impact on the obesity epidemic by generating fundamental changes in social norms.

Populations or individuals?

Whether we are talking about smoking, drugs, reckless driving or unhealthy eating, the basic conflict is the same. Most of us now have the knowledge that these behaviours have negative consequences and that stopping them would afford benefits and decrease risk for us as individuals and consequently for society. Yet changes in behaviour are very difficult to achieve for individuals, and it is even harder to trigger such changes on a bigger scale, for large sections of a population, which is typically the objective of public health policies.

At the centre of debates on the prevention of chronic diseases is the question of where to direct attention and funds in order to attain the largest possible health gain. Geoffrey Rose, a towering figure in epidemiology and public health, dedicated much of his career to the study of effective approaches to disease prevention. In a seminal article in the *British Medical Journal* published in 1981, he pointed out that:

> *The preventive strategy that concentrates on high-risk individuals may be appropriate for those individuals, as well as being a wise and efficient use of limited medical resources; but its ability to reduce the burden of disease in the whole community tends to be disappointingly small. Potentially far more effective, and ultimately the only acceptable answer, is the mass strategy, whose aim is to shift the whole population's distribution of the risk variable* (Rose, 1981).

Rose was writing about cardiovascular disease, but his conclusion that most cases of chronic disease occur in those members of the population at average rather than high risk is relevant to most relations between risk factors and chronic disease.

Rose's insights provide the foundations for a "population approach" to tackling numerous conditions, which seeks to understand the epidemiological and social contexts in which diseases develop, and how these contexts relate to individual behaviours. This is the prevailing public health approach to the prevention of chronic diseases. In Rose's analysis, the population approach is contrasted with an "individual", or "high-risk", approach, based on the targeting of those most at risk in the wider distribution of a given risk factor (adiposity, or BMI, in our case).

While it is true that obesity treatments, such as weight loss medications and bariatric surgery, work at least for some of those who are obese, health care systems do not have the means to offer treatments to everyone who could benefit from them, especially in the wake of rising numbers of potential beneficiaries, and even if they did have the resources, many for whom these remedies are unsuitable would still be left without an effective solution to their problem. A different type of individual approach to the prevention of chronic diseases linked to obesity is based on the delivery of lifestyle counselling to individuals at high risk, for instance in a primary care setting. This corresponds quite closely to one of the interventions assessed in Chapter 6, which proved extremely effective in our analysis, at least when delivered in an intensive form, involving physicians as well as dieticians, relative to other types of interventions.

Although the pathways of risk reduction that the latter approach and the population approach to prevention seek to pursue are virtually the same (persuading people to reduce calorie intake and/or increase exercise) the targets are different. Counselling in primary care focuses on a select group of individuals at high risk, some of whom will likely benefit substantially from the interventions. On the other hand, a population approach would perhaps seek less spectacular changes, but focusing on the entire population (as in mass media campaigns; food labelling regulation; or fiscal measures) or broad sub-groups (*e.g.* children in food advertising regulation; working-age adults in worksite health promotion interventions), no matter what the risk status of specific individuals within those groups may be.

As discussed throughout this book, the individual behaviour that leads to obesity is the result of complex interactions among multiple factors including socio-economic status, physical environment, ethnicity, gender, individual tastes, family history, transport options, town planning, fashion, and so on. A population approach would address some of these factors, targeting those that can be influenced to effect a change in attitudes and behaviour that made obesity less acceptable and thus less likely. A virtuous circle could then be created whereby unhealthy behaviours and products were rejected by a growing number of people, reducing the incentives to propose or adopt them. Rose summed it up thus:

> Once a social norm of behaviour has become accepted and (as in the case of diet) once the supply industries have adapted themselves to the new pattern, then the maintenance of that situation no longer requires effort from individuals (Rose, 1985).

Rose (1992) estimated that if the average weight in a population could be reduced by 1.25% (*e.g.* less than 900 grams for a person weighing 70 kg), the number of people who are obese in the same population would be reduced by one quarter. The relationship between average BMI and proportion of people who are obese in a population may or may not have changed since Rose produced his estimates, but what is most important is that the relative success of population *vs.* individual strategies depends crucially on the effectiveness of existing interventions at the two levels. What we know from existing evidence and from model-based analyses like the one presented in Chapter 6 is that none of the population prevention strategies assessed so far have shown the potential to generate a reduction in average weight for a whole population of the order mentioned above. On the other hand, the analysis jointly undertaken by the OECD and the WHO suggests that an individual strategy, although more expensive compared to others, can generate larger health gains than any of the population approaches assessed.

How can these findings be reconciled with Rose's theories of prevention? A dogmatic interpretation of the superiority of population approaches in chronic disease prevention would not help in the face of empirical evidence showing larger returns from high-risk strategies. Although Rose's theory and prescription are valid and work well for a potentially large number of risk factors, such as hypertension, it must be recognised that other risk factors, like BMI, may be different. This is not to dismiss population approaches in tackling obesity. On the contrary, our analyses show that population approaches are effective and can provide the most cost-effective means of addressing the obesity epidemic. What is needed is a "middle road" (Brown *et al.*, 2007) between individual and population approaches to prevention in the case of BMI and obesity, because targeting those most at risk can be at least as valuable as targeting the population at large and seeking to shift the overall distribution of BMI. On the other hand, population approaches come at a lower cost and are more efficient. Population approaches also provide greater chances to exploit social multiplier effects and to generate synergies between different actions, creating better opportunities to trigger long-lasting changes in social norms. In conclusion, a sensible approach to tackling obesity and preventing the chronic diseases which are linked to it could not do without either of the two main approaches to prevention, the population and the individual, or high-risk, approaches.

Changing social norms

A social norm is a perception that prescribes or influences behaviour – a definition of what most people would or should do in a given circumstance. The European Social Norms Repository at the University of Bradford explains the social norms approach to changing behaviour in these terms:

> *Social norms interventions are based on the simple idea that if individuals overestimate how common a behaviour is then correcting this misperception should reduce the pressure on the individual to engage in that behaviour. For example, if high school students think that the majority of their fellow*

pupils are drinking alcohol regularly and heavily – when in fact only a minority do so – then presenting this information in a credible way to the student body will correct their misperceptions and result in a reduction of their own alcohol consumption. In other words, a social norms intervention uses peer pressure to achieve a positive result [...] (www.normative beliefs.org.uk/about.htm#intervention; McAlaney, 2010).

How could this apply to obesity? As discussed in Chapter 4 in the context of social multiplier effects, there is at least some evidence that obesity is "socially contagious" (Christakis and Fowler, 2007), which means that you are more likely to be obese if you have a close friend who is obese, and also that you are more likely to become obese if someone else in your close social network is also gaining weight. Christakis and Fowler do not claim that social norms are the vector of the contagion, but other research suggests that it could play an important role, through either a "stigma effect" or a "complacency effect". In other words, in a group where obesity is rare and frowned upon, for instance upper class white women in the United States or Europe, an obese woman would be under far greater peer pressure to lose weight than a woman from a lower social class where obesity is far more widespread. A similar argument has been used to explain some of the differences in obesity between ethnic groups, such as those illustrated in Chapter 3. Research from the Brookings' Center on Social and Economic Dynamics, based on surveys of well-being, finds that in cohorts where obesity rates are high, obese people do not report being more unhappy than others, whereas in cohorts where obesity rates are low, obese people tend to be much unhappier than the mean (controlling for other factors such as age, gender and income). Computer simulations by the same researchers suggest that overall social norms about weight can shift dramatically as a result of even small changes by some members of the group (Felton and Graham, 2005; Graham, 2008).

Our evidence shows that obesity is most effectively and efficiently treated through a multi-faceted approach, or group of approaches that match the complexity of the problem at hand. Taking any of the interventions alone – even the most effective (and expensive) one of counselling in primary care – still does not solve the problem on any large scale.

The context in which the obesity epidemic has developed is particularly complex, since the agents at play, such as food manufacturers and retailers, or civil society organisations, such as consumer and patient organisations, are often complex systems in themselves. Consciously influencing such a wide range of relevant actors, often with conflicting interests, to achieve a tipping point that would trigger a reduction in obesity has so far proved impossible, although obesity rates are gradually levelling off in some groups in some countries. One of the problems is that although there is general recognition of the multiplicity of contributing factors, campaigns to tackle obesity have been too narrowly focused, and are often based on the assumption that individuals will consume food and take exercise in a healthy way if they are given the right information. So far, information and education have been the main pillars of government attempts to promote healthy lifestyles.

While the rationale for prioritising "soft" paternalism (actions involving persuasion, or the setting of default rules, as described in Chapter 5) over more intrusive measures at earlier stages of policy development is clear, the limitations of using only this approach in dealing with a complex issue like obesity are also apparent. Soft paternalism is seen by Glaeser (2005) as an "emotional tax on behaviour which yields no government revenues". Governments are not always equipped for delivering complex communication strategies, and in some cases there is also a risk that government action may be influenced by the very interests it attempts to counter. Governments may be hostages to lobbies and special interests (a phenomenon often referred to as "regulator capture") and may be themselves subject to judgement error and bounded rationality. When such situations occur, soft paternalism often proves more difficult to monitor and sanction by the public than hard paternalism (e.g. fiscal and regulatory measures of the types also described in Chapter 5). Glaeser concludes that it is undesirable for governments to engage in actions to influence individual choices through persuasion, not least because persuasion will eventually lead to the acceptance of "harder" paternalistic measures. A counterargument to Glaeser's point that governments should not engage in persuasion, and particularly in the setting of default rules, is that "paternalism is unavoidable" (Sunstein and Thaler, 2003). Governments will set default rules in any case, willingly or not. Even if they defined no rules at all, this would determine a default scenario.

However, it is worth repeating that all of the interventions discussed in this book are effective, even in isolation, but that combined, they could contribute to a shift in social norms. Turning the tide of risk factors and chronic diseases that have assumed epidemic proportions during the course of the 20th century requires more than a single preventive intervention and more than one approach, however effective and broadly based these may be. Fundamental changes in the social norms that regulate individual and collective behaviours can only be triggered by wide ranging prevention strategies addressing multiple determinants of health, strategies that are likely to develop incrementally, rather than through comprehensive planning.

Social norms cannot be engineered. They set the boundaries and the rules for a complex interplay of conflicting interests which we have interpreted here, using the tools of economics, as market dynamics. At the same time, it is precisely that interplay of interests that progressively adapts and changes social norms. The question of how to combine and successfully implement preventive interventions is as much a question of political economy and how decisions are made as it is of economics and health.

A multi-stakeholder approach

The approach adopted here recognises that people do not always make the choices that would maximise their own welfare, and do not always have the ability and possibility to make such choices, because their environment prevents them. Individual choices and habits regarding eating, physical activity and other aspects of lifestyles are shaped by factors partly or wholly beyond individual control, including: the range and availability of leisure activities; the organisation of work and free time; and the supply and composition of food. These are all largely influenced by market forces and the private sector, which are in turn influenced by laws and regulations. OECD governments, therefore, have tended to emphasise the importance of co-operation and partnership with business in preventing obesity. A range of actors, or stakeholders, are mentioned by governments as natural partners in the development of strategies to improve nutrition and physical activity. However, the precise terms in which such co-operation should take place and the respective roles of the different stakeholders often remain vague.

For their part, many business organisations engage in health-promoting production, marketing, and human resource management policies to fulfil the expectations and demands of consumers, government, and society at large. In April 2009 in the United Kingdom for example, 18 major supermarket and fast food chains signed up to a Food Standards Agency scheme to display the number of calories in dishes. Customers could thus learn that one kind of hamburger contained almost a thousand calories, compared with 266 for the same restaurant's standard burger.

Health and wellbeing is also an industry in itself, and has been developing at a very fast pace in recent years, driven by growing consumer demand. According to market researchers Marketdata Enterprises, in the United States alone, the weight loss and diet control market was worth USD 58.6 billion in 2008, an increase of almost USD 4 billion from a similar survey two years earlier. There appears to be little evidence that this is contributing to a reversal in obesity trends. Indeed, in February 2009, an editorial in the *Canadian Medical Association Journal* claimed that:

> The majority of commercial weight-loss providers manipulate vulnerable consumers with impunity, cultivating unrealistic expectations and false beliefs. Consequently, we regularly see preposterous claims [about vitamin injections and herbal supplements]... (Freedhoff and Sharma, 2009).

Increased attention to obesity and its consequences by the mass media has also contributed to changing consumer preferences, the most powerful driver of changes in the supply of lifestyle commodities. However, it is hard to say whether this has had a major, sustained impact on the behaviour of people who rely mainly on the mass media for information and entertainment. Socially disadvantaged groups continue to display lower levels of leisure-time physical activity (not compensated by work-related physical activity) and less healthy nutrition patterns. Furthermore, media interest is hard to sustain for long, particularly mass audience media such as the tabloid press and reality TV. Obesity may go out of fashion and lose media attention very rapidly.

Governments are often reluctant to use regulation because of the complexity of the regulatory process, the enforcement costs involved, and the desire to avoid confrontation with the food industry. They may prefer to cooperate with the food industry in developing guidelines to reformulate food by lowering sugar, salt and fats in processed food, and develop consistent nutritional advice on food labels. Cooperation between governments and the food industry is the single most critical link in the adoption of a multi-stakeholder approach. Neither party may have a choice. Every alternative to cooperation would likely bring heavy losses to both, including financial losses. But realising an effective and transparent co-operation is a daunting task because the potential for conflict, given the scale of the interests at stake, is vast. This is also the reason why failure to cooperate would most likely mean that government action may be substantially weakened.

There are many examples of conflict between governments and the food industry. In 2003, the WHO was almost brought to its knees by the sugar industry, following a recommendation in a WHO/FAO report to limit the intake of free sugars to 10% of total energy intake (Boseley, 2003). Arguably, this case set a precedent which induced many governments and international organisation to use special caution when considering regulation affecting people's diets. In fact, regulatory attempts in key areas of diet have been very timid.

Take the case of salt in US diets. An Institute of Medicine report produced recommendations on how to reduce the unhealthy amounts of sodium in food and thereby help prevent more than 100 000 deaths annually in the United States. The IOM states that:

> Regulatory action is necessary because four decades of public education campaigns about the dangers of excess salt and voluntary sodium cutting efforts by the food industry have generally failed [...] voluntary efforts have fallen short because [...] companies have feared losing customers who could switch to competing products or brands with higher salt content. Also, salt is so widespread and present in such large amounts in grocery store and menu items – including many foods and drinks that people do not think of

as salty – that it is difficult for people who want to reduce their sodium intake to succeed. (IOM, 2010)

The IOM concludes that a new, coordinated approach is needed to reduce sodium content in food, requiring new government standards for the acceptable level of sodium. However, without salt, the industry would have to use more expensive products to create textures and tastes. Salt producer and food conglomerate Cargill responded by producing a video called Salt 101 (*www.salt101.com/#/intro*) that encourages people to sprinkle salt on everything from fresh fruit to cookies. One of the key studies upon which the report was based, published in the *New England Journal of Medicine* only a few months before the IOM report, showed that reducing dietary salt by 3 g per day could reduce the new annual cases of coronary heart disease by 60 000 to 120 000, stroke by 32 000 to 66 000, and myocardial infarction by 54 000 to 99 000 (Bibbins-Domingo *et al.*, 2010). Virtually at the same time, a commentary was published in the *Journal of the American Medical Association* (JAMA), authored by an academic advisor to the Salt Institute, a salt industry organisation aimed at providing information on the benefits of salt, calling for caution in the interpretation of the evidence about links between salt intake and chronic diseases (Alderman, 2010). These are clear signs of a looming conflict, which could escalate to an open war should governments consider seriously the option of using regulation to reduce people's salt intake, similar to the war broken out between the current US administration and a coalition of industries led by the non-alcoholic beverage industry, on the prospect of including a soda-tax in the recent health care reform legislation.

If there is a market for healthier products, then the goal of healthy choices and profit can be aligned – the proliferation of lower salt and sugar products on store shelves is evidence of this. But adding healthier options to the range of unhealthy products that dominate the choice range of most food stores is unlikely to make much of a difference for obesity. Nonetheless, the simple expectation of government action may produce both direct and indirect effects on markets for health-related products, services and activities. If the food industry expects governments to impose new or stricter regulations, business organisations may seek to avoid or influence change through self-regulation and co-operation with governments, to obtain some control over the regulatory process.

The cases of trans fats and food advertising to children, both areas in which the industry has taken important steps, provide examples of the role played by expectations of government regulation in the food industry's production and marketing policies. In the case of trans fats, the prospect of government regulation was given support by initiatives such as those taken by the Danish Government, the City of New York, or the State of California, and by authoritative calls for regulation by bodies such as the UK National

Institute for Health and Clinical Excellence (NICE) in England and Wales. In addition, the prospect of legal action, such as the successful lawsuit brought to McDonald's for failing to correctly inform its customers about changes in cooking oils involving different levels of trans fats, which led to a multi-million dollar settlement mostly in favour of the American Heart Association, contributed to creating a convergence of interests between the relevant actors involved. In many instances, the food industry has been responding effectively through product reformulation aimed at reducing, or even eliminating, trans fats from processed food, thus holding back further government action. In the case of food advertising to children, an issue widely discussed in Chapter 6 and in the following Special Focus contributions, the prospect of government regulation has also become increasingly real, despite the difficulties involved in implementing an effective regulatory action. The industry has responded with a programme of "Pledges" (see contribution by Stephan Loerke), which again some governments may consider a sufficient protection for children against exposure to potentially harmful food advertising.

Regulation may seem like a clear-cut objective, but in fact it can also be a way for entrenched interests to reinforce their position by making it more difficult for new competitors to enter the market, especially if the older firms have the political experience to influence decisions ("regulatory capture"). In similar situations, advocacy groups would be expected to provide the necessary "checks and balances", but it can be difficult for advocacy groups to play this role effectively. Campaigns to prevent obesity suffer from the same weaknesses as other movements for social change or issues-based organisations. Coalition members may have widely differing motivations, goals and strategies for joining. A recent article in the *Atlantic Monthly* describes how the Robert Wood Johnson Foundation (RWJF), the largest philanthropy dedicated to improving health care in the United States, tried to become the "connective tissue" of the movement against child obesity in 2008:

> *[The RWJF] asked Robert Raben, a former assistant attorney general under Bill Clinton, for help. Raben and his team held meetings with the different interests: anti-poverty activists; leaders of the "green products" movement, which works to improve food quality in inner cities; academic health experts; advocates for better urban planning (they are known as the "Sidewalk people"); advocates for public transportation and bike use (the "Bike and bus people"); the anti-high-fructose-corn-syrup crowd; the nutrition labelers; and others. Raben got a good discussion going. But he found it difficult to figure out how to fuse this collection of interests into a coherent political movement. Successful advocacy campaigns have a clear agenda. Obesity activists had many different agendas: Reducing suffering? Food security? Health? Anti-poverty? And there were even more-basic*

questions: Should the foundation increase its cooperation with the food industry? Should it adopt a confrontational stance? (Ambinder, 2010).

However, even without the threat of tighter controls, business organisations may engage in health-promoting initiatives to fulfil broader societal expectations, as a form of corporate social responsibility or to counter a bad image. The food and beverage industry is often criticised for contributing to unhealthy eating habits, but it also finances, for instance, health education initiatives and programmes to promote physical activity among children. Employers' organisations participate in schemes to promote healthier workforces and workplaces. In many countries, a number of large employers have taken steps to promote healthy lifestyles among their employees, despite limited evidence that such initiatives generate positive returns for firms in terms of reduced sick leave and higher productivity.

How much individual choice?

Adding to the complexities of a policy arena crowded with powerful and often conflicting interests is the desire for governments to protect individual choice when seeking to prevent diseases linked to lifestyles. The political costs of a government being perceived as implementing a "nanny State", as telling people what to do in one of the most private spheres of their lives, as preventing people from enjoying products and activities viewed as unhealthy, are just too large for any government to be willing to constrain individual choice to any significant degree, unless a clear and uncontroversial case could be made in support for the measures to be adopted. Political ideology has a strong influence on how far a government may be willing to push the boundaries of individual choice, but more practical considerations, such as those discussed below, also play an important role in shaping government attitudes.

It is interesting to note that widespread concerns about possible restrictions on individual choice that may follow specific government policies are seldom matched by similar concerns about the environmental constraints that already limit individual lifestyle choices, which may have nothing to do with government action. Going back to Geoffrey Rose, he does share common concerns for individual choice in his work on prevention: "The first duty of governments in health promotion and environmental regulation is to protect the individual's freedom of choice" (Rose, 1992, p. 120). However, what Rose is most concerned about is limitations of individual choice created by the environment (essentially, by other economic agents). When Rose does mention examples of potential interference with choice by governments, here is the type of government actions he has in mind: "Heavy subsidies to farmers for producing milk and butter, but none for vegetable oils and soft margarines, creates an imbalance which distorts the freedom of consumers" (*op. cit.*,

p. 122). In Rose's analysis, public health actions promoted by governments for the sake of improving population health tend not to be viewed as a potential source of undue interference with individual choice. If there were interference, this would be justified by the health improvement brought about by the intervention. As discussed before, an economist may seek a stronger justification (social welfare should be improved, overall, once health gains and the consequences of interference with choice are both accounted for), but it remains clear that the argument in favour of individual choice may be overstated in the current debate on chronic disease prevention. There is no doubt that all parties which have an interest in minimising government action will use the choice argument to its full potential, and the popular media will often lend support to and amplify arguments in favour of individual choice, as "nanny State"-type news tend to make easy headlines.

A more balanced analysis of how far governments may push their actions when these involve limitations of individual choice should consider, above all, the nature of the lifestyle choices those actions are meant to influence and the characteristics of the individuals whose choices are to be influenced.

Of the types of actions discussed in the first part of Chapter 5, only those which have the effect of widening choice, or making healthy options more accessible, tend to be well accepted, although they may be expensive and the costs involved may fall disproportionally on those most in need. Finding support for other actions described in Chapter 5, which involve progressively higher degrees of interference with individual choice, is less straightforward.

An important distinction must be made between commodities whose consumption is invariably unhealthy, such as tobacco, and commodities whose impact on health depends on the modalities of consumption. An example of the latter is food. Certain forms of food consumption are hazardous, but most consumption is healthy, even essential for life, including some consumption of fats, sugars and salt. When consumption is not invariably unhealthy, interventions will be beneficial to those who tend to engage in unhealthy consumption (for whatever reasons) but will negatively affect those whose consumption is generally healthy, because the latter will have their choices limited by those interventions, or they will see the price of their consumption rise because of taxation or similar measures.

The concept of asymmetric paternalism (Camerer *et al.*, 2003) is a response to the tradeoffs arising with heterogeneous consumers. When some consumers are more able than others to handle the environmental pressures that influence their lifestyle choices, interventions with the largest potential for a welfare improvement are those that may change the behaviours of those who are most subject to environmental pressures without affecting, or minimally affecting, others. An example of these actions is the setting of default rules, discussed in Chapter 5. The same concept, however, can be applied to more intrusive interventions. O'Donoghue and Rabin (2003) provide an example of an optimal taxation model aimed at maximising the effects on those whose preferences are most present-biased, while minimising harm to other consumers. They tentatively propose a number of possible solutions to implement such a taxation model, involving, for instance, the advance purchase of coupons or licenses for the consumption of potentially unhealthy commodities, which would discourage inappropriate consumption by those with poorer self-control.

In conclusion, actions that widen choice or make certain options more accessible are generally well accepted. Opportunities for adopting actions of these types find their main limits in their financial costs. The use of actions involving higher degrees of interference with individual choice may be met with increasing degrees of hostility, especially when only certain forms of consumption of a commodity are unhealthy and consumers differ in terms of the nature of their consumption. Persuasion and other non-price devices such as default rules are often advocated as minimally intrusive interventions responding to the ideal of asymmetric paternalism, as they do not significantly harm rational consumers. However, there are risks involved in relying on governments to deliver persuasion effectively and in the best interest of individuals, and it is difficult to monitor whether governments are able to do this. Taxes and consumption bans are more transparent and contestable, although they may lead to potentially severe welfare losses in the presence of heterogeneous consumers with varying degrees of rationality. Actions involving higher than minimal degrees of interference with individual choice become more acceptable when the consumption of a commodity is invariably unhealthy and bears a large potential for self-harm; in the presence of important externalities; when actions may be targeted to population groups that deserve greater protection, such as children, or groups that are particularly exposed to external influences that may trigger unhealthy behaviours (*e.g.* disadvantaged socio-economic groups).

Key messages

- Comprehensive strategies involving multiple interventions to address a range of determinants are required to reach a "critical mass" and have a meaningful impact on the obesity epidemic by generating fundamental changes in social norms.

- A minor reduction in the average weight of a population would cut dramatically the number of people who are obese in the same population, but the effectiveness of existing population-level approaches to tackling obesity, when assessed in isolation, is limited.

- Population approaches must be implemented alongside individual, or high-risk, approaches, as the latter have shown a greater potential for health gain in our analysis, while the former offer greater opportunities for exploiting synergies between interventions and possible social multiplier effects.

- Turning the tide of risk factors and chronic diseases that have assumed epidemic proportions requires fundamental changes in the social norms that regulate individual and collective behaviours.

- Social norms cannot be engineered. A coordinated action by multiple agents is required to trigger incremental changes, but consciously influencing a wide range of actors, often with conflicting interests, to achieve a tipping point that would trigger a reduction in obesity has so far proved impossible.

- The best chances of success lie in the adoption of a multi-stakeholder approach, involving cooperation and compromise between governments and other agents who may bear conflicting interests, in the pursuit of a common goal.

- Co-operation between governments and the food industry is the single most critical link in the adoption of a multi-stakeholder approach. Neither party may have a choice. Every alternative to cooperation would likely bring heavy losses to both, including financial losses.

- Realising an effective and transparent cooperation is a daunting task because the potential for conflict, given the scale of the interests at stake, is vast. This is also the reason why failure to cooperate would most likely mean that government action may be substantially weakened.

- The political costs potentially involved are too large for any government to be willing to constrain individual choice to any significant degree, unless a clear and uncontroversial case could be made in support for the measures to be adopted. However, the argument in favour of individual choice may be overstated in the current debate on chronic disease prevention.

- Widespread concerns about possible restrictions on individual choice that may follow specific government policies are seldom matched by similar concerns about existing constraints and environmental pressures impinging on individual lifestyle choices.

Bibliography

Alderman, M.H. (2010), "Reducing Dietary Sodium. The Case for Caution", *JAMA*, Vol. 305, No. 5, pp. 448-449.

Ambinder, M. (2010), "Beating Obesity", *The Atlantic Magazine*, May 2010.

Bibbins-Domingo, K., G.M. Chertow, P.G. Coxson *et al.* (2010), "Projected Effect of Dietary Salt Reductions on Future Cardiovascular Disease", *New England Journal of Medicine*, Vol. 362, No. 7, pp. 590-599.

Boseley, S. (2003), "Political Context of the World Health Organization: Sugar Industry Threatens to Scupper the WHO", *International Journal of Health Services*, Vol. 33, No. 4, pp. 831-833.

Brown, W.J., R. Hockey and A. Dobson (2007), "Rose Revisited: A 'Middle Road' Prevention Strategy to Reduce Non-Communicable Chronic Disease Risk", *Bulletin of the World Health Organisation*, Vol. 85, No. 11, pp. 886-887.

Camerer, C. *et al.* (2003), "Regulation for Conservatives: Behavioural Economics and the Case for 'Asymmetric Paternalism'", *University of Pennsylvania Law Review*, Vol. 151, pp. 1211-1254.

Christakis, N.A. and J.H. Fowler (2007), "The Spread of Obesity in a Large Social Network Over 32 Years", *New England Journal of Medicine*, Vol. 357, No. 4, pp. 370-379.

Felton, A. and C. Graham (2005), "Variance in Obesity Across Cohorts and Countries: A Norms-Based Explanation Using Happiness Surveys", Working Paper, Brookings Institution, Washington.

Freedhoff, Y. and A.M. Sharma (2009), "Lose 40 Pounds in 4 Weeks: Regulating Commercial Weight-Loss Programs", *Canadian Medical Association Journal*, Vol. 180, p. 367.

Glaeser, E. (2006), "Paternalism and Psychology", *University of Chicago Law Review*, Vol. 73, pp. 133-156.

Graham, C. (2008), "Happiness and Health: Lessons – and Questions – for Public Policy", *Health Affairs*, Vol. 27, pp. 72-87.

Institute of Medicine (2010), *Strategies to Reduce Sodium Intake in the United States*, National Academy of Sciences, Washington.

McAlaney, J. (2010), B.M. Bewick and J. Bauerle, "Social Norms Guidebook: A Guide to Implementing the Social Norms Approach in the UK", University of Bradford, University of Leeds, Department of Health, West Yorkshire, UK.

O'Donoghue, T. and M. Rabin (2003), "Studying Optimal Paternalism, Illustrated by a Model of Sin Taxes", *American Economic Review*, Vol. 93, No. 2, pp. 186-191.

Pezzullo, L. (2008), *The Growing Cost of Obesity in 2008: Three Years on Melbourne*, Access Economics for Diabetes Australia.

Rose, G. (1981), "Strategy of Prevention: Lessons from Cardiovascular Disease", *British Medical Journal*, Vol. 282, pp. 1847-1851.

Rose, G. (1985), "Sick Individuals and Sick Populations", *International Journal of Epidemiology*, Vol. 14, pp. 32-38.

Rose, G. (1992), "The Strategy of Preventive Medicine", Oxford University Press, Oxford.

Sunstein, C.R. and R.H. Thaler (2003), "Libertarian Paternalism is Not an Oxymoron", *University of Chicago Law Review*, Vol. 70, No. 4, pp. 1159-1202.

ANNEX A

Supplementary Figures and Tables

1. Supplementary tables and figures associated with Chapters 2 and 3

Table A.1. **Description of the national health survey data used in the analyses reported in Chapters 2 and 3**

	Name of the survey	Organisation undertaking the survey	Type of survey	Years used in the analyses
Australia	National Health Survey	Australian Bureau of Statistics	Health interview survey	1989, 1995, 2001, 2004/05
Austria	Mikrozensus + Health Interview Survey	Statistics Austria	Health interview survey	1983, 1991, 1999, 2006/07
Canada	National Population Health Survey + Canadian Community Health Survey	Statistics Canada	Health interview survey	1994/95, 2000/01, 2003, 2005
England	Health Survey for England (HSE)	Office for Population Censuses and Surveys (1991-93), then the Joint Survey Unit of the National Centre of Social Research and the Department of Epidemiology and Public Health at University College London (since 1994)	Health examination survey	1991 to 2007
France	Enquête Santé et Protection Sociale	Institute for Research and Information in Health Economics	Health interview survey	1990, 1991, 1992, 1993, 1994, 1995, 1996, 1997, 1998, 2000, 2002, 2004, 2006
Hungary	National Health Interview survey	Johan Béla National Center of Epidemiology	Health interview survey	2000, 2003
Italy	Condizione di Salute	Istituto Nazionale di Statistica	Health interview survey	1994/95, 2000, 2005
Korea	Korean National Health and Nutrition Examination Survey (KNHANES)	Jointly carried out by the Korea Institute for Health and Social Affairs and the Korea Health Industry Development Institute	Health examination survey	1998, 2001, 2005
Spain	Encuesta Nacional de Salud de Espana	Ministry of Health and Consumers in collaboration with the Centre of Sociological Investigations	Health interview survey	1993, 1995, 1997, 2001, 2003, 2006
Sweden	Swedish Level of Living Survey (LNU)	Statistics Sweden	Health interview survey	1991, 2000
United States-NHANES	National Health and Nutrition Examination Survey (NHANES)	National Center for Health Statistics	Health examination survey	NHANES I, NHANES II, NHANES III (1988-94), 1999/2000, 2001/02, 2003/04, 2005/06, 2007/08
United States-NHIS	National Health Interview Survey (NHIS)	National Center for Health Statistics	Health interview survey	1997 to 2005

Figures A.1 and A.2 present odds ratios of obesity and overweight, respectively, by socio-economic condition, and the associated confidence intervals. Mixed patterns emerge in men with a risk of obesity increasing in lower socio-economic groups in Austria and France and decreasing in countries such as Canada and Korea (Figure A.1, Panel A), and a risk of being overweight increasing in Austria and decreasing in Australia, Canada, Korea and the Unites States (Figure A.2, Panel A). Social gradients are found more consistently in women (Panel B in both figures).

Figure A.1. **Obesity by household income or occupation-based social class, selected OECD countries**

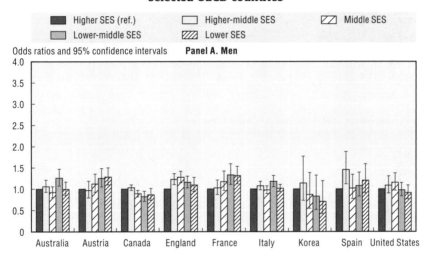

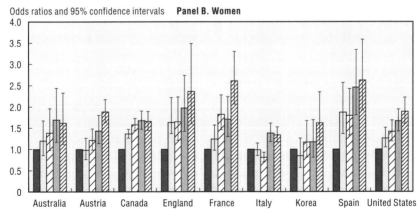

Note: SES is based on household income in Australia, Canada, Korea and the United States, and on occupation-based social class in other countries.

Source: OECD analysis of national health survey data.

StatLink ◤◢◤ http://dx.doi.org/10.1787/888932316210

Figure A.2. **Overweight by household income or occupation-based social class, selected OECD countries**

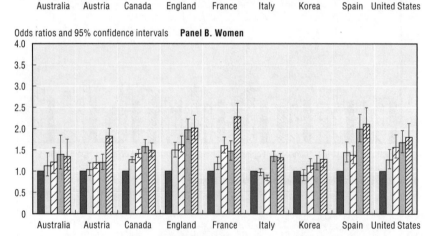

Note: SES is based on household income in Australia, Canada, Korea and the United States, and on occupation-based social class in other countries.

Source: OECD analysis of national health survey data.

StatLink ⟨☰⟩ http://dx.doi.org/10.1787/888932316229

Figures A.3 and A.4 present odds ratios of obesity and overweight, respectively, by education level, and the associated confidence intervals. The risks of obesity and overweight increase at lower levels of education in both men and women, except in men in Korea and in the United States (overweight only). Gradients are generally larger in women (Panel B in both figures) than in men (Panel A, both figures).

Figure A.3. **Obesity by education level, selected OECD countries**

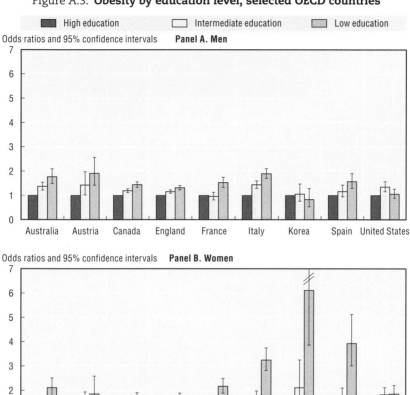

Note: The bar of the upper confidence interval is truncated for Korea. Its value is 8.4.

Source: OECD analysis of national health survey data.

StatLink ⧉ http://dx.doi.org/10.1787/888932316248

Figure A.4. **Overweight by education level, selected OECD countries**

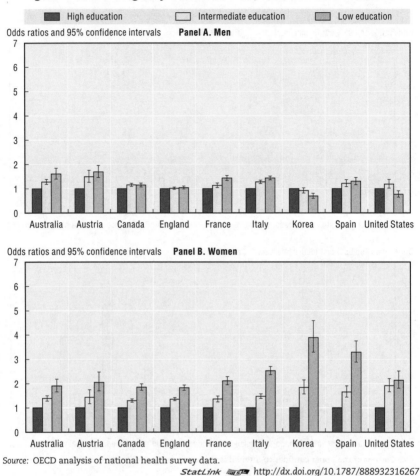

Source: OECD analysis of national health survey data.

StatLink [logo] http://dx.doi.org/10.1787/888932316267

2. Supplementary tables and figures associated with Chapter 6

Table A.2 provides a list of the main input parameters used in the model-based analyses presented in Chapter 6, along with references to the respective sources. References are listed at the bottom of the table.

Table A.2. **Main input parameters used in CDP model-based analyses and relevant sources**

Parameters	References		
	All other countries	Canada	Japan
RRa of incidence of IHD relative to high blood pressure		Lim *et al.* (2007)	
RRa of incidence of IHD relative to high cholesterol			Healthy Japan 21
RRa of incidence of IHD relative to diabetes	van Baal *et al.* (2008)		
RRa of incidence of IHD relative to obesity			van Baal *et al.* (2008)
RRa of fatality of IHD relative to high blood pressure	Hu *et al.* (2005b); Stevens *et al.* (2004); Hart *et al.* (1999)		
RRa of fatality of IHD relative to high cholesterol	Hart *et al.* (1999); Boshuizen *et al.* (2007)		
RRa of fatality of IHD relative to diabetes	Hu *et al.* (2005a); Hu *et al.* (2006); Hu *et al.* (2005b); Hart *et al.* (1999)		
RRa of fatality of IHD relative to obesity	Batty *et al.* (2006); Pardo Silva *et al.* (2006)		
RRa of incidence of stroke relative to high blood pressure			
RRa of incidence of stroke relative to high cholesterol		Lim *et al.* (2007)	
RRa of incidence of stroke relative to diabetes			
RRa of incidence of stroke relative to obesity	van Baal *et al.* (2008)		Healthy Japan 21
RRa of fatality of stroke relative to high blood pressure	Stevens *et al.* (2004); Boshuizen *et al.* (2007); Menotti *et al.* (2003)		
RRa of fatality of stroke relative to high cholesterol	Boshuizen *et al.* (2007); Menotti *et al.* (2003)		
RRa of fatality of stroke relative to diabetes	Hu *et al.* (2005a); Wannamethee *et al.* (2004)		
RRa of fatality of stroke relative to obesity	Batty *et al.* (2006); Pardo Silva *et al.* (2006)		
RRa of incidence of cancer relative to fibre consumption	Lock *et al.* (2005)		
RRa of incidence of cancer relative to obesity	van Baal *et al.* (2008)		
RRa of fatality of cancer relative to fibre consumption	Skuladottir *et al.* (2006); Pierce *et al.* (2007); Jansen *et al.* (1999)		
RRa of fatality of cancer relative to obesity	Calle *et al.* (2003)		
RR of high cholesterol relative to obesity	OECD calculculations on Health Survey for England		
RR of high systolic blood pressure relative to obesity	OECD calcuilculations on Health Survey for England		
RR of diabetes relative to obesity	van Baal *et al.* (2008)		
RR of obesity relative to fat diet	OECD calculations on US National Health and Nutrition Examination Survey		NIPH calculations on National Health and Nutlition Survey in Japan
RR of obesity relative to physical activity		PHAC calculations on Canadian Community Health Survey	NIPH calculations on National Health and Nutlition Survey in Japan
RR of obesity relative to fibre consumption			NIPH calculations on National Health and Nutlition Survey in Japan
Factors for disability-adjusted life years		Lopez *et al.* (2006)	

Table A.2. **Main input parameters used in CDP model-based analyses and relevant sources** (cont.)

Parameters	References		
	Canada	England	Italy
Starting population distribution	Statistics Canada	Office of National statistics	ISTAT
Total mortality	Statistics Canada	Office of National statistics	ISTAT
Incidence of IHD	Lopez et al. (2006)	OECD calculations using Dismod II	Gruppo di Ricerca del Progetto Registro per gli Eventi Coronarici e Cerebrovascolari, 2005
Prevalence of IHD	PHAC calculations using DISMOD II	MoH calculations on Health survey for England	OECD calculations using Dismod II
Mortality of IHD	Statistics Canada, Vital Statistics 2005	Office of National statistics	OECD calculations on database ISTAT Cause di Morte
Incidence of stroke	Lopez et al. (2006)	OECD calculations using Dismod II	Palmieri et al., 2009
Prevalence of stroke	PHAC calculations using DISMOD II	MoH calculations on Health survey for England	OECD calculations using Dismod II
Mortality of stroke	Statistics Canada, Vital Statistics 2005	Office of National statistics	OECD calculations on database ISTAT Cause di Morte
Incidence of cancer	Statistics Canada 2006	Office of National statistics	IARC
Prevalence of cancer	PHAC calculations using DISMOD II	OECD calculations using Dismod II	OECD calculations using Dismod II
Mortality of cancer	Statistics Canada, Vital Statistics 2005	Office of National statistics	WHO cancer mortality database
Prevalence of low physical activity	PHAC calculations on Canadian Community Health Survey, 2007/08 share file	OECD calculations on Eurobarometer 183-6/wave 58.2	
Prevalence of low fibre consumption	PHAC calculations on Canadian Community Health Survey, 2004 share file, wave 2	MoH calculations on Health survey for England	OECD calculations on Leclercq et al. (2009)
Prevalence of fat consumption	PHAC calculations on Canadian Community Health Survey, 2004 share file, wave 2	MoH calculations on Health survey for England	OECD calculations on FAOStat
Incidence of obesity	PHAC calculations using DISMOD II	OECD calculations using Dismod II	OECD calculations using Dismod II
Prevalence of obesity	PHAC calculations on Canadian Community Health Survey 2007/08 share file	MoH calculations on Health survey for England	OECD calculations on Indagine Multiscopo
Incidence of diabetes	PHAC calculations using DISMOD II	OECD calculations using Dismod II	OECD calculations using Dismod II
Prevalence of diabetes	PHAC calculations on National Diabetes Surveillance System	MoH calculations on Health survey for England	OECD calculations on Health for All – Italy
Incidence of high systolic pressure	PHAC calculations using DISMOD II	OECD calculations using Dismod II	OECD calculations using Dismod II
Prevalence of high systolic pressure	Lawes et al. (2004a)	MoH calculations on Health survey for England	OECD calculations on Indagine Multiscopo
Incidence of high cholesterol	PHAC calculations using DISMOD II	OECD calculations using Dismod II	OECD calculations using Dismod II
Prevalence of high cholesterol	Lawes et al. (2004b)	British heart foundation	OECD calculations on Progetto Cuore

Table A.2. **Main input parameters used in CDP model-based analyses and relevant sources** (cont.)

Parameters	References	
	Japan	Mexico
Starting population distribution	NIPH calculations on Vital Statistics in Japan	CONAPO
Total mortality	NIPH calculations on Vital Statistics in Japan	SS-DGIS 2007
Incidence of IHD	Yoshida et al. (2005)	MoH'S calculations on SS-DGIS-SAEH 2004-08; IMSS 2004-05
Prevalence of IHD	NIPH calculations on Patient Survey in Japan	OECD calculations using Dismod II
Mortality of IHD	OECD calculations employing Dismod II	SS-DGIS-SEED 2004-08
Incidence of stroke	Nagura et al. (2005)	WHO (2008)
Prevalence of stroke	NIPH calculations on Patient Survey in Japan	OECD calculations using Dismod II
Mortality of stroke	OECD calculations employing Dismod II	SS-DGIS-SEED 2004-08
Incidence of cancer	NIPH calculations on Cancer Statistics in Japan	MoH'S calculations on SS-DGIS-SAEH 2004-08; IMSS 2004-05
Prevalence of cancer	NIPH calculations on Cancer Statistics in Japan	OECD calculations using Dismod II
Mortality of cancer	OECD calculations employing Dismod II	SS-DGIS-SEED 2004-08
Prevalence of low physical activity	NIPH calculations on National Health and Nutrition Survey in Japan	MoH's calculations based on National Health and Nutrition Survey in Mexico 2006
Prevalence of low fibre consumption	NIPH calculations on National Health and Nutrition Survey in Japan	MoH's calculations based on National Health and Nutrition Survey in Mexico 2006
Prevalence of fat consumption	NIPH calculations on National Health and Nutrition Survey in Japan	MoH's calculations based on Mundo-Rosas et al. (2009); Rodriguez-Ramirez et al. (2009); Barquera et al. (2009)
Incidence of obesity	OECD calculations using Dismod II	OECD calculations using Dismod II
Prevalence of obesity	NIPH calculations on National Health and Nutlition Survey in Japan	Olaiz-Fernández et al. (2006); Shamah-Levy et al. (2007)
Incidence of diabetes	OECD calculations employing Dismod II	Olaiz et al. (2003); Villalpando et al. (2010)
Prevalence of diabetes	NIPH calculations on National Health and Nutlition Survey in Japan	Villalpando et al. (2010)
Incidence of high systolic pressure	OECD calculations employing Dismod II	OECD calculations using Dismod II
Prevalence of high systolic pressure	NIPH calculations on National Health and Nutlition Survey in Japan	Barquera et al. (2010)
Incidence of high cholesterol	OECD calculations employing Dismod II	OECD calculations using Dismod II
Prevalence of high cholesterol	NIPH calculations on National Health and Nutlition Survey in Japan	Aguilar-Salinas et al. (2010)

Table A.2. **Main input parameters used in CDP model-based analyses and relevant sources** (cont.)

References:

Aguilar-Salinas, C.A., F.J. Gómez-Pérez, J. Rull, S. Villalpando, S. Barquera and R. Rojas (2010), "Prevalence of Dyslipidemias in the Mexican National Health and Nutrition Survey 2006", *Salud Pública Mex* 2010, Vol. 52, pp. 44-53.

Barquera, S., L. Hernández-Barrera, I. Campos-Nonato, J. Espinosa, M. Flores, J.A. Barriguete and J. Rivera (2009), "Energy and Nutrient Consumption in Adults: Analysis of the Mexican National Health and Nutrition Survey 2006", *Salud Pública Mex* 2009, Vol. 51-4.

Barquera, S., I. Campos-Nonato, L. Hernández-Barrera, S. Villalpando, C. Rodríguez-Gilabert, R. Durazo-Arvizú and C.A. Aguilar-Salinas (2010), "Hypertension in Mexican Adults: Results from the Mexican Health and Nutrition Survey 2006", *Salud Pública Mex* 2010, Vol. 52, pp. 63-71.

Batty, G.D., M.J. Shipley, R.J. Jarrett, E. Breeze, M.G. Marmot and G. Davey Smith (2006), "Obesity and Overweight in Relation to Disease-Specific Mortality in Men With and Without Existing Coronary Heart Disease in London: The Original Whitehall Study", *Heart*, Vol. 92, No. 7, pp. 886-892, July.

Boshuizen, H.C., M. Lanti, A. Menotti, J. Moschandreas, H. Tolonen, A. Nissinen, S. Nedeljkovic, A. Kafatos and D. Kromhout (2007), "Effects of Past and Recent Blood Pressure and Cholesterol Level on Coronary Heart Disease and Stroke Mortality, Accounting for Measurement Error", *American Journal of Epidemiology*, Vol. 165, No. 4, pp. 398-409, 15 Feb.

British Heart Foundation website, *www.heartstats.org*, accessed on 2 March 2010.

Calle, E.E., C. Rodriguez, K. Walker-Thurmond and M.J. Thun (2003), "Overweight, Obesity, and Mortality from Cancer in a Prospectively Studied Cohort of US Adults", *New England Journal of Medicine*, Vol. 348, No. 17, pp. 1625-1638, 24 Apr.

CONAPO – Consejo Nacional de Población, "Proyecciones de la población de México 2005-2050", website, *www.conapo.gob.mx*, accessed on 19 April 2010.

FAOStat food supply database, website, *http://faostat.fao.org/site/609/default.aspx#ancor*, accessed on 18 June 2010.

Gruppo di Ricerca del Progetto Registro per gli Eventi Coronarici e Cerebrovascolari (2005), "Registro nazionale Italiano degli evento coronarici maggiori: tassi di attacco e letalità nelle diverse aree del paese", *Giornale Italiano di Cardiologia*, Vol. 6, pp. 667-673.

Hu, G., P. Jousilahti, Q. Qiao, S. Katoh and J. Tuomilehto (2005a), "Sex Differences in Cardiovascular and Total Mortality Among Diabetic and Non-Diabetic Individuals With or Without History of Myocardial Infarction", *Diabetologia*, Vol. 48, No. 5, pp. 856-861, May.

Hu, G., C. Sarti, P. Jousilahti, M. Peltonen, Q. Qiao, R. Antikainen and J. Tuomilehto (2005b), "The Impact of History of Hypertension and Type 2 Diabetes at Baseline on the Incidence of Stroke and Stroke Mortality", *Stroke*, Vol. 36, No. 12, pp. 2538-2543, Dec.

Hu, G., P. Jousilahti, C. Sarti, R. Antikainen and J. Tuomilehto (2006), "The Effect of Diabetes and Stroke at Baseline and During Follow-Up on Stroke Mortality", *Diabetologia*, Vol. 49, No. 10, pp. 2309-2316, Oct.

Hart, C.L., D.J. Hole and G.D. Smith (1999), "Risk Factors and 20-Year Stroke Mortality in Men and Women in the Renfrew/Paisley Study in Scotland", *Stroke*, Vol. 30, No. 10, pp. 1999-2007, Oct.

IARC – Cancer Incidence in Five Continents – Vol. IX, website *www-dep.iarc.fr/CI5_IX_frame.htm*, accessed on 2 March 2010.

IMSS – Instituto Mexicano del Seguro Social, "Egresos Hospitalarios 2004-2005", Dirección de Finanzas, México.

ISTAT website, *www.istat.it*, accessed on 18 June 2010.

ISTAT, "Cause di morte website", *www.istat.it/dati/dataset/20080111_00/*, accessed on 18 June 2010.

Jansen, M.C., H.B. Bueno-de-Mesquita, R. Buzina, F. Fidanza, A. Menotti, H. Blackburn, A.M. Nissinen, F.J. Kok and D. Kromhout (1999), "Dietary Fiber and Plant Foods in Relation to Colorectal Cancer Mortality: The Seven Countries Study", *International Journal of Cancer*, Vol. 81, No. 2, pp. 174-179, 12 Apr.

Lawes, C.M.M., S. Vander Horn, M.R. Law and A. Rodgers (2004b), "High Cholesterol", in M. Ezzati, A.D. Lopez, A. Rodgers and C.J.L. Murray (2004b), *Comparative Quantification of Health Risks. Global and Regional Burden of Diseases Attributable to Selected Major Risk Factors*, World Health Organisation, Geneva.

Lawes, C.M.M., S. Vander Horn, M.R. Law, P. Elliot, S. Mac Mahon and A. Rodgers (2004a), "High Blood Pressure", in M. Ezzati, A.D. Lopez, A. Rodgers and C.J.L. Murray (2004a), *Comparative Quantification of Health Risks. Global and Regional Burden of Diseases Attributable to Selected Major Risk Factors*, World Health Organisation, Geneva.

Leclercq, C., D. Arcella, R. Piccinelli, S. Sette, C. Le Donne and A. Turrini (2009), "The Italian National Food Consumption Survey INRAN-SCAI 2005-06: Main Results in Terms of Food Consumption", *Public Health Nutrition*, Vol. 12, No. 12, pp. 2504-2532.

Lim, S.S., T.A. Gaziano, E. Gakidou, K.S. Reddy, F. Farzadfar, R. Lozano and A. Rodgers (2007), "Prevention of Cardiovascular Disease in High-Risk Individuals in Low-Income and Middle-Income Countries: Health Effects and Costs", *The Lancet*, Vol. 370, No. 9604, pp. 2054-2062, 15 Dec.

Table A.2. **Main input parameters used in CDP model-based analyses and relevant sources** (cont.)

Lock, K., J. Pomerleau, L. Causer, D.R. Altmann and M. McKee (2005), "The Global Burden of Disease Attributable to Low Consumption of Fruit and Vegetables: Implications for the Global Strategy on Diet", *Bulletin of the World Health Organisation*, Vol. 83, No. 2, pp. 100-108, Feb.

Lopez, A.D., C.D. Mathers, M. Ezzati, D.T. Jamison and C.J.L. Murray (2006), *Global Burden of Disease and Risk Factors*, Oxford University Press/The World Bank, New York.

Menotti, A. and M. Lanti (2003), "Coronary Risk Factors Predicting Early and Late Coronary Deaths", *Heart*, Vol. 89, No. 1, pp. 19-24, Jan.

Mundo-Rosas, V., S. Rodríguez-Ramírez and T. Shamah-Levy (2006), "Energy and Nutrient Intake in Mexican Children 1 to 4 Years Old. Results from the Mexican National Health and Nutrition Survey 2006", *Salud Publica Mex* 2009, Vol. 51-4.

Nagura, J. et al. (2005), "Stroke Subtypes and Lesion Sites in Akita, Japan", *Journal of Stroke and Cerebrovascular Diseases*, Vol. 14, No. 1, Jan-Feb, pp. 1-7.

Office of National Statistics website, *www.statistics.gov.uk*, accessed on 2 March 2010.

Olaiz, G., R. Rojas, S. Barquera, T. Shamah, C. Aguilar, P. Cravito, P. López, M. Hernández, R. Tapia and J. Sepúlveda (2003), "Encuesta Nacional de Salud 2000. Tomo 2. La salud de los adultos", Instituto Nacional de Salud Pública, Cuernavaca, México.

Olaiz-Fernández, G., J. Rivera-Dommarco, T. Shamah-Levy, R. Rojas, S. Villalpando-Hernández, M. Hernández-Avila and J. Sepúlveda-Amor (2006), "Encuesta Nacional de Salud y Nutrición 2006", Instituto Nacional de Salud Pública, Cuernavaca, México.

Palmieri, L., A. Barchielli, G. Cesana, E. de Campora, C.A. Goldoni, P. Spolaore, M. Uguccioni, F. Vancheri, D. Vanuzzo, P. Ciccarelli and S. Giampaoli (2007), "The Italian Register of Cardiovascular Diseases: Attack Rates and Case Fatality for Cerebrovascular Events", *Cerebrovascular Diseases*, Vol. 24, pp. 530-539.

Pardo Silva, M.C., C. De Laet, W.J. Nusselder, A.A. Mamun and A. Peeters (2006), "Adult Obesity and Number of Years Lived With and Without Cardiovascular Disease", *Obesity (Silver Spring)*, Vol. 14, No. 7, pp. 1264-1273, Jul.

Pierce, J.P., L. Natarajan, B.J. Caan, B.A. Parker, E.R. Greenberg, S.W. Flatt, C.L. Rock, S. Kealey, W.K. Al-Delaimy, W.A. Bardwell, R.W. Carlson, J.A. Emond, S. Faerber, E.B. Gold, R.A. Hajek, K. Hollenbach, L.A. Jones, N. Karanja, L. Madlensky, J. Marshall, V.A. Newman, C. Ritenbaugh, C.A. Thomson, L. Wasserman and M.L. Stefanick (2007), "Influence of a Diet Very High in Vegetables, Fruit, and Fiber and Low in Fat on Prognosis Following Treatment for Breast Cancer: The Women's Healthy Eating and Living (WHEL) Randomized Trial", *Journal of the American Medical Association*, Vol. 298, No. 3, pp. 289-298, 18 Jul.

Rodriguez-Ramírez, S., V. Mundo-Rosas, T. Shamah-Levy, X. Ponce-Martínez, A. Jiménez-Aguilar and T. González-de Cossío (2009), "Energy and Nutrient Intake in Mexican Adolescents: Analysis of the Mexican National Health and Nutrition Survey 2006", *Salud Publica Mex* 2009, Vol. 51-4.

Shamah-Levy, T., S. Villalpando-Hernández and J.A. Rivera-Dommarco (2007), *Resultados de Nutrición de la ENSANUT 2006*, Instituto Nacional de Salud Pública. Cuernavaca, México.

Skuladottir, H., A. Tjoenneland, K. Overvad, C. Stripp and J.H. Olsen (2006), "Does High Intake of Fruit and Vegetables Improve Lung Cancer Survival?", *Lung Cancer*, Vol. 51, No. 3, pp. 267-273, Mar.

SS – INSP Secretaría de Salud and Instituto Nacional de Salud Pública, "National Health and Nutrition Survey in Mexico 2006".

SS – Secretaría de Salud, Dirección General de Información en Salud (DGIS), "Base de datos del Sistema Estadístico Epidemiológico de las Defunciones (SEED) 2004-2008", México.

SS – Secretaría de Salud, Dirección General de Información en Salud (DGIS), "Base de datos del Sistema Automatizado de Egresos Hospitalarios (SAEH) 2004-2008", México.

Statistics Canada website, *www.statcan.gc.ca*, accessed on 18 June 2010.

Stevens, R.J., R.L. Coleman, A.I. Adler, I.M. Stratton, D.R. Matthews and R.R. Holman (2004), "Risk Factors for Myocardial Infarction Case Fatality and Stroke Case Fatality in Type 2 Diabetes, UKPDS 66", *Diabetes Care*, Vol. 27, No. 1, pp. 201-207, Jan.

Van Baal, P.H., J.J. Polder, G.A. de Wit, R.T. Hoogenveen, T.L. Feenstra, H.C. Boshuizen, P.M. Engelfriet and W.B. Brouwer (2008), "Lifetime Medical Costs of Obesity: Prevention No Cure for Increasing Health Expenditure", *PLoS Medicine*, Vol. 5, No. 2, e29, Feb.

Villalpando, S., V. De la Cruz, R. Rojas, T. Shamah-Levy, M.A. Ávila, B. Gaona, R. Rebollara and L. Hernández (2010), "Prevalence and Distribution of Type 2 Diabetes Mellitus in Mexican Adult Population. A Probabilistic Survey", *Salud Pública Mex* 2010, Vol. 52, pp. 27-35.

Wannamethee, S.G., A.G. Shaper and L. Lennon (2004), "Cardiovascular Disease Incidence and Mortality in Older Men with Diabetes and in Men with Coronary Heart Disease", *Heart*, Vol. 90, No. 12, pp. 1398-1403, Dec.

WHO Cancer Mortality database website, *www-dep.iarc.fr/WHOdb/WHOdb.htm*, accessed on 18 June 2010.

Yoshida, M. et al. (2005), "Incidence of Acute Myocardial Infraction in Takashima, Shiga, Japan", *Circulation Journal*, Vol. 69, No. 4, April.

Table A.3 shows the cost per capita (per unit of population) and the potential coverage of the interventions assessed in the OECD/WHO analysis. Costs include only the costs of delivering the interventions, and are expressed in USD PPPs. Coverage figures reflect the proportions of national populations which would be given the opportunity to benefit from preventive interventions, without accounting for individual uptake rates, estimated separately.

Table A.4 shows the magnitude of health gains associated with preventive interventions. This is expressed as a ratio between the total number of statistical lives lived during the course of the simulation analysis and the total number of DALYs/LYs gained during the course of the same simulation. The figures in each box of Table A.3 (n) should be interpreted as: "The intervention generates a gain of one DALY/LY for every n individuals, over their lifetime". The lower the value of n, the larger the effectiveness of the intervention.

Figure A.5 shows the cumulative effectiveness of interventions over time. The vertical axis shows the number of disability-adjusted life years gained per million population, while the horizontal axis corresponds to the time frame of the analysis. DALYs are discounted at a 3% rate.

Figure A.6 describes the cumulative impact of interventions on health expenditure over time. The vertical axis shows the cumulative impact of interventions on health expenditures in terms of USD PPPs per capita. The horizontal axis reflects the time frame of the analysis. Figures are discounted at a 3% rate.

Figure A.7 shows the cumulative effectiveness of a multiple intervention strategy over time in the five countries concerned. The vertical axis shows the number of disability-adjusted life years gained per million population, while the horizontal axis corresponds to the time frame of the analysis. DALYs are discounted at a 3% rate.

Figure A.8 describes the cumulative impact of a multiple intervention strategy on health expenditure over time in the five countries concerned. The vertical axis shows the cumulative impact of interventions on health expenditure in terms of USD PPPs per capita, while the horizontal axis corresponds to the time frame of the analysis. Figures are discounted at a 3% rate.

Figure A.9 presents the cost-effectiveness of a multiple intervention strategy over time in the five countries concerned. The vertical axis shows cost-effectiveness ratios in terms of USD PPPs per DALY gained, while the horizontal axis corresponds to the time frame of the analysis. Both costs and DALYs are discounted at a 3% rate.

Table A.3. Costs and coverage of selected preventive interventions

		School-based interventions	Worksite interventions	Mass media campaigns	Fiscal measures	Physician counselling	Physician-dietician counselling	Food advertising regulation	Food advertising self-regulation	Food labelling	Multiple-intervention strategy
Canada	Target as % of population	2.4%	15.6%	78.3%	100.0%	12.7%	12.7%	21.0%	21.0%	100.0%	100.0%
	Cost/capita (USD PPPs)	1.78	5.59	1.36	0.13	9.26	19.74	0.55	0.04	1.10	24.03
England	Target as % of population	2.3%	15.7%	78.5%	100.0%	14.7%	14.7%	20.4%	20.4%	100.0%	100.0%
	Cost/capita (USD PPPs)	1.02	3.49	1.85	0.09	6.52	13.80	0.24	0.02	0.84	17.52
Italy	Target as % of population	1.9%	8.2%	82.9%	100.0%	10.2%	10.2%	16.2%	16.2%	100.0%	100.0%
	Cost/capita (USD PPPs)	1.36	2.73	1.56	0.09	6.82	14.42	0.42	0.02	0.93	18.29
Japan	Target as % of population	1.9%	12.7%	83.6%	100.0%	5.8%	5.8%	15.6%	15.6%	100.0%	100.0%
	Cost/capita (USD PPPs)	1.41	4.28	0.84	0.09	4.32	8.82	0.46	0.02	0.99	12.07
Mexico	Target as % of population	4.2%	12.6%	63.5%	100.0%	14.1%	14.1%	34.7%	34.7%	100.0%	100.0%
	Cost/capita (USD PPPs)	1.78	2.48	0.65	0.03	6.42	13.61	0.14	0.01	0.33	16.38

Note: Figures should be interpreted as follows: The intervention generates a gain of one DALY/LY for every N individuals over their lifetime. The multiple-intervention strategy is a sum of the following: Food labelling; food advertising self-regulation; school-based intervention; mass media campaign; and physician-dietician counselling in primary care.

Source: CDP model-based analysis relying on input data from multiple sources, listed in Table A.2.

StatLink 〰 http://dx.doi.org/10.1787/888932316571

Table A.4. **Magnitude of health gains associated with preventive interventions (population per DALY/LY gained)**

	Disability-adjusted life years						Life years					
	Canada	England	Italy	Japan	Mexico		Canada	England	Italy	Japan	Mexico
School-based interventions	98	105	127	62	235		197	272	237	101	647
Worksite interventions	38	44	70	37	107		63	85	104	46	272
Mass media campaigns	97	79	93	81	172		127	130	100	101	398
Fiscal measures	26	31	26	22	83		43	69	37	40	185
Physician counselling	31	25	33	37	50		50	57	51	49	142
Physician-dietician counselling	9	6	8	10	13		14	17	12	14	41
Food advertising regulation	35	29	94	33	98		57	52	134	40	181
Food advertising self-regulation	64	55	180	59	181		100	95	260	74	340
Food labelling	55	47	47	51	131		82	80	61	63	233
Multiple-intervention strategy	7	4	6	10	11		10	9	9	9	30

Note: Figures should be interpreted as follows: The intervention generates a gain of one DALY/LY for every *N* individuals, over their lifetime. The multiple-intervention strategy is a sum of the following: Food labelling; food advertising self-regulation; school-based intervention; mass media campaign; and physician-dietician counselling in primary care.

Source: CDP model-based analysis relying on input data from multiple sources, listed in Table A.2.

StatLink http://dx.doi.org/10.1787/888932316590

Figure A.5. **Cumulative DALYs saved over time (per million population)**

DALYs (per million population)

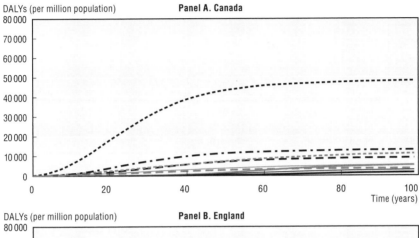

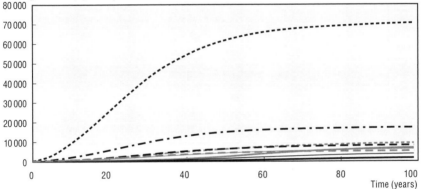

Source: CDP model-based analysis relying on input data from multiple sources, listed in Table A.2.
StatLink http://dx.doi.org/10.1787/888932316286

Figure A.5. **Cumulative DALYs saved over time (per million population)** *(cont.)*

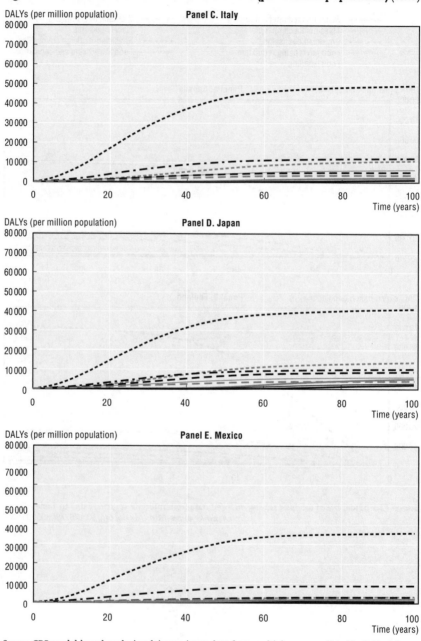

Source: CDP model-based analysis relying on input data from multiple sources, listed in Table A.2.
StatLink http://dx.doi.org/10.1787/888932316286

Figure A.6. **Cumulative impact on health expenditure over time**

Impact on health expenditure (USD PPPs/capita)   **Panel A. Canada**

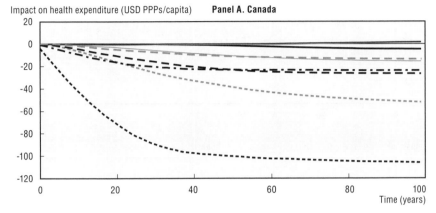

Impact on health expenditure (USD PPPs/capita)   **Panel B. England**

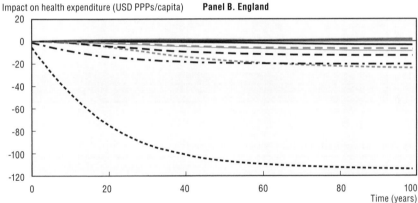

Source: CDP model-based analysis relying on input data from multiple sources, listed in Table A.2.
StatLink http://dx.doi.org/10.1787/888932316305

Figure A.6. **Cumulative impact on health expenditure over time** (*cont.*)

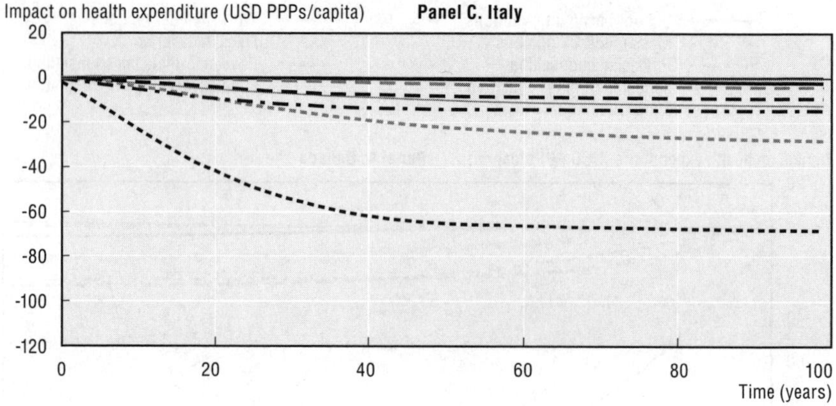

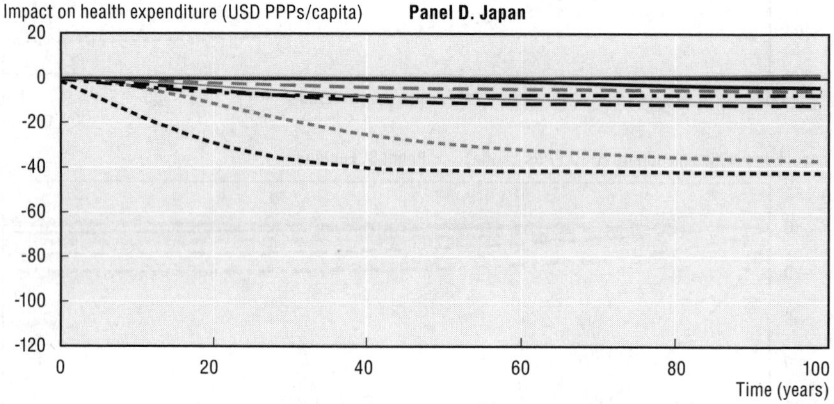

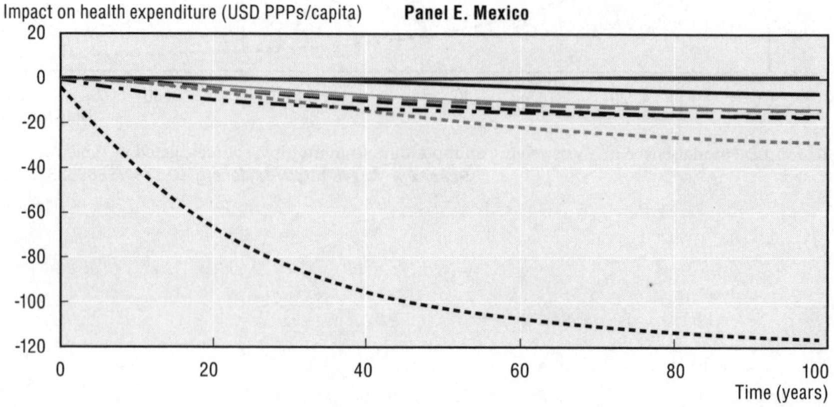

Impact on health expenditure (USD PPPs/capita)　　　**Panel C. Italy**

Time (years)

Impact on health expenditure (USD PPPs/capita)　　　**Panel D. Japan**

Time (years)

Impact on health expenditure (USD PPPs/capita)　　　**Panel E. Mexico**

Time (years)

Source: CDP model-based analysis relying on input data from multiple sources, listed in Table A.2.
StatLink ⟨⟨⟩⟩ *http://dx.doi.org/10.1787/888932316305*

Figure A.7. **Cumulative DALYs saved with a multiple-intervention strategy over time**

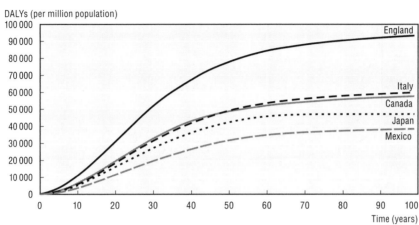

Note: The multiple-intervention strategy is a sum of the following: food labelling; food advertising self-regulation; school-based intervention; mass media campaign; and physician-dietician counselling in primary care.

Source: CDP model-based analysis relying on input data from multiple sources, listed in Table A.2.

StatLink ㅡ http://dx.doi.org/10.1787/888932316324

Figure A.8. **Cumulative impact on health expenditure of a multiple-intervention strategy over time**

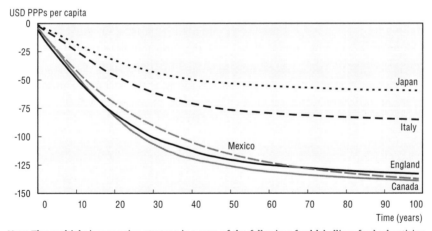

Note: The multiple-intervention strategy is a sum of the following: food labelling; food advertising self-regulation; school-based intervention; mass media campaign; and physician-dietician counselling in primary care.

Source: CDP model-based analysis relying on input data from multiple sources, listed in Table A.2.

StatLink ㅡ http://dx.doi.org/10.1787/888932316343

Figure A.9. **Cost-effectiveness of a multiple-intervention strategy over time**

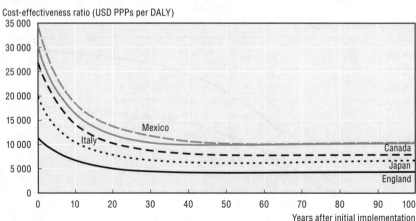

Cost-effectiveness ratio (USD PPPs per DALY)

Note: The multiple-intervention strategy is a sum of the following: food labelling; food advertising self-regulation; school-based intervention; mass media campaign; and physician-dietician counselling in primary care.

Source: CDP model-based analysis relying on input data from multiple sources, listed in Table A.2.

StatLink 🖧 *http://dx.doi.org/10.1787/888932316362*

Figures A.10 to A.14 illustrate average annual cost-effectiveness ratios of different interventions after they have been in place for 30 years. The vertical axis shows intervention costs in millions of USD PPPs, while the horizontal axis shows intervention effects in thousands of DALYs. Clouds of points for each intervention reflect the uncertainty surrounding cost and effect estimates. Clouds resting mostly or entirely beneath the threshold lines correspond to the interventions with the most favourable cost-effectiveness profiles.

Figures A.15 to A.19 illustrate the average annual cost-effectiveness ratios of different interventions after they have been in place for 100 years. These figures have the same characteristics as Figures A.10 to A.14.

Figure A.10. **Canada: Probabilistic sensitivity analysis of the cost-effectiveness of interventions at 30 years**

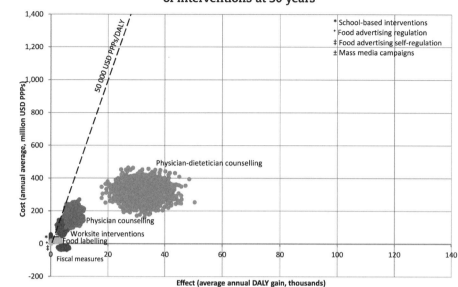

Source: CDP model-based analysis relying on input data from multiple sources, listed in Table A.2.

StatLink http://dx.doi.org/10.1787/888932316381

Figure A.11. **England: Probabilistic sensitivity analysis of the cost-effectiveness of interventions at 30 years**

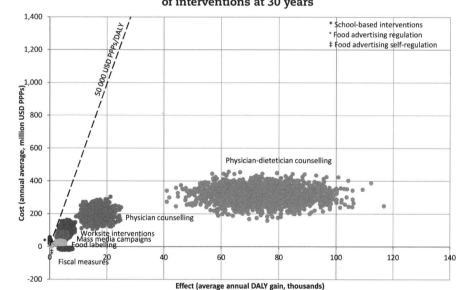

Source: CDP model-based analysis relying on input data from multiple sources, listed in Table A.2.

StatLink http://dx.doi.org/10.1787/888932316400

Figure A.12. **Italy: Probabilistic sensitivity analysis of the cost-effectiveness of interventions at 30 years**

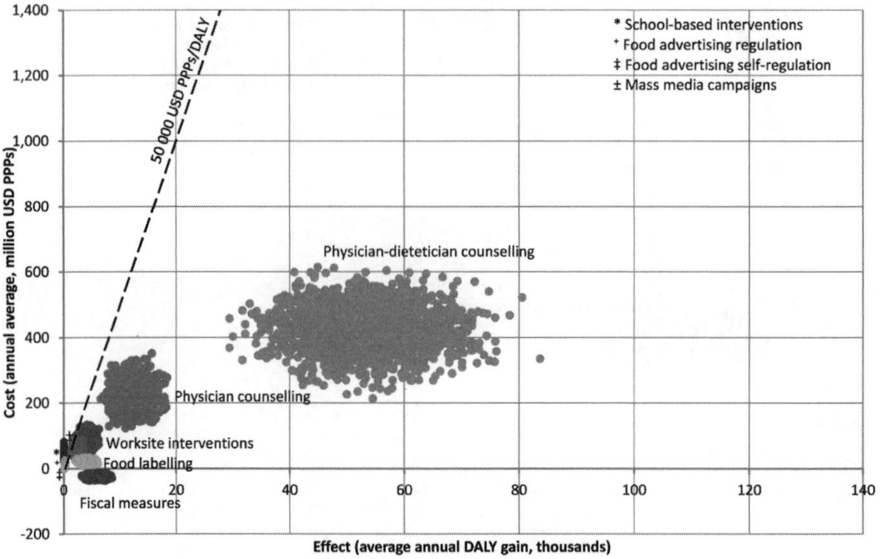

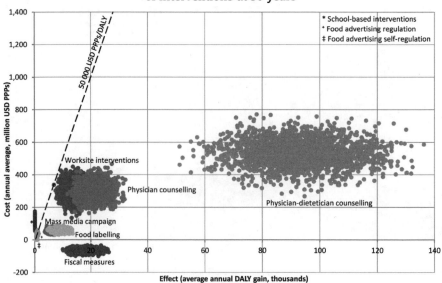

Source: CDP model-based analysis relying on input data from multiple sources, listed in Table A.2.

StatLink http://dx.doi.org/10.1787/888932316419

Figure A.13. **Japan: Probabilistic sensitivity analysis of the cost-effectiveness of interventions at 30 years**

Source: CDP model-based analysis relying on input data from multiple sources, listed in Table A.2.

StatLink http://dx.doi.org/10.1787/888932316438

Figure A.14. **Mexico: Probabilistic sensitivity analysis of the cost-effectiveness of interventions at 30 years**

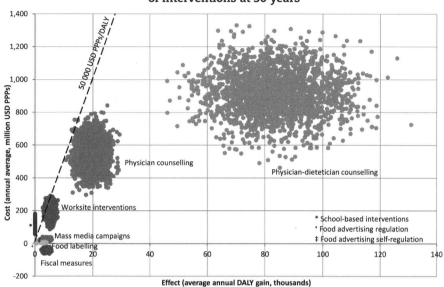

Source: CDP model-based analysis relying on input data from multiple sources, listed in Table A.2.

StatLink ⎈🖎 http://dx.doi.org/10.1787/888932316457

Figure A.15. **Canada: Probabilistic sensitivity analysis of the cost-effectiveness of interventions at 100 years**

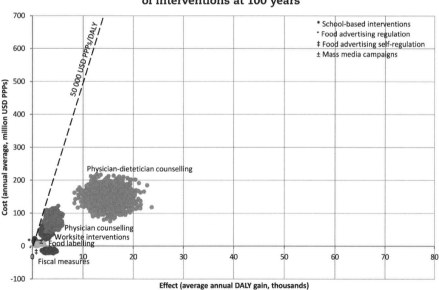

Source: CDP model-based analysis relying on input data from multiple sources, listed in Table A.2.

StatLink ⎈🖎 http://dx.doi.org/10.1787/888932316476

Figure A.16. **England: Probabilistic sensitivity analysis of the cost-effectiveness of interventions at 100 years**

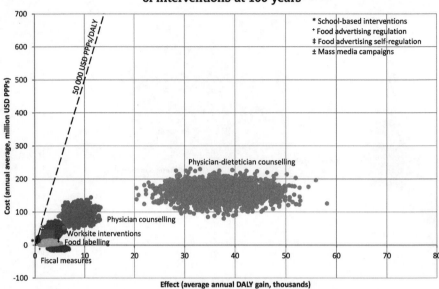

Source: CDP model-based analysis relying on input data from multiple sources, listed in Table A.2.

StatLink ⟪⟫ http://dx.doi.org/10.1787/888932316495

Figure A.17. **Italy: Probabilistic sensitivity analysis of the cost-effectiveness of interventions at 100 years**

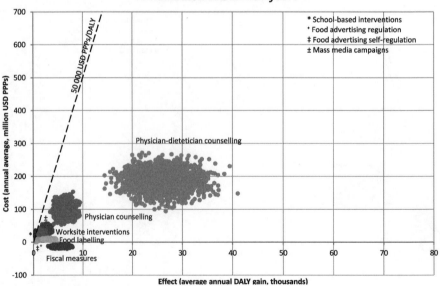

Source: CDP model-based analysis relying on input data from multiple sources, listed in Table A.2.

StatLink ⟪⟫ http://dx.doi.org/10.1787/888932316514

Figure A.18. **Japan: Probabilistic sensitivity analysis of the cost-effectiveness of interventions at 100 years**

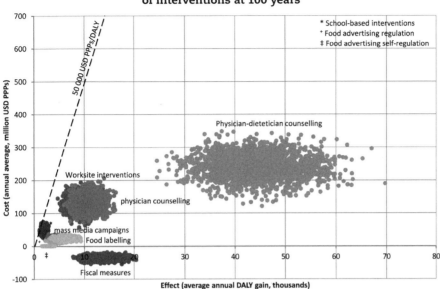

Source: CDP model-based analysis relying on input data from multiple sources, listed in Table A.2.
StatLink ⎯⎯ http://dx.doi.org/10.1787/888932316533

Figure A.19. **Mexico: Probabilistic sensitivity analysis of the cost-effectiveness of interventions at 100 years**

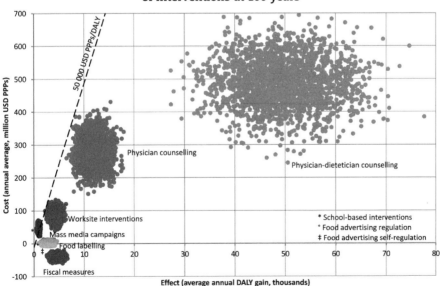

Source: CDP model-based analysis relying on input data from multiple sources, listed in Table A.2.
StatLink ⎯⎯ http://dx.doi.org/10.1787/888932316552

ANNEX B

Author's and Contributors' Biographies

Franco Sassi is responsible for the OECD Economics of Prevention project and is the author of this book. He is a senior health economist in the OECD Health Division. Previously, he was a senior lecturer in health policy at the London School of Economics and Political Science (LSE), where he was based since 1995. He was director of the graduate programme in Health Policy, Planning and Financing, one of the longest established health policy programmes worldwide, run jointly by the LSE and the London School of Hygiene and Tropical Medicine, for eight years. Franco has an undergraduate degree from Bocconi University (Milan) and obtained his doctorate in health economics from the University of London. The overarching theme of his research and publications, throughout his career, has been the evaluation of health interventions. He holds an adjunct professor position at the Université de Montréal and held visiting positions at a number of universities in the United States, including University of California at Berkeley, Harvard University, University of California at San Francisco, and Duke University, as well as at the Catholic University of Rome. He served as a temporary advisor to the European office of the World Health Organisation on a range of issues including cost-effectiveness of health care services, reshaping health systems towards health outcomes, health care quality management. He was awarded a 2000-01 Commonwealth Fund Harkness Fellowship in Health Care Policy.

Michele Cecchini is a health economist/policy analyst in the OECD Health Division, where he has been working on the economics of prevention project. In particular, he contributed to the design of the CDP micro-simulation model and conducted analyses aimed at assessing the cost-effectiveness and distributional impacts of alternative strategies to tackle obesity and related chronic diseases. He also contributed to the analysis of past trends and future projections of overweight and obesity. After obtaining a degree in Medicine and Surgery at the University of Genoa, Michele completed his specialist training in Public Health at the University of Siena. He obtained a masters degree in health policy, planning and financing from the London School of

Economics and the London School of Hygiene and Tropical Medicine. Before joining the OECD, Michele's research focused on patient mobility in relation to perceived quality of care and on equity of access to health services.

Marion Devaux is a statistician in the OECD Health Division. She holds a masters degree in statistics from the École Nationale de la Statistique et Analyse de l'Information (ENSAI, France). She previously worked on the intergenerational transmission of health inequalities at the Institute for Research and Information in Health Economics (IRDES, Paris), and published in academic journals. At the OECD, she has contributed to a range of projects on the prevention of obesity, the health care financing and the health systems characteristics. Her main contribution to the OECD Economics of Prevention project consisted in the analysis of trends over time in obesity and overweight in OECD countries, including attempts to disentangle age, period and cohort effects. She also examined existing disparities in obesity among socio-economic groups, the relationship between education and obesity, and social multiplier effects on the spread of obesity, using household-based national health survey data.

Francesco Branca is director of the Department of Nutrition for Health and Development at the World Health Organisation, Geneva, and is responsible for strategic and managerial guidance in the areas of Growth Assessment and Surveillance; Nutrition Policies and Scientific Advise; Reduction of Micronutrient Malnutrition; Nutrition in the Life Course. Francesco graduated in medicine and surgery and specialised in diabetology and metabolic diseases at the Catholic University of Rome. He obtained a PhD in nutrition from Aberdeen University. He was a senior scientist at the Italian Food and Nutrition Research Institute where he was responsible for the design and implementation of studies on the effects of food and nutrients on human health at different stages of the life cycle, and for the design, management and evaluation of public health nutrition programmes. Francesco was president of the Federation of the European Nutrition Societies in 2003-07.

Donald S. Kenkel is a professor in the Department of Policy Analysis and Management at Cornell University, Ithaca, United States, where he has been based since 1995. He received his PhD in economics from the University of Chicago in 1987. Most of Don's research is on the economics of disease prevention and health promotion. He is the author of the chapter on prevention in the Handbook of Health Economics (2000). He conducted a series of studies on the economics of public health policies, including: alcohol taxes and other policies to prevent alcohol problems (*Journal of Applied Econometrics*, 2001; *American Economic Review Papers and Proceedings*, 2005); cigarette taxes to prevent youth smoking (*Journal of Political Economy* 2002); and advertising to promote smoking cessation (*Journal of Regulatory Economics*, 2007, and *Journal of Political Economy*, 2007). Another area of research and teaching interest is in cost-benefit analysis of public policies, especially policies that affect health. He is a Research Associate at the National Bureau of Economic Research. In 2005 he was commissioned a Kentucky Colonel.

Tim Lobstein is Director of Policy and Programmes at the International Association for the Study of Obesity (IASO), based in the United Kingdom, and policy co-ordinator for the International Obesity Task Force (IOTF). He was previously Director of the UK Food Commission, and a consultant on food and nutrition policy to the European Commission, the World Health Organisation and several national and international non-governmental organisations. Professor Lobstein is a visiting fellow at the University of Sussex Science Policy Research Unit, United Kingdom, a Rudd Visiting Fellow at Yale University, United States, and adjunct professor of public health advocacy at Curtin University, Western Australia.

Marc Suhrcke is a professor of public health economics at the University of East Anglia in Norwich, United Kingdom. He is also the health economics lead in the new UKCRC funded centre of excellence in public health research, the Centre for Diet and Activity Research (CEDAR), a collaboration of the Universities of Cambridge and East Anglia. Previously he worked as an economist at the WHO European Office for Investment for Health and Development (Venice), where he was in charge of work on Health and Economic Development. His other former professional experiences include: the UNICEF Innocenti Research Centre (Florence), Hamburg University, the European Bank for Reconstruction and Development (London), the Centre for European Policy Studies (Brussels), and the European Commission (Brussels). His background is in economics and his main current research interests are: health and economic development, economics of prevention, socio-economic determinants and inequalities of health.

Tracey Strange contributed to the editing and writing of the book. She is a freelance writer and media consultant. She is co-author of Sustainable Development in the OECD Insights series and has collaborated on other titles in the series as editorial advisor. Tracey manages the OECD Insights blog and is developing social media applications and communications material for several OECD activities. She is participating in the OECD Future Global Shocks project, working on the emerging risk landscape. Tracey also has a background in user-driven innovation research for multinational clients in France and the United States with a focus on qualitative research, analysis, concept and prototype development for clients from the medical and lifestyle-related sectors.

Index

accumulation model of long-term
  health 120
addictive behaviours 128–9
adiposity 59, 61, 107–9
advertising *see* food advertising
  regulation; self-regulation of
  food advertising
age, and obesity 17, 65–7, 68,
  81–2, 119–20
  see also children
age-period-cohort (APC) analysis
  65–7
Aghion, P. 52
alcohol abuse 24, 50–51, 83
Allais, O. 203
ANGELO framework (Analysis Grid
  for Environments Linked to
  Obesity) 171
Arendt, J.N. 86
asymmetric paternalism 233–4
Australia
  child overweight 108, 112
  community interventions 168
  data sources 238
  education and obesity 84, 85,
    93, 241–2
  future trends 68, 69, 70
  gender and obesity 80
  obesity rates 58, 59, 60, 62, 63, 64
  self-regulation of food advertising
    218
  social disparities and obesity 92
  socio-economic status and
    obesity 94, 239–40
Austria
  child overweight 108
  data sources 238
  education and obesity 92, 93,
    241–2
  future trends 68, 70
  obesity rates 60, 62, 63, 64

socio-economic status and
  obesity 94, 239–40
Avery, R. 142

bans on unhealthy behaviours
  152–3, 156
Becker, G.S. 129, 130
behavioural economics 126, 127
Belgium 60, 100, 108
Bhattacharya, J. 124
body mass index (BMI)
  formula 75
  trends in 16, 25, 44, 67–9, 75
  use in measuring obesity 59–61
Bogalusa Heart study 110
Branca, Francesco 43, 264
Brazil 58, 60, 108, 161, 218
Brunello, G. 86, 102, 123, 125
Buller, D.B. 180
business 41, 228
  see also food industry

Canada
  age and obesity 82
  child overweight 108
  cohort patterns 65–7
  community interventions 166
  cost-effectiveness of
    interventions 256, 257, 259
  cost of interventions 249
  data sources 238, 243, 244
  distributional impacts of
    interventions 202
  education and obesity 84, 85,
    93, 241–2
  effectiveness of interventions
    191, 193, 195, 197, 250,
    251, 253, 255
  future trends 68, 70
  gender and obesity 80
  multiple-intervention strategies
    200, 201